The Rorschach Technique

The Rorschach Technique

Perceptual Basics, Content Interpretation, and Applications

Edward Aronow

Montclair State College and
Psychologist in Private Practice
Cedar Grove, New Jersey

Marvin Reznikoff

Fordham University and
The New York Hospital–Cornell University
Medical Center, Westchester Division

Kevin Moreland

Fordham University and
The New York Hospital–Cornell University
Medical Center, Westchester Division

Allyn and Bacon

Boston · London · Toronto · Sydney · Tokyo · Singapore

Library of Congress Cataloging-in-Publication Data

Aronow, Edward.
    The Rorschach technique: perceptual basics, content
interpretation, and applications / Edward Aronow, Marvin Reznikoff,
Kevin Moreland.
        p.   cm.
    Includes bibliographical references and index.
    ISBN 0-205-14912-X
    1. Rorschach Test.   I. Reznikoff, Marvin.   II. Moreland, Kevin.
III. Title.
BF698.8.R5A764   1994
155.2'842—dc20   93-38065
                                                                 CIP

Printed in the United States of America

10 9 8 7 6 5 4 3 2 1   98 97 96 95 94

To the late Dr. Joseph Zubin,
a true pioneer in projective techniques

About the Authors

Dr. Edward Aronow has been a Professor at Montclair State College in New Jersey for the past 20 years. He also served as Senior Clinical Psychologist at St. Vincent's Hospital in New York City. Dr. Aronow has been engaged in the private practice of psychology in New Jersey.

Dr. Aronow is the author of two previous books on the Rorschach. These were *Rorschach Content Interpretation*, published in 1976, and *A Rorschach Introduction: Content and Perceptual Approaches*, published in 1983. Dr. Aronow has also authored a number of articles on projective techniques and other topics in clinical psychology.

Dr. Marvin Reznikoff has been a Professor for the past 25 years at Fordham University, where he also served as chair of the Psychology Department and Director of the Doctoral Program in Clinical Psychology. He has been a clinical consultant for the State of Connecticut, and is Adjunct Professor of Psychology in the Department of Psychiatry, The New York Hospital–Cornell Medical Center, Westchester Division. He was formerly Director of Psychology at The Institute of Living, Hartford.

Dr. Reznikoff has authored over 110 professional articles and 6 books. He is a Diplomate of the American Board of Professional Psychology (Clinical).

Dr. Kevin Moreland is currently on the faculty at Fordham University and Cornell University Medical College. He has worked for National Computer Systems in Minneapolis. During his six years at NCS, Dr. Moreland was involved in research and development on many psychological tests, including the Rorschach, MMPI-2, and MCMI-II. Dr. Moreland has published over 50 book chapters and articles in professional journals. He co-authored the text *Responsible Test Use: Case Studies in Human Behavior.* He is especially well known for his publications about computer-based psychological assessment. Dr. Moreland also presents MMPI-2 workshops throughout the country.

Contents

Foreword

"*The* Rorschach" refers to any of a number of approaches to clinical psychological assessment that center about subjects' responses to the 10 inkblots bequeathed to us by Hermann Rorschach. Several of these approaches have been identified as systems, each of which sets forth its author's particular recommendations for administration, scoring, and interpretation. Adding to these variations, most Rorschachers permit themselves some latitude in the application of their chosen technique.

The most commonly accepted use of the blots is as an instrument based on the interpretation of how these blots are perceived. The blot areas where the subject reports percepts and the various characteristics cited by the subject as contributing definition to these percepts form the main basis for gaining knowledge of his or her personality. Rorschach considered the content of responses as of minor value for this purpose. Only in his posthumous publication with Oberholzer did he discuss the insights into personality functioning that may be derived from studying the subject's response content. This aspect of the Rorschach has received little emphasis in the leading texts, which build on the perceptual basis of the instrument, though most Rorschachers have long included content analysis in their practice.

The Rorschach, conceived of solely as a perceptual tool, fitted nicely into the empirical, physicalistic, S-R, nomothetic, and psychometric psychological climate into which it was introduced—except for the validity problem it posed. It was assigned a place alongside the then extant measures of psychological functioning, though it never entered the psychometrician's sweetest dreams.

Further developments in the technique followed upon a half-century's evolution in psychological theory and climate. The new ambiance is less mechanistic, proportionately less nomothetic and more idiographic. The Rorschach is viewed by many as not so much of a test—or psychometric tool—but as more of a transaction or an interview. Personality theory, particularly psychoanalytic theory, shares the stage with psychometric concerns. Cognitive concepts—personal construct theory, constructivism, the central role of meaning, and the key representations of the individual all have taken on a position of importance alongside perceptual factors.

The contribution that the Rorschach as a clinical instrument can make to therapy is a basic concern. The perceptual-psychometric approach yields data that are relevant to this need, such as qualitative and quantitative features of the individual's controls, tendencies to abstract or concrete thinking, and respect for reality. The method falls short, however, in the ability to supply information in a number of other key areas pertinent to therapy where analysis of content frequently is helpful. Personality dynamics, defensive structures, fantasies, and object relations are some of these.

The subject matter of this book represents a clinical-idiographic approach, a balanced account of both perceptual and content roles of the Rorschach against a background of recent theoretical advances. The authors, long experienced as clinicians, Rorschach researchers, and teachers, have selected for their text what is most relevant to beginning Rorschach students. Moving from a gentle introduction to location and the scoring of determinants, they proceed to a responsible discussion of content interpretation, avoiding what Rapaport called the "dream book" approach.

Another of the highlights particularly worth mentioning is the authors' treatment of the always difficult problem of validity. The topic is approached in a realistic way that avoids the idiographic (square peg)–nomothetic (round peg) trap. This and other features of presentation that students can grasp and relate to will both instruct them and let them feel good about the Rorschach.

Norman Tallent
Northhampton, Massachusetts

Preface

An important distinction in approaches to the Rorschach is that between the nomothetic and the idiographic. This draws on a distinction made by Gordon Allport (1937, 1961) in relation to personality evaluation in general. *Nomothetic methods* have as their aim the discovery of general laws. *Idiographic methods* pertain to the intensive study of the particular case.

As initially presented by Hermann Rorschach in 1921, the Rorschach test was conceived largely as a perceptual instrument, with the personality of the subject revealed through scoring categories such as location, determinants, and form-level. Rorschach clinicians such as Beck, Klopfer, and Piotrowski continued this perceptual emphasis, with content considerations typically given short shrift. These authors considered the Rorschach to be a *psychological test* having to meet the usual standards for a nomothetic instrument (norms, reliability, validity, freedom from response style, etc.). This approach might therefore be called the "perceptual–nomothetic model" for the Rorschach.

Later, however, content interpretation began to receive more attention, as it became evident that the validity literature was much more promising for content than for perceptual categories (e.g., Aronow & Reznikoff, 1976; Eron, 1965) and that clinicians relied quite heavily on content in interpreting Rorschach records (Potkay, 1971). In this approach, content and accompanying verbalizations are used either in empirical scales or to try to enter the unique idiographic world of each individual. For example, Blatt (1990) has written of the distinction between the Rorschach as a measure of perception or as an evaluation of the representational or "meaning systems" of the unique individual. This approach to the Rorschach technique might most appropriately be dubbed the "content–idiographic" model. Here, scoring is typically relegated to a secondary position, and the Rorschach is used as a clinical "technique" to reveal the unique pattern of psychodynamics and world views of each individual. As Potkay (1971) has shown, this is the approach to which experienced clinicians typically gravitate in any case.

A major purpose of this text is to lessen the chasm that has for many years existed between Rorschach training and experienced Rorschach practice. A further and related intent of this book is to provide a more appropriately balanced presentation of the two approaches to Rorschach work than is available in other contemporary introductory Rorschach texts, which without exception are based largely on an analysis of the perceptual components of the procedure. As can be seen from the title of this text, in the tradition of Zubin, Eron, and Schumer (1965), we refer to the Rorschach as a *technique* rather than a *test*, underscoring the essentially idiographic nature of the instrument. As noted by Murstein (1968), a technique, as oppposed to a test, is best viewed as "an aid in arriving at information . . . and its keynote is flexibility" (p. 229).

> *When we consider projective techniques as tests, we cause some of our projective forefathers to experience a dyspeptic moment or two because the original* cause celebre *of projective techniques was to free psychology from its preoccupation with numbers and have it instead embrace the whole individual. Nomotheticists, or individuals concerned with quantitative measurement, had left the individual no place to sit but on his continuum—but projective technique adherents attempted to restore the concept of the unity of the individual. Yet, like it or not, the . . . more research oriented clinical psychologist has attempted to justify the continued use of the instrument by treating it as a test. (Murstein, 1968, p. 229)*

A certain amount of conceptual clarity in the field of assessment might be achieved if we consistently reserved the term "test" for those procedures that are largely nomothetic with the term "technique" used for instruments that primarily provide idiographic information. This would essentially result in referring to *objective tests* of personality and *projective techniques*.

We also believe that researchers would do well not to underestimate the intelligence and practical experience of the psychologists "in the trenches," those clinical, counseling, and school psychologists who administer test batteries on a regular basis. These applied psychologists have over time gravitated to making maximum use of the psychometric properties of nomothetic "tests" (such as the Wechsler intelligence tests, the MMPI, the MAPI, etc.), while either ignoring scoring entirely or relegating it to a secondary position when dealing with projective techniques that yield rich idiographic data (Figure Drawings, the TAT, the Rorschach Technique, etc.).

As contrasted with an accepted nomothetic test of personality, the MMPI-2, the Rorschach technique gives the subject tremendous freedom of response.

Instead of answering either true or false to written statements, the subject can report seeing anything from an aardvark to a zebra on the Rorschach inkblots. The subject may even choose the number of responses given to a Rorschach inkblot. While these characteristics of the procedure undermine its psychometric use, they are clearly linked with the idiographic strength of the technique. *More than any other psychological instrument, the Rorschach technique reveals the idiographic, idiosyncratic dynamics of the individual case.* We believe that our idiographic and less psychometric approach to the Rorschach is thus more congruent with the nature of the instrument. We are in fundamental agreement with Zubin's dictum that "inkblots do not a test make" (1984, p. 153).

The fact that the Rorschach deals in visual images increases the value of this procedure for revealing psychodynamic aspects of the individual. As can be seen with dreams, the unconscious is very comfortable in expressing itself in representational visual images. Rorschach images are thus ideally suited to revealing unconscious aspects of functioning during the waking life. The unstructured nature of the task may also serve to facilitate regression (Aranow & Cooper, 1984).

Financial constraints in the clinical and school context also militate against expensive, protracted inquiry and overemphasis on scoring and tabulation practices that make the Rorschach technique one of the most time-consuming of psychological instruments. Unless we can free ourselves from these procedures, it seems possible that the Rorschach will be consigned to history's dustbin, particularly in the current "Age of Managed Care." As noted by Tallent (1992), "the money squeeze is likely to get worse, not better. . . . Such considerations rule out the unhurried pace of psychological assessment characteristic of an earlier time" (p. 74). Rather than seeking ever more complex scoring systems, we should be seeking to use to maximum advantage the time that we spend administering and interpreting the Rorschach, to obtain the richest and most revealing idiographic and clinical information. Any procedure or innovation suggested by "Rorschachers" must fit in the time-effectiveness frame of reference if it is to be widely used.

Thus, as discussed in this text, we suggest the possibility of abandoning the traditional inquiry in favor of a content inquiry with pre-adolescent, adolescent, and adult subjects and substituting a "forced confabulation" inquiry with child subjects under age 9. The Consensus Rorschach Technique is presented for use in the growing marital and family psychotherapy context, with emphasis on optimal use of clinical time through maximization of the dynamic interpretation of content. Additionally, we suggest a relaxation of the boundaries between evaluation and psychotherapy, with the Rorschach technique actively used as a tool in the therapeutic process. We also urge fellow clinicians to experiment with the Rorschach and other projective techniques to find additional paths to advancing clinical knowledge. Now is a time when creativity is needed in expanding the usefulness of the Rorschach technique.

In essence, with regard to an individual Rorschach administration as presented in this text, there are three possibilities that clinicians may use. In the first, a traditional inquiry is conducted as presented in Chapter 2, with subsequent scoring and tabulation. The process of administration, scoring, tabulation, and interpretation will likely consume 2½ hours. A second possibility involves substitution of a content-oriented inquiry for the traditional inquiry; scoring and tabulation are again done, but not for determinants. The time involved for this approach is likely to average 1¾ hours. The third possibility involves conducting a content-oriented inquiry with no scoring or tabulation. In this incarnation the Rorschach Technique and its interpretation can be expected to consume 1 to 1¼ hours. Theoretical as well as practical considerations will influence which administration is chosen. When the Rorschach technique is used as a tool in psychotherapy, the third, briefer form of administration will probably be most relevant. We believe that the time involved in all three types of administration and interpretation compares quite favorably with the Rorschach Comprehensive System.

It should also be noted that the atmosphere of a Rorschach administration will also strongly influence the extent to which the subject is willing to "open up" and reveal the self. As remarked by Murstein (1968), "it makes a big difference who administers the [technique]" (p. 229). If the subject trusts the examiner, sees the evaluation as a valuable process that will be of benefit to him or her, and particularly if the examiner is already the subject's psychotherapist (as will be the case in examples presented later), the Rorschach process can be remarkably revealing and can become a useful tool in the therapy. On the other hand, if the examiner concentrates on mechanically administering a "standardized test," the subject is much more likely to give the Rorschach equivalent of name, rank, and serial number—bats, butterflies, and the like—with almost nothing projective or personal revealed. The examiner should therefore be highly motivated to establish a "collaborative" relationship with the subject (see Leventhal, Slepian, Gluck, & Rosenblatt, 1962). It is our belief that the Rorschach technique will come to be used more as a psychotherapeutic tool than as an assessment technique per se, both because of its great utility in psychotherapy and its ability to shorten the length of therapy.

As we discuss in Chapter 1, we are deeply concerned that the currently popular Comprehensive System approach (e.g., Exner, 1986a, 1991) is pushing the Rorschach in the wrong direction. We also believe that because of different types of administration that would be appropriate and because of time pressures it is not possible to have a Rorschach that is both a strong psychometric instrument and a powerful idiographic technique. Untimately one has to choose between the two. As Willock (1992) observed, psychodynamic interpretation is also a time-consuming process that cannot be "just an afterthought to a psychometric, structural analysis of a protocol" (p. 111). For a host of reasons, including the availability of many simple-to-use and time-effective objective tests of personality, the psychometrics-hostile nature of the Rorschach terrain, and the incredible richness of idiographic information that the Rorschach can provide, we favor concentrating on maximizing the idiographic qualities of the Rorschach technique. We advocate relegating psychometrics to a secondary position.

This book represents further development of our previous positions to encompass such subjects as more practical use of the consensus technique and the integration of the Rorschach with the psychotherapy process. It should be noted that many of the chapters in the present text are continued from an earlier edition, *A Rorschach Introduction* (Aronow & Reznikoff, 1983). Portions of Chapter 1, Chapter 8, and Chapter 13 are continuations of topics first broached in our book *Rorschach Content Interpretation* (Aronow & Reznikoff, 1976). This text also benefits from the contributions of Dr. Kevin Moreland, who lends particular expertise in personality assessment, with emphasis on psychometric issues.

The present text is organized as follows. Chapter 1 presents a brief history and review of the current status of inkblot techniques. Chapter 2 discusses traditional administration techniques and what is known about the blot stimulus characteristics. Chapter 3 defines the response and the scoring of locations. Then the major perceptual scoring categories will be summarized to provide grounding for the student in the traditional Rorschach procedure. The heart of traditional perceptual interpretation, the determinants category, is presented in Chapter 4, while form-level, the scoring of populars, and the simple content categories are discussed in Chapter 5. Tabulation and traditional perceptual interpretation are presented in Chapter 6. Chapter 7 is a brief summary of normative data pertinent to the scoring categories. Chapter 8 deals with the scoring of pathological verbalizations, a category that may be seen as a hybrid between the nomothetic and the idiographic approach.

In the discussion of the traditional perceptual categories, we have chosen primarily to follow the Klopfer approach, bringing in contributions by other workers when indicated, such as the list of populars developed by Beck. We have also elected to simplify perceptual scoring and tabulation in an effort to make the presentation more understandable to the student and to eliminate the many convoluted aspects of scoring and tabulation that contribute to the psychometric deficiencies of the Rorschach technique. We are aware that our perceptual scoring is less sophisticated than that used by the Comprehensive System and that many of the psychometric deficiencies that plague the Comprehensive System apply to our scoring system as well. However, our approach is less scoring-driven than is the Comprehensive System; as already noted, we believe that a choice has to be made between having a strong nomothetic or a strong idiographic instrument.

In the second half of this book the content-idiographic approach to Rorschach interpretation is presented. Chapter 9 first discusses the theoretical underpinnings of content interpretation in general, and idiographic content interpretation in particular. Chapter 10 discusses the weaknesses and problems of this approach and guidelines for making idiographic content interpretation more productive and for reducing the occurrence of "wild analysis." Chapter 11 elucidates the important area of content sequence analysis. Chapter 12 discusses content-oriented methods of administration, in particular the Content Rorschach Technique that we have developed. Chapter 13 discusses the Consensus Rorschach Technique, a fascinating use of the Rorschach with more than one subject that is particularly useful in marriage and family counseling settings.

Chapter 14 discusses the use of the Rorschach and other projective techniques not merely as assessment devices, but as tools in the psychotherapeutic endeavor. Individual and marital case examples are presented. Chapter 15 presents report writing, and Chapter 16 contains three complete protocols, two obtained by the traditional administration technique and one obtained by the Content Rorschach Technique.

As previously stated, the perceptual chapters of this book precede the content-idiographic chapters so that the student initially becomes familiar with the traditional technique. This order does not imply that we regard the perceptual categories as of primary importance in interpretation. The major emphasis in arriving at interpretations about subjects must be placed on content-idiographic analysis. Quantitative and perceptual evaluation of the Rorschach record must therefore play a complementary, rather than a primary, role in clinical Rorschach work.

The authors approach the Rorschach technique from a primarily psychoanalytic frame of reference (combined, it is hoped, with common sense). This should be obvious throughout the latter part of the book. This stands in contrast to the perceptual-nomothetic approach of Exner (1986a) and his co-workers, who largely view the Comprehensive System as free of theoretical commitment. We believe that our approach to the Rorschach technique will prove clinically useful not only to those who are psychoanalytically oriented but also to those of other theoretical orientations, such as followers of Jungian, gestalt, existential, humanistic, object relations, and self theory.

Ziskin and Faust (1988) have suggested that our approach is almost a diametric opposite of the Comprehensive Rorschach System. However, we would note that the Exner system incorporates pathological verbalizations, which is certainly in the "content and accompanying verbalizations" camp as well as being amenable to quantification. Further, our approach, while it does not emphasize scoring, does include traditional though simplifed Rorschach scoring. Clearly, our view of the Rorschach differs from the Comprehensive System in many respects, emphasizing the content-idiographic approach in contrast to what we see as a regimentation of the Rorschach into an objective test.

In our view, the Rorschach should be used primarily as it usually has been by clinicans, not as a test in the classical sense but as a projective technique for the intensive study of the individual case. As expressed by Vincent and Harman (1991), "The alternative [to the Comprehensive System approach] is to use the Rorschach as it has always been: a clinical instrument, useful in exploring the idiographic world of an individual's personal mythology in the fashion of [the] Content Rorschach" (p. 599). The present text is designed to educate within this conceptual framework.

The authors would like to extend thanks to those who have reviewed an earlier edition of this manuscript: Dr. Vincent Guarnaccia, Hofstra University; Dr. Norman Tallent, private practice, Northampton, Massachusetts; and Dr. Franklin Shontz, University of Kansas (Emeritus) and Greater Kansas City Mental Health Foundation.

E.A.
M.R.
K.M.

Acknowledgments

Reproduction of the Rorschach blots in the location sheets is by permission of Verlag Hans Huber Publishers, Bern, Switzerland.

Reproduction of the Klopfer location areas is by permission of Harcourt Brace Jovanovich, Publishers.

Reproduction of the Beck list of populars is by permission of Grune & Stratton, Inc.

1

History and Current
Status of the
Rorschach Technique

EARLY HISTORY OF INKBLOT TECHNIQUES

The Pre-Rorschach Period

The pre-Rorschach use of inkblots and similar ambiguous stimuli has a long history (Tulchin, 1940; Zubin et al., 1965). Zubin and Eron (cited in Holtzman, Thorpe, Swartz, & Herron, 1961) divide the history of inkblot usage into three distinct periods. In the pre-experimental period, inkblot usage was character-ized by "occasional observations that inkblots and other vague, formless stimuli were useful to the artist, the poet, and the spiritualist to stimulate the imagination, foretell the future, or communicate with spirits" (Holtzman et al., 1961, p. 3). In the 15th century, Leonardo da Vinci quoted Botticelli as stating that when a sponge full of various colors is thrown against a wall, a blot is produced in which figures of people, various animals, etcetera may be perceived. Da Vinci suggested the use of such perceptions for artistic inspira-tion (Zubin et al., 1965). Da Vinci did not limit the use of ambiguous stimuli to "inkblots." He stated:

> Don't take my advice lightly when I advise you, even though it may appear boring to stop and gaze at wall spots, or at the ashes in the fire, in the clouds, or in the mud and at similar things; you will, if you consider it carefully, discover in it many wonderful things. For the

painter's spirit is aroused to new things by it, be it in composition of battles, of animals and men, or in the various compositions of landscapes and of unusual things such as devils, and their like, which are calculated to bring you honor. Through the indescribable and indefinite things, the spirit becomes awakened to new discoveries. (DaVinci, quoted in Zubin et al., 1965, p. 167)

Presumably these perceptions of the artist drew from unconscious symbolic images, similar to what is seen with the Rorschach technique.

Shakespeare, as usual hundreds of years ahead of his time in psychological insight, briefly included an interaction between Hamlet and Polonius on the shapes to be seen in a cloud.

The 19th-century poet Kerner produced inkblots by folding paper over drops of ink. The figures so produced stimulated him to poetry. Many of these poems were printed with their accompanying blots. The inkblots became popular as a parlor game, with each person trying to use the blots to foretell the future (Zubin et al., 1965).

The Experimental Period

The second stage delineated by Zubin and Eron, the experimental period, began when Binet and Henri (1896) took a psychometric approach to inkblots, utilizing them as a test of imagination in their search for a valid test of intelligence. In America, Dearborn (1897, 1898) used inkblots to study the "content of consciousness"—that is, memory, imagination, after-images, and associative processes. He also used inkblots to test for differences of reaction time. Kirkpatrick (1900) found that young children and older children were more certain in their responses to an inkblot task than were children in grades four to six. Pyle (1913, 1915) noted that dull children responded in the same manner as younger children—they were uncritical and gave many responses. Whipple (1910) and Sharp (1899) used inkblots as measures of imagination. Bartlett (1916) and Parsons (1917) analyzed inkblot responses primarily on the basis of content. Bartlett distinguished between specific responses (i.e., personal reminiscences) and general responses. Parsons classified her subjects' responses into such categories as animal associations, human beings, and architecture.

Hermann Rorschach

The third period in inkblot usage discussed by Zubin and Eron began with the work of Hermann Rorschach. Rorschach was born in 1884, in Zurich, Switzerland, the son of an art teacher. In school, Rorschach was nicknamed "Klex," meaning "inkblot" or "painter," an appellation possibly indicating his classmates' expectation that he would follow his father's profession (Zubin et al., 1965). Rorschach decided in favor of medicine and attended universities between 1904 and 1909. From 1909 to 1913 he worked as a resident in psychiatry at an asylum. He received his M.D. in 1912, having written a dissertation under Eugen Bleuler entitled "On Reflex-Hallucinations and Kindred Manifestations." During this time Rorschach carried out several inkblot studies, but he was primarily interested in psychoanalysis.

In 1913 Rorschach worked in Russia, his wife's native country. But a year later he returned to Switzerland, where he began to experiment with his patients' inkblot perceptions. Rorschach worked with many inkblots, which he administered to a variety of patients with varying diagnoses. On the basis of his observations, Rorschach incorporated into his scoring system response categories that seemed to differentiate between diagnostic groups. He further refined his scoring categories by administering the test to individuals of supposedly known characteristics, such as mental defectives and artists. "Rorschach's methodology thus represented an early, informal, and relatively subjective application of criterion keying" (Anastasi, 1976, p. 560). Rorschach was so encouraged by his results that he decided to write a monograph describing his findings. However, before Rorschach completed his work, a report by Hens was published in 1917 dealing with the use of inkblots with children, normal adults, and the mentally ill. Rorschach was critical of this approach because of its emphasis on content and the relation of responses to such factors as vocational interest and current events.

Rorschach's monograph, *Psychodiagnostik*, was published in 1921. His initial experimentation had been done with 15 blots, but he was only able to have his work printed by agreeing to limit the test to 10. The printer also reduced the blot cards in size, eliminated parts of blots, and altered their colors. In addition, an imperfect printing process resulted in varieties of shading that were not originally intended by Rorschach (Ellenberger, 1954). These altered and imperfect reproductions of Rorschach's plates constitute what is now known as the Rorschach test or, as we prefer to term it, the *Rorschach technique*. This incredible and almost accidental formation of the final form of the blots contrasts strikingly with the subsequent devotion of many Rorschachers to Hermann Rorschach's categories and interpretations.

Rorschach presented his test before the Swiss Psychiatric Society and the Swiss Psychoanalytic Society, but not many of his colleagues were interested in his work. Few copies of the book were sold. The test was described to the German Society of Experimental Psychology, but it was attacked by Wilhelm Stern. Hermann Rorschach died in 1922 at the age of 38, never to know of the extraordinary and widespread success of his instrument. In his entire lifetime, Rorschach earned approximately five dollars from the Rorschach test (Ellenberger, 1989).

RORSCHACH'S TEST

Rorschach wrote that "in scoring the answers given by subjects, the content is considered last. It is more important to study the function of perception and apperception" (Rorschach, 1921/1942, p. 19). Rorschach thus held that the procedure was essentially perceptual in nature. Four types of questions were to be asked with respect to Rorschach protocols (Rorschach, 1921/1942, p. 19):

1. How many responses are there? What is the reaction time? How frequently is refusal to answer encountered for the several plates?
2. Is the answer determined only by the form of the blot, or is there also appreciation of movement or color?
3. Is the figure conceived and interpreted as a whole or in parts? Which are the parts interpreted?
4. What does the subject see? Rorschach's preliminary answers to these questions and sample protocols make up the bulk of the *Psychodiagnostik.*

Rorschach concluded that the answers to the questions would reveal which of the so-called "types" the subject belonged to (e.g., introversive versus extratensive experience type). Rorschach further held that the formal characteristics of the responses revealed aspects of the individual under study. For example, "the more color responses predominate over kinaesthetic responses, the more unstable the affectivity of the subject" (Rorschach, 1921/1942, p. 182). Finally, Rorschach asserted that the test was very useful in diagnosis and as a measure of intelligence.

The Rorschach in America

Emil Oberholzer, a coworker of Rorschach, introduced the procedure to David Levy, an American psychiatrist studying in Switzerland. In 1921 Levy brought a set of Rorschach blots home with him to America. While working as chief of staff at the Institute for Child Guidance in New York, Levy taught the procedure to Samuel Beck, a psychology trainee. At about the same time, Manfred Bleuler, a psychiatrist, introduced the Rorschach at the Boston Psychopathic Hospital.

In 1930 Beck published a Rorschach study involving the diagnosis of the feebleminded; it was the first published Rorschach research in the United States. Beck received a fellowship in 1934 that enabled him to study the test with Oberholzer in Zurich. Beck was soon joined by Marguerite Hertz and Bruno Klopfer in intensive efforts at developing and encouraging the use of the Rorschach in America. Major Rorschach scoring systems in the United

States were put forward over the years by Beck, Klopfer and Piotrowski. Other systems include those of Hertz and of Rapaport and Schafer.

Changing Attitudes Toward the Rorschach

After the death of Hermann Rorschach, his technique gradually came to assume prominence among instruments used by clinicians in the United States and in other parts of the world. However, it was subject to a number of criticisms even during the early period of use. The present authors surveyed book reviews dealing with the Rorschach (Aronow & Reznikoff, 1973) and found a number of trends. In early reviews, dating from before World War II to soon after the war, considerable optimism characterized the field of Rorschach psychology. In some instances the Rorschach was compared favorably with the Stanford-Binet in importance and usefulness. The major criticism of the instrument in the early reviews accused its users of being a "cult of the initiated" who employed complex terminology undecipherable to outsiders. A need for comprehensive norms was also voiced in the early reviews, as was a somewhat defensive posture toward criticism from the academic community. As stated by Holtzman et al. (1961), "The mainstream of academic psychology looked askance at the Rorschach movement, criticizing its cultist character and lack of scientific discipline" (p. 4).

World War II brought with it a great need for psychodiagnostic evaluation in the armed services. The Rorschach became the major psychodiagnostic tool during the war; training manuals were rushed into print and many people were trained in Rorschach procedure. Following the war, graduate training in psychology increased tremendously, and the Rorschach became one of the major clinical tools.

In the postwar period, however, failure to validate many of Rorschach's hypotheses became increasingly known in the field. Thus, later book reviews surveyed by Aronow and Reznikoff (1973) show a shift from optimism to pessimism about the test's value. The Rorschach was described by many reviewers as flatly invalid. Rorschachers were criticized for their resistance to modifying their interpretive systems in light of new research findings, for the rivalry that existed between the major Rorschach schools (e.g., Beck versus Klopfer), for the overemphasis on scoring, and for the lack of links with theoretical psychology as a whole.

Consequently, use of the Rorschach in research began a period of decline, as did that of other projective instruments. This decline in popularity was documented by a survey of test references in the psychological literature carried out by Buros (1970). Rorschach references as a percentage of all test references went from 18.4% in 1939 to a high of 36.4% in 1954. After this peak the percentage gradually dropped to 11.3% in 1968. Thelen, Varble, and Johnson (1968) observed that projective techniques declined substantially in use and importance among academic clinical psychologists. In a later survey of a similar sample reported by Thelen and Ewing (1970), the respondents favored an emphasis on instruction in research and therapy in lieu of diagnosis. Biederman and Cerbus (1971) noted a corresponding decrease in the number of Rorschach courses offered in clinical training programs.

The decline of the Rorschach technique has also been apparent, although less pronounced, in the clinical sector of psychology. Sundberg (1961) surveyed 185 clinical settings and reported that the Rorschach was used in 92% of them; 59% reported that the Rorschach was used "in a majority of cases." Lubin, Wallis, and Paine (1971) repeated the Sundberg survey on 251 clinical settings. This later survey found that although 91% still used the Rorschach, only 35% used it with a majority of cases. As stated by Holt (1968), there are a number of reasons for this decline of the Rorschach and of projective techniques in general, including the expansion and acceptance of the clinical psychologist's role to include functions other than diagnosis. However, it is also likely that discouraging validity evidence played a prominent role in the decline of the Rorschach.

Dana (1978) noted that the clinical usage of the Rorschach is "no longer ubiquitous or routine" (p. 1041), with the Rorschach reported to be third in frequency of test usage in 1971. Peterson (1978) stated, "The general lack of predictive validity for the Rorschach raises serious questions about its continued use in clinical practice" (p. 1042).

However, some recent studies have indicated that news of the death of the Rorschach and other projective techniques "has been greatly exaggerated." For example, Wade, Baker, Morton, and Baker (1978) found that in clinical contexts both objective and projective tests were used with great frequency. Similarly, Piotrowski (1984, 1985), Piotrowski, Sherry, and Keller (1985), and Piotrowski and Keller (1978, 1989a, 1989b) found that practicing clinicians viewed projective techniques "with favor." This has proven to be less the case, however, in more academic settings (Durand, Blanchard, & Mindell, 1988; Piotrowski, 1984, Piotrowski and Keller, 1984b) and among adherents of behavior therapy (Piotrowski and Keller, 1984a; Wade et al., 1978).

Lubin, Larsen, Matarazzo, and Seever (1985) found the Rorschach to be the fourth most frequently used test behind the MMPI, WAIS, and Bender-Gestalt across various clinical settings, again suggesting that the procedure's demise is far from having occurred. The work of Exner in the popularization of the Comprehensive System has doubtless been instrumental in preventing the end of the Rorschach.

The Holtzman Inkblot Technique

Although a number of inkblot scales have been proposed since the advent of the Rorschach—for example, the Bero test (Zulliger, 1941/1969) and the

Howard Inkblot Test (Howard, 1953)—the Holtzman inkblot technique has been by far the most successful of these other inkblot sets. Wayne Holtzman and his coworkers published *Inkblot Perception and Personality* in 1961. This book presented the Holtzman inkblot technique (HIT), an inkblot test specifically designed to avoid the psychometric deficiencies of the Rorschach. The HIT has two parallel forms, A and B. Each form contains a series of 45 cards. The parallel forms make it possible to assess the temporal stability of the HIT and also facilitate the test's use as a before-and-after measure in experimentation. The HIT permits only one response per card and thus, unlike the Rorschach, holds test productivity constant for all subjects.

Other problems of the Rorschach that were specifically dealt with in the development of the HIT were the lack of objectivity in the inquiry period and the frequent lack of agreement on scoring criteria, particularly with respect to the determinants. The HIT provides for an inquiry immediately after each response. This inquiry invariably consists of three standard questions, and the scoring procedures are standardized in terms of rating scales. Each response is scored for 22 variables. The HIT manual presents extensive data on reliability, and validity data are also available (Gamble, 1972; Holtzman, 1968). Anastasi (1988) describes both the reliability and the validity data for the HIT as "promising."

The major criticism of the HIT pertains to the loss of information that may be entailed in limiting the subject to one response per blot. "The clinician accustomed to subjective analysis may feel that something vital has been lost if he cannot observe a sequence of responses to a single stimulus" (Coan, 1965, p. 440). Martin (1968) has also pointed to the loss of potential for sequence analysis. Hayslip and Darbes (1974) administered the HIT under an altered procedure requiring five responses per blot. These researchers found that there was a tendency for responses from the first through the fifth to become more dissimilar, a finding implying that information may be lost through the established HIT procedure.

THE CONTENT APPROACH

Hermann Rorschach's neglect of content led to little interest in the content approach for many years, although it appears that Rorschach's own attitude toward content interpretation was undergoing a change prior to his untimely death (Brown, 1953, 1960). In a posthumous monograph published by Rorschach's colleague Oberholzer (Rorschach & Oberholzer, 1924), Rorschach discussed at length the application of the Rorschach technique to a psychoanalytic understanding of the individual case. He compared the Rorschach percept to a dream, noting that the Rorschach percept is analogous to the manifest dream content, requiring interpretation as to latent content. Correspondences between Rorschach technique content and dream content of various clients are highlighted. Much of Rorschach's discussion seems contemporary and content-based.

For example, in one instance Rorschach described the protocol of a politician:

> [This record] had as the only kinesthetic interpretation two gigantic idols clinging to something. Combined with these were several . . . answers which always repeated the same theme: . . . the core of the earth and the like. At the same time . . . there were some abstract interpretations . . . which, again, are variations of a certain theme: the germ out of which everything is to be developed. . . . [These] interpretations lead us at least to suspect that there are world-creative phantasies present, and which betray how the man came to be a politician . . . Such experiences have . . . demonstrated that the contents of the interpretations given to the experiment can be of some importance. (pp. 368–369)

A number of similar interpretations by Rorschach of inkblot content appear in this monograph. It is interesting to speculate if Rorschach's increased interest in content would have continued and progressed had he not died so young. It is clear that content is presented in this monograph in a much more important light than in Rorschach's original *Psychodiagnostik*.

A shift to increased interest in content began in the late 1940s. Lindner (1946) wrote of the possible symbolic meaning of specific Rorschach responses; Hertzman and Pearce (1947) published a quasi-experimental study demonstrating types of personality interpretations that can be made from the content of certain test responses. Rapaport et al. (1946) emphasized the importance of the subject's verbalizations during testing.

Rapaport et al. (1946) published as part of their text a now famous exposition on the analysis of pathological verbalizations on the Rorschach. As noted in Aronow and Reznikoff (1976) this analysis has held up well in the research literature. Pathological verbalizations were included in both the HIT and the Comprehensive System. This type of Rorschach interpretation is discussed intensively in Chapter 8.

In 1949, two major content approaches were published: the anxiety and hostility scales of Elizur and the Wheeler signs of homosexuality. In 1950, Sen published an article reporting a study in which content scales developed by Burt (1945) demonstrated considerable validity in contrast to Rorschach perceptual scales. De Vos (1952) produced a series of scales of affective symbolism, and Schafer (1954) published his well-known exposition of Rorschach interpretation from a psychoanalytic perspective. In 1958, Fisher and Cleveland published their Barrier and Penetration scales, which were conceptualized as measures of permeability of body boundaries. Other major content and contextual scales developed over the years include the elaborations of the

Zubin scales (Zubin et al., 1965), Holt's Primary and Secondary Process scoring (Holt & Havel, 1960), the Rorschach Index of Repressive Style (Levine & Spivack, 1964), the Endicott scales of depression and suspiciousness (Endicott, 1972), and the Singer and Wynne (1966) Communication Defects and Deviances system for use with families.

With the availability of a wide variety of content scales, research interest in the Rorschach shifted toward content and the analysis of verbalizations. As noted by Ogdon (1975), many Rorschach research studies in the 1960s and 1970s dealt at least in part with the interpretation of content. Anastasi (1976), Eron (1965), Klopfer (1968), and Zubin et al. (1965) have pointed out that the validity evidence thus far developed on content scales is quite impressive. This circumstance has led several investigators to suggest that the analysis of content and verbalization may indeed offer the most productive approach to the Rorschach (Aronow & Reznikoff, 1973; Eron, 1965; Zubin et al., 1965). Unfortunately, while nomothetic content scales have frequently been shown to be valid for research purposes, Aronow and Reznikoff (1976) concluded that they were not sufficiently reliable for use in the clinical context.

In the last two decades a number of authors have focused on the development of scales to measure various aspects of "object relations." Many of these scales have been heavily based on content and "pathological verbalizations." These scales include the Lerner (1991) approach, Urist's 1977 work on the assessment of object relations, and the work of Blatt and his coworkers on the quality of object representation on the Rorschach (e.g., Blatt, 1990; Blatt, Brenneis, Schimek, & Glick, 1976; Blatt & Lerner, 1983; Blatt, Tuber, & Auerbach, 1990). In the latter series of studies, Blatt and his colleagues worked on developing a Rorschach scoring system roughly based on Werner's concept of differentiation. The scoring system has been used to measure the degree of normal development of the concept of the object. The scale includes both formal and content-based categories. The scale shows developmental change from adolescence to adulthood (Blatt et al., 1976) and discriminates significantly between various clinical groups (e.g., Blatt et al., 1976; Ritzler, Wyatt, Harder, & Kaskey, 1980).

In very recent years, while content-based scoring systems have been put forward, the bulk of research publications on the Rorschach has shifted to studies dealing with the Comprehensive System, which is, of course, largely perceptually based.

THE RORSCHACH AS AN IDIOGRAPHIC INSTRUMENT

As noted in the Preface, the terms *idiographic* and *nomothetic* were first coined by Allport (1937, 1961) to describe two approaches to the study of personality, the first emphasizing the uniqueness of the individual, the latter studying how the subject compares with others on common dimensions. Allport (1962) later substituted the term *morphogenic* for *idiographic*, based on his belief that the relative uniqueness of the individual is based on differences in pattern. However, the term *morphogenic* has never really "caught on," and it is for this reason that the term *idiographic* is used in this text.

Tallent (1992) describes the Rorschach as "an instrument with polymorphous potential" (p. 50), that is, an instrument that can be used to derive scores as one does on a classic psychological test or to tap the individual's idiographic views of the self and the world from a phenomenological frame of reference.

Zubin et al. (1965) are usually credited as being the first to suggest that the Rorschach can best be viewed not as a test, but as a type of interview. "Its correct evaluation, like the correct evaluation of any interview, depends on its content and the characteristic ways of thinking which it reveals" (p. 312).

Blatt (1986) has similarly approached the Rorschach as something of an idiographic instrument, noting the historical shift away from the "objective" approach. How the individual uniquely constructs his or her world is seen as the dominant issue. He further states:

> Psychology has begun to shift from the view that reality is well defined and that we must understand how individuals come to perceive this reality veridically, to a view that reality is constructed by each individual based on his relative position and assumptions. (p. 345)

Anastasi (1976), Hock (1992), Korchin and Schuldberg (1981), Frank (1990), and numerous other authors have gravitated to the position that the Rorschach is most productive when viewed as an idiographic technique rather than a test per se. Even Exner (1986a) has written that the term *scores* may be inappropriate for Rorschach scoring categories, preferring the term *coding*.

THE COMPREHENSIVE SYSTEM

In a book published in 1969, John Exner summarized the differences between the various major Rorschach systems then extant (e.g., Beck, Klopfer). In 1974, he presented his own amalgamation and enlargement of Rorschach scoring categories in his own system, called the Comprehensive System. The Comprehensive System has attempted to answer many of the criticisms pertaining to the lack of standardization in administration and scoring procedures. Extensive norms are also provided. The Comprehensive System quickly established dominance, currently seen by its use in over 80% of psychology training programs (Ritzler & Alter, 1986). It has been an evolving and changing system, not to mention complex, dealing with as many as 313 structural features of the test. As noted by Anastasi (1988), "the availability of this system and its accompanying research have injected new life into the Rorschach as a potential psychometric instrument" (p. 599). Parker, Hanson, and Hunsley (1988) essentially concluded that the Comprehensive System has succeeded in demonstrating both adequate reliability and validity for the Rorschach. Shontz and Green (1992) reported recent personal communication from I. B. Weiner stating, "Anyone who currently believes that the Rorschach is an unsound test with limited utility has not read the relevant literature of the last 20 years or, having read it, has not grasped its meaning." Shontz and Green further noted that the Comprehensive System "promises to introduce a hitherto unfamiliar consistency into the research literature if not into actual clinical practices" (p. 150).

Exner's psychometric use of the Rorschach even extends to computer interpretation of the instrument, with the introduction of the Rorschach Interpretation Assistance Program (RIAP), with coded responses producing a three-section report approximately five pages in length (Exner, 1985).

However, the Comprehensive System has not gone without criticism. Vincent and Harman (1991) statistically analyzed the Exner scoring categories and determined that there is insufficient variability to justify their use in a clinical context, with the exception of pathological verbalizations. They criticize validation studies of the system for their small sample sizes given the large number of variables analyzed, possibly leading to spurious significance. They note that cross-validation studies have rarely been forthcoming. Frank (1990) stresses that formal scoring even with the Comprehensive System is insufficient for clinical purposes. Gregory (1992) describes the preponderance of research as pointing to low reliability, with the Exner system failing to tackle "the most urgent topic of external validity" (p. 456). Blatt and Berman (1984) do not believe that the complex data integration recommended by Exner is even possible.

In a more systematic critique of the Comprehensive System, Ziskin and Faust (1988) have noted that temporal stability, while much better than earlier systems, is often below the .80 cutoff seen as necessary for clinical use. They remarked that Exner also seems to arbitrarily dismiss low coefficients as indicative of changes in "state" and that validity studies have been quite mixed. They also questioned the ability of clinicians to integrate such a large number of quantitative findings and further noted that many psychologists trained in the Comprehensive System use only part of the system or gravitate to an idiosyncratic "Exner-influenced" scoring, despite Exner's injunction that the system should be used *in toto* or not at all.

The present authors also see certain technical and other issues concerning the Comprehensive System that have not yet been sufficiently addressed; we believe that conclusions as to the reliability, validity, and general usefulness of the system are premature.

First, with regard to the issue of reliability, one should be aware that Exner bases his estimate of temporal stability of the instrument on test-retest coefficients. These coefficients are the evidence for the reliability of the Comprehensive System. While the absence of alternate forms has not infrequently led test researchers to compute test-retest coefficients, this sometimes common practice is not a particularly justifiable one. As stated in the *Standards for Educational and Psychological Testing* published by the American Psychological Association, "Estimates of stability based on a retest with the same form . . . may be spuriously inflated due to the effects of memory" (1985, p. 21). Anastasi (1988) similarly notes that "the test-retest technique [of determining reliability] presents difficulties when applied to psychological tests. . . . For the large majority of psychological tests . . . retesting with the identical test is not an appropriate technique for finding a reliability coefficient" (p. 118).

We believe that the Rorschach in particular, even more than other psychological assessment instruments, is susceptible to memory effects even over very long periods of time. As we have previously stated:

> In our own experience, Rorschach percepts have a high degree of salience for many subjects, which results in their remembering and associating percepts with the particular Rorschach cards over extended periods of time. If such is the case, one might expect a spuriously high estimate of temporal stability based on test-retest reliability coefficients. (Reznikoff, Aronow, & Rauchway, 1982, p. 98)

Schlesinger (1973) has also commented on the extraordinary amounts of time over which a subject can still recall his or her Rorschach percepts. For these reasons, we have recommended against the clinical use of inkblot content scales, given the misleading quality of available test-retest coefficients and the clear unreliability of the same scales when alternate-form reliability has been assessed via the HIT (Reznikoff et al., 1982). In short, the reliability of the Comprehensive System is far from proven.

We also believe that it is a mistake to assume that the notorious psychometric problems of the Rorschach have disappeared because of the advent of the Comprehensive System. For instance, many of the variables of the Comprehensive System continue to have problems of skewness and kurtosis of distributions, which present all kinds of difficulties. The issue of controlling for response productivity is a rather important case in point in this regard. In an article entitled "R in Rorschach Research: A Ghost Revisited," Exner (1992a) argues that changes introduced in the Comprehensive System have in most cases reduced the issue of R to the point where it is no longer a major problem. Other articles, however, view the problem as still being substantial. For example, Meyer (1992a) has noted that R is consistently and highly correlated with many scoring categories of the Comprehensive System. He notes that pre–Comprehensive System factor-analytic studies suggest that the proportion of variance among Rorschach scores accounted for by R is generally as high as 50%. At one point Meyer suggests that "it may be that variable R is like Achilles' heel in the normative use of structural data" (p. 242).

In a further article, Meyer (1992b) reports on a factor-analytic investigation of the Comprehensive System. In this study the first two dimensions were found to be aspects of response productivity. Again, Meyer reports that even using the Comprehensive System, the R factor accounts for about 50% of what is measured by the scoring system. "Unfortunately this role is inconsistent with the minimal significance that is generally afforded to R when interpreting a protocol" (p. 130). Meyer also notes, disturbingly, that "the Rorschach's internal structure does not clearly correspond to that which would be expected from traditional variable interpretation" (p. 132).

It is certainly not Exner's fault that the Rorschach lacks an alternate form, or that the subject is generally free to choose the number of responses given. To change this latter characteristic might well limit the idiographic information provided by the instrument. However, we believe that it is fair to say that the test-retest coefficients reported for the Comprehensive System must be considered highly suspect, and the problem of R remains thorny and unresolved. Should one want for some reason to develop a refined psychometric inkblot test, one might do better to start with the Holtzman inkblot technique (test?), which already has an alternate form, controls for number of responses, and so forth.

A further criticism of the Comprehensive System concerns the exclusion of the many categories of content scoring systems that have shown a remarkable relationship to variables of psychological interest in the real world (Aronow & Reznikoff, 1976). In recognition of this fact, Holtzman and his coworkers included four thematic contact variables in the HIT (viz., Anxiety, Hostility, Barrier, and Penetration). Few content variables are included in the Comprehensive System (although pathological verbalizations are an integral part). Exner does score for Aggressive Movement, Cooperative Movement, and Morbid Content. These scoring categories, however, intermingle determinant and content categories and are descriptive rather than psychodynamic.

Further issues concerning the Comprehensive System deal with theoretical and also practical themes. Kleiger (1992a) has asserted that the development of the Comprehensive System would have benefited from clearer theoretical underpinnings. It is commonly agreed that an empirical finding predicted by a theory is likely to prove more robust and have greater explanatory power than an empirical observation that is not embedded in a theoretical context.

As Exner (1986a) describes it, the approach to building the Comprehensive System was data-based, beginning with an exhaustive examination of the empirical literature on the perceptual-nomothetic systems that were developed between 1920 and 1970 in the spirit of Hermann Rorschach's original approach to the test. We believe that this implicit reliance on Rorschach's original observations may not have been the best way to proceed. A specific example of our concern in this regard is the development of the scoring ("coding" in Comprehensive System terminology) for developmental level employed in the Comprehensive System.

Initially, attempts were made to integrate Friedman's (1952, 1953) developmental level scoring into the Comprehensive System. Friedman's method was based on Werner's (1948, 1957) theory of cognitive development and has received much empirical support (cf. Goldfried, Stricker, & Weiner, 1971). Several problems arose in this effort, including "possibly most important, one of [Friedman's] developmentally low categories is directly correlated with . . . the form quality of response. The developmental quality codes relate [to] the levels of cognitive functioning, whereas the coding for form quality relates to perceptual accuracy or conventionality" (Exner, 1986a, p. 95). Here Exner seems to have accepted Rorschach's original interpretation of form quality, without considering whether Werner's more comprehensive theory might offer an even more useful conceptualization. (How can perceptual accuracy not be a level of cognitive functioning?) Indeed, the efforts to overcome the shortcomings of Friedman's approach appear to have been largely empirical and inductive (Exner, 1986a). For the reasons already noted, an effort to better operationalize Werner's theory might have been a more fruitful approach to this problem. This concern is reinforced by the observation that many of the empirical findings cited in support of the Comprehensive System have not been cross-validated (cf. Ziskin & Faust, 1988).

We also feel that much of the published empirical support for the Comprehensive System is somewhat removed from everyday clinical concerns. A number of the studies can best be described as basic, as opposed to applied, science. For example, Exner (1986a) reviewed 23 elegant, fascinating studies of the process of responding to the Rorschach stimuli that he conducted with his students and colleagues at Long Island University and the Rorschach Research Foundation. However, it is difficult to see the practical import of the observation that individuals typically scan an entire blot even if they choose to respond to only a portion of it. A number of the studies that more directly inform the interpretation of the Comprehensive System codes have also taken a construct validation approach of uncertain external validity. The development and interpretation of the "Four Square" and related derivations (i.e., relationships among color, movement, shading, and achromatic codes; see Exner 1986a, chapter 14), for example, appear to rest heavily on two laboratory studies of problem-solving style (Exner, 1978; 1991; Wiener-Levy & Exner, 1981). While such studies are undoubtedly useful, studies that deal with the implications of the codes employing indices of real-life stress tolerance and coping are needed. Do well-adjusted individuals experiencing a given number of negative life events have a more flexible problem-solving style, as indexed by the Comprehensive System, than do less effective copers who are experiencing the same level of stress?

Perhaps partly as a result of these validation strategies, some of the Comprehensive System interpretations are couched in language that lacks concrete, intervention-relevant referents (Kleiger, 1992a, 1992b). For example:

> Her personality organization is somewhat less mature than might be expected. . . . [T]he impact of stress is diffuse. . . . [S]he is considerably more complex now than she has been previously. . . . She appears to be willing to process emotional stimuli. . . . [S]he is prone to experience frequent difficulties when interacting with the environment. . . . [A]lthough she is more conservative in her processing effort, the process is reasonably consistent and sophisticated. (Exner, 1991, pp. 411–417)

Another sign that the Comprehensive System is somewhat removed from everyday clinical concerns is the fact that there have been no studies addressing the clinical bottom line. That is, there have been no studies of whether the finished, Comprehensive System–based interpretation makes a positive contribution to patient care. This is of obvious practical importance given the ever mounting pressure to justify the use of clinical procedures in order to receive third-party reimbursement. It is of particular concern with the Comprehensive System because, as Ziskin and Faust (1988) have pointed out, the system has grown to be so large and so complex that clinicians may not be able to use it in a reliable and valid way. Exner's (cf. 1991, pp. 233–423) numerous, extraordinarily detailed examples of his interpretative approach may inadvertently contribute to this problem by fostering a test-based rather than a client-based approach to Rorschach interpretation. That is, the examples do not approach interpretation by first posing the question "What hypotheses do I have about this individual that I need help from the Rorschach to confirm or disconfirm," examining the data pertinent to those hypotheses, and concluding the interpretation. Rather, the interpretative process is kicked off by examining 11 "key" Comprehensive System variables that guide the remainder of the interpretative process. The interpretation then proceeds, albeit in different sequences, through all the 300-plus variables yielded by the Comprehensive System (Exner, 1991). This approach results in a comprehensive description of the individual, but we fear that it may also yield a lot of error. It may also be too time-consuming and expensive for mental health practice in the 21st century.

In our opinion, psychometric issues are not the major problem of the

Comprehensive System. Exner and his colleagues have clearly done an incredible job, accomplishing much more than anyone would have deemed possible
in making the Rorschach a true "test." Our concern is primarily with the
neglect of what we see as the idiographic and psychodynamic richness of this
instrument. We view it as a fundamental mistake to try to "regiment" this
clinically sensitive procedure into some sort of inkblot version of an MMPI.
Too much is lost in the process, and too little gained as a result. Psychological
assessment of personality should include both nomothetic and idiographic—
objective and projective—approaches in combination. This brings the unique
strengths of each to bear. If one wants an objective test, there are many more
suitable instruments available, with time demands on the psychologist far
more modest. Why sacrifice the clinically sensitive and versatile Rorschach
technique in such a quest?

A major difficulty, as we see it, has to do with the fact that the Rorschach
technique is a "psychoanalytic tool par excellance" in psychology (Willock,
1992). Peterson (1978) has noted that the extraordinary popularity of the
Rorschach among clinicians has been due not to the scoring categories, but to
the procedure's ability to generate psychodynamic associations (although
Peterson himself is hardly a proponent of this approach). Exner, however,
does not see the Rorschach this way. Despite the best of intentions and
prodigious efforts, the Comprehensive System significantly "misses the boat"
on maximizing the Rorschach. In a 1989 article entitled "Searching for Projection in the Rorschach," Exner goes so far as to state, "Unfortunately, the
Rorschach has been erroneously mislabeled as a projective test for far too
long" (p. 527). As noted by Willock (1992):

> The title [of Exner's article] reveals how different his perspective is
> from the psychoanalytic psychologist's for whom this title would be
> analogous to announcing an intention of searching for trees in the
> forest. To the psychoanalytic psychologist, one does not have to hunt
> for projection as if it were as rare as a five-leaf clover. Projection is
> ubiquitous in the Rorschach. (p. 100)

The Comprehensive System is thus, ironically, singularly non-compre-
hensive: For the most part it does not make use of the Rorschach's principal
strength, that is, its ability to yield incredibly rich psychodynamic and idiographic data. As stated by Willock (1992):

> Non projective tests may yield important information about aspects
> of mental functioning. They will not, however, reveal the essence of
> the psyche. They cannot go to the heart of the patient's problems. It
> is only in being creative that the individual discovers the self, and it
> is only through creative, projective media, such as the Rorschach, that

psychologists can discover the selves of their patients in all their multifaceted complexity. (p. 115)

Shontz and Green (1992) have commented that the Comprehensive System's emphasis on uniformity of administration and scoring—treating the Rorschach as a standardized "test"—"may have transformed the instrument into something that its originator and many of its users might not wish it to be" (p. 150). They further state:

Students may be gaining the impression that the Rorschach is valued mostly for its quantitative analyses and that interpretations derived from qualitative analyses are less valuable than or may even be replaced by quantitative indexes. If this is the case, students may be losing much of the richness that is inherent in Rorschach records. (p. 152)

Leslie Phillips, the author of *Rorschach Interpretation: Advanced Technique* (1953) has likewise suggested that the recent strong psychometric focus of the Rorschach is a mistake.

I'm unhappy with the recent "Americanization" of the Rorschach test and its reconstruction as simply an objective, formal test of perceptual and personality functioning. Within this orientation no unitary theory of personality provides a coherent framework for the understanding of Rorschach performance. Rather, a hodgepodge of formulations are drawn upon for test interpretation that range from the descriptive to the psychoanalytic. Personally, I prefer to treat the Rorschach not so much as a *test*, but as a situation in which the client is actively and intensely involved.
        . . . Exner and most writers on the Rorschach appear to prefer to start Rorschach interpretation with the scoring summary. I do not. I believe that personality is most directly expressed and is most directly observed in the moment-to-moment behavioral manifestations of the client as he responds to the Rorschach blots. (Phillips, 1992, p. 9)

The present authors are similarly concerned that the Comprehensive System approach to the Rorschach may be leading a generation of American Rorschachers in the wrong direction. It is our hope that this text can help redirect American Rorschach efforts in a more idiographic and clinically relevant direction.

It should be noted that outside the United States the psychometric approach to the Rorschach is generally not as highly regarded. In a summary of the Congress of the International Rorschach Society held in Paris in 1990, Smith (1992) notes:

> The most memorable aspect of the meetings . . . was the intense (and at times acrimonious) debate between psychoanalytic and empirical Rorschachists. This was all the more polarized as it represented essentially a split between North Americans and Europeans. . . . The majority of the contributions from this side of the Atlantic were empirical in nature and based upon John Exner's Comprehensive System. Cultural stereotypes seemed to fuel the debate, and the Americans were frequently dismissed as obsessed with numbers and conceptually bankrupt. (p. 5)

Shontz and Green (1992) have similarly noted the dichotomy between recent English-language (largely American) and non–English-language publications on the Rorschach. They found that while English-language publications emphasized psychometric issues, non–English-language Rorschach references were more concerned with diagnostic and theoretical issues. Shontz and Green concluded that the most likely reason for this discrepancy is that "researchers who write in languages other than English are less concerned with psychometric issues than are English-writing investigators" (p. 151).

THE SCIENCE OF CONTENT-IDIOGRAPHIC PERSONALITY INTERPRETATION

Content-idiographic personality interpretation is clearly different from assessment based on the perceptual-nomothetic approach, but, as noted by Lipgar (1992) with respect to idiographic interpretation in particular, "the distinction . . . should not be used to dismiss the need to meet the standards of scientific method" (p. 226). Content-idiographic personality interpretation based on the Rorschach technique or on other projective techniques or sources of information must be under the umbrella of science.

In general, we find three general types of content-idiographic information revealed by the Rorschach technique, which, though they often overlap and merge, have different implications for scientific validation.

The first type we might call "informational." This essentially involves declarative statements by the subject about his or her life, history, or feelings. This type of information is particularly prevalent when our altered inquiry procedure is used to garner associations to the Rorschach percepts. An example would be a female patient's associations on Card VII to the percept "two women talking": "It makes me think of how I don't talk to women much—I don't like them as people. (Why?) Girls never keep confidences." In this response, information about the patient is directly communicated as in an interview. Inferences about more subtle aspects of personality functioning are not made *at this level*. In our view, issues of scientific validation are therefore not relevant.

The second type of content-idiographic information might be called "thematic." This involves responses and associations given by the patient indicating the presence of a personality "theme" largely expressed symbolically. The theoretical substructure of this type of interpretation is psychoanalytic; it is also nomothetic (despite the interwoven presence of idiographic elements). This might involve a response of "chain saws, upside down" in the top of Card VII. The associations were: "All I can think of is the *Texas Chain Saw Massacre*." This response might be interpreted as symbolically indicating the presence of hostility.

As noted in an earlier volume (Aronow & Reznikoff, 1976), the empirical validity evidence pertaining to nomothetic content interpretation of the Rorschach technique is overwhelmingly favorable. This is true despite the fact that many of the early Rorschach studies were characterized by methodological problems and small sample sizes, which some have blamed for the generally poor validity evidence for perceptual scales. The psychoanalytically oriented content scales prove to be particularly robust—in particular, Schafer's 1954 content themes. It is interesting to note that of the empirical studies carried out to date on the 14 Schafer themes, "not one study has yet been reported which has found evidence militating against the validity of the Schafer themes" (Aronow & Reznikoff, 1976, p. 62). Clearly, far more research of this type needs to be done, and the Rorschach practitioner should be conversant with those themes that hold up well empirically and those found not to be valid. Familiarity with the Lerner (1991) system and the empirical work of Blatt on the topic of object representation are also likely to be particularly helpful. As Lipgar (1992) remarks, "Assessment of individual personality functioning. . . . [requires the] use of normative data in order to reject or defend most clinically relevant hypotheses and assessments" (pp. 226–227). Thus, while we cannot at this time recommend clinical use of content *scales* for nomothetic purposes largely because of the psychometric deficiencies of the Rorschach technique, the practitioner should be grounded in the empirical findings relating to such psychodynamic approaches. However, judgments as to the strength or extent of a theme should be avoided inasmuch as such judgment of degree requires a psychometrically sound measuring instrument.

The third type of personality interpretation that is available through the content-idiographic approach is in our view the most interesting, the most specific to the individual, and, unfortunately, the most difficult in terms of scientific validation. This might be dubbed the "complex idiographic image" interpretation. In this situation the subject presents a complex symbolic image that is a very poignant and striking representation of how the self, significant others, or important issues are viewed in the world (see also Chapter 9). This might be seen, for example, in the response of a female patient to Card V: "Some kind of insect—it's not pretty enough to be a butterfly." Her associations: "It's an ugly, black butterfly—no colors." (What does that make you think of in your own life?) "You probably want me to say myself. Well, that's probably how I thought of myself when I was younger—I never thought of myself as attractive—my sister was the attractive one. I was the ugly duckling—I did get more attractive as I got older."

In this response and associations we are vividly presented with the poor self-concept, its origin in childhood, her half-hearted attempt to avoid insight but ultimate ability to achieve it, and also some sense that this self-concept remnant from childhood is no longer accurate, if it ever was—all presented as a "gestalt."

In such responses the idiographic qualities are foremost; the individual is telling you how he or she uniquely views the self and the world. As Allport (1937, 1961) has pointed out, while other things that are studied in science also have their unique qualities, it is only in the field of personality interpretation that the unique aspects are so central in understanding the object of study.

The meaning of such responses is often transparently obvious to the psychodynamically oriented psychologist; further, the patient him- or herself may well confirm the interpretation. In addition, it should be noted that the interpretative process is quite similar to what is seen in psychoanalytic dream interpretation. Nonetheless, it would be desirable if this type of interpretation could be brought more firmly within the realm of science than is possible from the clinical case study approach, which would not be easy. The traditional psychometric methods of reliability and validity have been developed for use with nomothetic assessment and are largely irrelevant for such purely idiographic purposes. As we have noted (Aronow, Reznikoff, & Rauchway, 1979), the complex idiographic image presents special statistical problems because one is dealing with essentially nominal data. As stated by Tolman (quoted in Allport [1962]), "I know I should be more idiographic in my research, but I just don't know how to be" (p. 414).

In a reply to an article by Exner, Kleiger (1992b) warns against the danger of "scientism," in which "scientific knowledge, understanding, and methodology become confused with scientific techniques" (p. 302). He concludes that the profession of psychology has evolved "through both objective-positivist as well as subjective-rationalist traditions" (p. 302).

Our approach to this issue is somewhat different, in that we view the clinical case study itself as a scientific tool, though inherently less dependable in reaching scientific conclusions than the experimental or correlational methods of science. Just as one turns to the correlational method when it is impractical to use the experimental method (despite the lower degree of confidence one has in conclusions reached by this method), similarly, when it is impractical to use the correlational method (as is currently the case with most idiographic issues), one must turn to the clinical case study. The case study does not test hypotheses, having more of an explorative nature. As noted by Holt (1962), "the method of clinical judgment has a great deal in common with the hypothesis forming and theory building phases of work in all the sciences" (p. 401). We do not recommend being content with this state of affairs but, rather, being committed to advancing the scientific understanding of idiographic aspects of personality functioning by the development of appropriate, scientifically sound techniques.

To start with, it should certainly be possible to develop techniques to determine the extent to which adequately trained assessors agree on the idiographic meaning of responses. Other research possibilities might involve the use and further development of statistics for the individual case, where N = 1 (e.g., Chassan, 1960, 1961). Hertzman and Pearce (1947) presented a statistical analysis of what is essentially idiographic information provided by Rorschach responses (though they do not use the term *idiographic*). They concluded that the self-concept is foremost in such information. Allport (1962) had suggested a number of ways in which idiographic methods may be employed more scientifically.

In order for an approach to be considered rigorously scientific, quantification and hypothesis testing must be brought to bear. However, it should be recognized that quantification and hypothesis testing may occur at the macro rather than the micro level, as demonstrated by Finn and Tonsager (1992); Hayes, Nelson, & Jarrett, (1987). Thus, an empirical demonstration that idiographic Rorschach interpretation speeds the psychotherapy process might well be considered sufficient validation to bring this type of interpretation most firmly within the scientific orbit.

It should also be noted that the clinical case study, despite its inferior scientific ability to test hypotheses, should not be sold short as an investigative technique. For example, the entire science of psychoanalysis was in essence built upon clinical case study. In recent years, efforts have also been made to apply the more dependable scientific methods to psychoanalysis with encouraging results (e.g., Fisher & Greenberg, 1977, 1978).

If current research efforts directed at developing the nomothetic qualities of the Rorschach could be redirected toward creative empirical research on idiographic inkblot interpretation, it might well be possible to bring such interpretation more firmly within the realm of science. Until then, idiographic personality interpretation will remain "the laggard end of our science" (Allport, 1962).

Ziskin and Faust (1988) have suggested that if our approach to the Rorschach is correct, the process of strict empirical investigation of the technique has only just begun. While this is certainly not true with respect to the first two types of information noted above, it is largely true with regard to the third type, the more purely idiographic information provided by the Rorschach technique.

Psychology is a new science, barely a hundred years old. Its object of study often presents special difficulties not evident in the older sciences, with such issues as unconscious mental processes and the uniqueness of the individual raising methodological and statistical issues not presented in other fields. However, to ignore such aspects of psychology because they are difficult to research is reminiscent of the old joke about looking for an object lost in one place somewhere else because the light is better there. While it may be natural for psychology to defensively assume a posture of "more scientific and quantitative than thou" in an effort to prove to ourselves and others our scientific credentials, it is not productive.

If psychology is to progress as a science, we must not neglect to pursue those areas that are precisely the most difficult to explore empirically. This includes in particular idiographic aspects of personality functioning. To restrict psychology to the study of the areas that can be most easily examined scientifically would be in the truest sense an unscientific path.

THE TESTING ENVIRONMENT

As Tallent (1992) has pointed out, assessment with the Rorschach is now being carried out in an environment that is far different—economically, legally, politically, and socially—from the environment in which the technique and the procedures for using it were originally developed. From a fiscal standpoint, the annual cost of health care in the United States increased 17-fold from 1960 to 1986, far outpacing the rate of inflation (American Hospital Association, 1987). Over all, mental health care is the fastest rising component of health care costs (Winslow, 1989). From a societal viewpoint, on the other hand, health care has been increasingly viewed as a basic right for all Americans (Callan & Yeager, 1991). These trends have led to vigorous efforts to contain these costs, especially mental health care costs (Kessler, 1986).

The push to contain costs does not bode well for traditional psychological assessment practices given the ambivalent view of the utility of assessment expressed in an authoritative review: "It seems self-evident that [treatment] interventions are more rational, faster, and more effective if based on prior diagnosis of the problem. . . . However, . . . [o]bjective evidence is slim" (Korchin & Schuldberg, 1981, p. 1154).

How might the current socio-political milieu affect psychological assessment? It is possible to make some educated predictions by examining legislation that is under active consideration and regulations recently developed to implement federal legislation. In 1992 a prominent psychologist told a Senate hearing that Senator (now Secretary of the Treasury) Lloyd Bentsen's national health care bill provided inadequate mental health care coverage. We fear that psychological assessment may be one of the first aspects of mental health care jettisoned in the face of inadequate funding. Discussions with experts on managed care—settings in which costs are closely scrutinized—suggest that testing is rarely employed in those settings even now.

Even more disquieting is the prospect that psychological assessment might be explicitly curtailed by legal regulations. At this writing the Social Security Administration is poised to announce new rules for determining eligibility for mental disability benefits (Freiberg, 1992). While the current rules indicate that the Rorschach may be useful in establishing the existence of a mental disorder, the proposed rules comment that projective techniques are of uncertain reliability and validity. A less extreme but still problematic outcome might be the reduction of assessment to the status of mere testing. This distinction is made in the Medicare fee schedule proposed in 1992: Psychological assessment is reimbursed as a "technical service," like a blood test, rather than as a "professional service" requiring expert knowledge to perform and interpret (DeAngelis, 1992).

We believe that a major implication of these trends is that the use of the Rorschach and other psychological assessment techniques will continue to be funded only if they are rigorously proven to help contain health care costs. That is, assessment techniques must be shown to do one or more of the following:

1. Predict who will respond to a particular treatment (e.g., Perry & Viglione, 1991)
2. Predict who will respond better to one form of treatment as opposed to another
3. Predict when, during a course of treatment, new therapeutic maneuvers should be implemented
4. Document when therapy should be discontinued
5. Contribute directly to client improvement

Furthermore, assessment techniques must also be shown to be cost-effective in performing these functions. In other words, the Rorschach must also function more cheaply than other assessment methods.

Note that we were able to cite a study (there are many others) demonstrating that the Rorschach can predict positive response to a treatment. We could find no study documenting the Rorschach's usefulness for the other four tasks. Nor could we find studies demonstrating the cost-effectiveness of the Rorschach.[1]

A discussion of all of the types of Rorschach research that needs to be done is beyond the scope of this book. Readers who wish to help document the utility of the Rorschach should consult the excellent article by Hayes et al. (1987) for methodological tips. However, we would like to assert our belief that the Rorschach technique when administered and interpreted with an emphasis on idiographic interpretation is likely to contribute directly to client improvement and to do so in a cost-effective way. Since cost-effectiveness will be a driving force of mental health practice in the 21st century, there is no surer way to justify use of the Rorschach technique than to go straight to the bottom line: Does use of the technique have a direct positive impact on the client and is it cheaper than simply forging ahead with treatment?

Finn and Butcher (1991) listed the putative benefits of incorporating test feedback into the therapeutic process as (a) an increase in self-esteem, (b) increased hope, (c) decreased symptomatology, (d) reduced feelings of isolation, (e) greater self-awareness and understanding, and (f) increased motivation for treatment. We believe that all these benefits will accrue from use of the Rorschach, especially the cost-effective use of the Rorschach technique as described in this text. Of course, we recognize that this belief is in need of empirical verification. The methodology Finn and Tonsager (1992) used to study the therapeutic benefits of the MMPI-2 is readily adaptable to the Rorschach.

As Hayes et al. (1987) trenchantly noted, "It is useful to recognize that there may even be times when an assessment could have treatment utility without the assessment having any reliability or validity whatsoever" (p. 972).

Anastasi (1988) describes two major approaches to the Rorschach, one nomothetically based, the other idiographically and more clinically based. The first approach is best represented by the Comprehensive System, with the latter represented in part by the current authors, viewing the Rorschach technique:

> as a semi-standardized clinical interview. [Focusing] on the interpretations of content [and accompanying verbalizations] rather than on structural scoring systems . . . [they] recommend a strictly clinical application of the Rorschach as a means of embracing the idiographic understanding of the individual case—and they observe that this is, in fact, how most clinicians use the Rorschach. (pp. 559–600)

It remains to be seen whether these two approaches to the Rorschach can, in fact, exist side by side, or if one will prevail in this country as well as around the world in coming decades.

▲2

Technique Administration and Blot Characteristics

TECHNIQUE ADMINISTRATION

Materials

Only a few materials are necessary for the Rorschach technique.

1. The Rorschach blots. A reasonably new set of blots should be used. The examiner should avoid using smudged or otherwise damaged inkblots.
2. Stopwatch. A stopwatch that is calibrated to seconds is desirable for purposes of calculating the reaction time to each blot.
3. Recording paper. Blank 8½" × 11" paper—5–15 sheets for each administration will be necessary, depending on the length of the record and the recording style of the examiner. The examiner may wish to use a clipboard for holding the recording sheets.
4. Forms. One or two location sheets, one summary sheet, and one tabulation sheet (see Chapter 7) will be necessary for each administration.

Setting

The procedure should be done in a comfortable, well-lighted room. The examiner should ensure that interruptions and distractions (e.g., a telephone ringing, someone knocking on the door) will not interfere with the session.

There is some controversy among psychologists as to the proper seating arrangement for Rorschach administration. Some psychologists prefer sitting to the right or left, slightly behind the subject, analogous to a psychoanalytic psychotherapy session. The present authors prefer sitting naturally at a desk with the subject at the corner. This has the advantage of not differentiating the Rorschach from other tests in the battery (intelligence test, etc.), thus avoiding the arousal of undue anxiety in the subject. This arrangement also prevents the desk being used as a barrier between examiner and subject (Fig. 2-1).

The blots are kept face down in a pile in front of the examiner, with Card I on top. The completed blots are also kept face down, with the subject placing them in the face-down position after the responses to the blot are obtained.

Rapport Considerations

The attitude the subject has about the procedure is important and can have a strong influence on the quality of the responses. If a subject perceives the procedure to be threatening or a waste of time, this will have a detrimental effect on what is elicited. It is vital, therefore, that the subject understand the purpose of the procedure, as far as is possible or practical.

It is often helpful to first ask the subject how he or she felt about coming for the session. This question can be used as a lead-in to a discussion of the subject's feelings regarding the procedure and his or her understanding of its purpose. Distortions in the subject's understanding can then be corrected, and the subject can be told, very generally or more specifically, how the session will be helpful to him or her.

This discussion with the subject must, of course, be conducted with discretion. If a subject is referred for assessment because a therapist suspects a possible underlying psychosis, for example, it would be quite inappropriate for the examiner to impart this information. Often, a very general explanation will suffice: "In order for us to help you, we would first like to know as much about you as we can."

It is important that the Rorschach technique in particular, and projective tests in general, not be regarded as procedures in which the subject can be

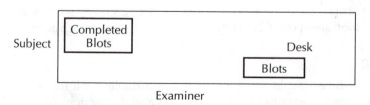

FIGURE 2-1   Suggested Seating Arrangement for Rorschach Administration

treated in a detached, mechanical, and rigid manner and "tested." While standardization of administration is of some relevance, the nature and quality of the relationship between the examiner and the subject are central to the Rorschach. It is vital that the subject experience the examiner as a helping party, someone to be trusted. Establishing such a "set" in the subject is, therefore, an important part of the testing in general and the pretest conversation in particular (Leventhal et al., 1962).

There are subjects, however, who remain resistive to and suspicious of the evaluation despite the efforts of the examiner. The administration should not necessarily be abandoned under such circumstances, but it should be recognized that the subject will likely be minimally productive on the Rorschach and other projective techniques.

Administration of the Rorschach Technique

Traditional Rorschach administration procedure involves two distinct phases of the test: the *Association phase*, in which the subject states what he or she sees in the blots, and the *Inquiry phase*, in which the examiner asks clarifying questions about the subject's responses. As will be discussed in a subsequent chapter, the examiner may wish to substitute a *Content Inquiry* for the more traditional type of inquiry. Furthermore, some examiners also use a third phase of testing, usually called *Testing-the-Limits*. This will be discussed later in this chapter. The present discussion will focus on the two traditional phases of Rorschach administration, Association and Inquiry.

Association Phase

In the Association phase, the subject is asked to state what he or she sees on all 10 blots. It is often helpful for neophyte examiners to prepare a 5" × 8" index card with the Association and Inquiry instructions and questions written on the two sides of the card. This instruction card can be kept with the Rorschach blots.

The instructions that precede the Association phase should be as follows:

I'm going to show you 10 inkblots, and I would like you to tell me what each inkblot looks like or resembles. They are not designed to look like anything in particular, so there are no right or wrong answers. Different people see different things. Now, what does this first blot look like to you?

The first blot is then handed in an upright position to the subject. It is frequently useful to encourage the subject to hold the blot in his or her hand—this seems to bring about a more active involvement on the part of the subject. If the subject is resistant to doing so, however, it is not necessary to insist.

Subjects will sometimes ask questions in an attempt to get the examiner to further structure the situation for them: e.g., "How many things should I see?" "Can I turn the card?" The response to such questions should be an indication that these decisions are up to the subject—e.g., "That's entirely up to you."

Timing is begun as soon as the blot is presented to the subject. The reaction time is recorded when the subject begins verbalizing *a scorable response.* Thus, if the subject makes a comment such as, "It doesn't look like much to me," timing continues since this is not a scorable response. If the subject then states, "It could be a bat," the timing should cease with the first word of this sentence. The notion of a scorable response will be developed further in Chapter 3.

The examiner should try to record all responses verbatim, including side comments. Although this will be difficult for novice examiners, use of a shorthand method of recording, as discussed later in this chapter, is helpful. We do not favor tape recording of responses as a substitute for the written record. Tape recording Rorschach responses greatly increases the length of time required because all tapes must be transcribed, and it does not help the novice examiner learn the skill of writing down the patient's exact comments. In the long run, the examiner usually will need to learn this anyway.

If the subject speaks too quickly for the examiner to record responses verbatim, the subject may be asked to speak more slowly, or the last few words that the subject has spoken may be repeated by the examiner while he or she records them. Such "slowing down" of the subject should be done sparingly, however, so as not to unduly affect spontaneity.

If the subject gives only one response to Card I and indicates that he or she is finished with the blot, the examiner should then say to the subject: "Some people see more than one thing. Do you see anything else?" It should be noted that this is *only* done with Card I. If more responses then follow, the examiner should continue to record them. If the patient indicates that nothing further is seen, this should be accepted. Generally, a maximum of six responses per card is sufficient. Beyond this number, a subject is likely to be repetitious and/or overly immersed in minor details of the blots. As a rule of thumb, therefore, we will stop the subject if he or she is continuing to give responses to a blot after already having offered six.

Following completion of the subject's responses to Card I, Cards II through X are presented to the subject. As each card is given to the subject, it is useful to make comments such as, "And what might this blot look like or resemble?" The presentation of the blots should be done in a relaxed and comfortable rather than a stilted and rigid manner, in keeping with the very clinical nature of the Rorschach technique.

Inquiry Phase

Following the completion of the subject's responses to the 10 blots, the Inquiry phase begins. The purpose of the Inquiry phase is to make the scoring of the traditional Rorschach categories—location, determinants, content, populars, and form-level—possible (see Chapters 3, 4, and 5).

The instructions used with the Inquiry phase begin as follows:

> There is one more part to this procedure. I'm going to go through your responses with you, and I would like you to tell me where you saw the various things that you mentioned and what about the blots made them look like that to you. Now, on the first blot (blot shown to the subject) you saw _____. Please circle on this location sheet where you saw it.

This first question of the Inquiry phase seeks to pinpoint location. On subsequent responses during the inquiry, the examiner also repeats the subject's responses from the Association phase.

The subject will circle his or her percept on the location sheet. The examiner should then label the circled percept with the appropriate number— 1, 2, and so on. If many overlapping responses to the same blot might make the location sheet difficult to decipher, a second location sheet should be used.

Sometimes subjects will misunderstand and try to circle the percept on the blot itself. The examiner should be alert to this possibility and stop the subject before the blot is damaged. The examiner may also wish to ask the subject to label parts of the response (e.g., wings, head, body, etc, of the bat), particularly if it is an atypical percept or if it is difficult for the examiner to perceive it in the blot.

Once the location of a percept is ascertained, the inquiry then turns to the question of determinants. At this point the examiner wishes to know whether the shape, the color, and/or the shading of the blots helped to determine the response, and whether movement is perceived. It should be noted that movement is the one determinant that derives essentially from the subject's imagination, in contrast to form, color, and shading, which are actual elements of the stimulus that the individual chooses to utilize or ignore. The examiner might, thus, introduce this part of the inquiry on a particular percept with a question such as: "What on the blot suggested _____ to you?" However, there is no standard set of inquiry questions.

The purpose of the inquiry is to enable the examiner to score the protocol. Thus, if the determinants of the response are clear from the Association phase, for example, there may be no need to pursue determinants in the inquiry. The simple repeating of the subject's response as a stimulus often produces verbalizations from the subject that are sufficient for scoring purposes. This is particularly the case as the inquiry progresses, and the subject understands the general direction of the inquiry.

If the examiner deems it necessary to probe for the presence of movement in connection with a percept, the examiner may wish to ask the subject to "tell me how you see (the bat)." The examiner may sometimes ask how the subject sees the arms or legs of a figure if movement is suspected as a possible determinant.

At times, the examiner may also wish to probe very generally for further information relevant to scoring—asking, for example, "Tell me more about (the bat) you saw."

An important point is that when inquiring as to determinants, the examiner must be careful *not* to directly indicate the relevant determinants. Thus, it is incorrect to ask such questions as, "Does the color of the blot make it look like _____ to you?" or "Do you see it moving?" However, more subtle aids in the inquiry are possible. Thus, if chromatic color is suspected as a possible determinant, the examiner may ask the subject if the same percept is seen on the (achromatic) location sheet. If it isn't, then color may be assumed to be a determinant of the response, even though it was not stated by the subject.

The examiner must also avoid asking questions like, "Why do you see (a bat)?" Such questions call upon the subject to *justify* his or her response. It should be clear at all times that the examiner accepts the subject's responses and is merely seeking further information about them.

A perusal of the material on determinants (see Chapter 4) will probably be necessary at this point in order for the examiner to conduct an adequate determinant inquiry. Once the inquiry is completed for all of the responses, the standard Rorschach administration is completed. It should be noted that subjects will sometimes give further responses during the Inquiry phase (i.e., perceive more percepts) that were not perceived during the Association phase. If this occurs, these responses (called additional responses), are also recorded and an Inquiry carried out if necessary for scoring. The distinction between main and additional responses will be discussed in subsequent chapters on scoring.

Testing-the-Limits

The Testing-the-Limits procedure is sometimes used by the examiner to explore the extent to which the subject is *capable* of giving certain categories of response that are largely absent from the record. For example, if there is a dearth of popular responses or of whole responses in the record, is the subject nonetheless able to perceive whole or popular responses? A further question answered in the Testing-the-Limits procedure is how much leading on the part of the examiner is necessary in order to elicit such a response from the subject.

When using this optional procedure after the Association and Inquiry phases have been completed, the examiner again presents certain Rorschach blots to the test subject, beginning with very general questions. If there is an absence of whole responses in the test record, for example, the examiner may present blots that lend themselves readily to whole responses, such as Cards IV and V. A general question might then be asked, such as, "Sometimes, people use all of the blot in seeing things—can you do that?" The subject's responses are then observed and recorded, thereby indicating whether he or she is capable of using the inkblots in this manner. If the subject cannot respond with a whole response at this juncture, questioning might then become more specific—suggesting a common percept, for example, a bat on Card V. If the subject is still unable to see such a percept, the examiner might then point out specific parts of the percept (the wings, the head, etc.). How much aid the subject requires naturally constitutes very relevant information regarding the subject's capacities and orientation.

Recording the Rorschach Responses

The paper used to record the Rorschach technique performance is simply 8½"×11" paper turned sideways. The paper is then divided into four columns. The first column is narrow and used to record card numbers, response numbers, and reaction times. The second and third columns are wide and are used to record the Association and Inquiry verbalizations, respectively. The last column is narrow and is used for scoring the responses. (See Fig. 2-2 and sample protocols in Chapter 16 for examples of our response forms.)

The examiner should try to line up each response in the Association phase with the corresponding Inquiry questions and answers. It is preferable to use one page for each inkblot; thus five pages and the backs of those pages are used for the full procedure. Of course, further pages may be used if necessary. Roman numerals are used to represent the blot numbers, with Arabic numerals representing the response number on each blot. We use the lowercase letters (a), (b), (c), and (d) to represent the examiner asking the four most common types of inquiry questions, pertaining respectively to location (a), determinants in general (b), movement in particular (c), and the more general probing type of question (e.g., "tell me more about [the bat])," (d). Other questions and comments the examiner makes should also be recorded in parentheses. We use the notation (>1) to represent the examiner telling the subject on the first blot that some people see more than one thing. If the blot is not upright when a response is given, the position in which the subject is holding the blot is indicated by a carat (v, <, or >), with the point indicating the location of the top of the card. If the subject turns the card around, this is indicated by an arrow ↻ . If additional responses occur, these are labeled A1, A2, and so on for each blot.

1.5"	1.	It ll a bat $(>I)$	1. (a) Just the whole thing. (b) The wings and the black color.	W	FC'	A	+ P
	2.	It also cd be a woman in the middle, doing a dance. She has on a transparent dress.	2. (a)	D	M	H	+ P
	3.	V I also c 2 animals moving around.	3. They're at the side, w their mouths open. (b) Just the shapes and posture.	D	FM	A	+
			A1. I also c 2 people w wings, holding onto st in the middle.	W	M	(H)	+
			Here they are. (b) These r the people–they just ll it. (d) They might be pulling on the thing in the middle.				

FIGURE 2-2   Sample Recording Sheet for Card I

The recording paper for Card I responses for a hypothetical subject might resemble Fig. 2-2. This subject gave one response to the first blot, then gave two more after being told that some people see more than one thing. The card was rotated 360 degrees prior to the second response; the third response was with the card in an inverted position. In the second response, the subject gave sufficient information in the Association phase (with reference to transparency shading and movement) so that further inquiry was superfluous. The subject gave one additional response on Card I, which was then inquired for. In both the third and the additional responses, the location of the response was clear; no location question was asked. For the additional response, the examiner chose to ask a further probing question: "Tell me more about the people with wings." The fourth column is used for scoring (see Chapters 3, 4, and 5).

It should be noted that the responses to Cards II through X would be labeled, 1, 2, 3, and so on, as they were on Card I.

To aid in recording verbalizations quickly, the examiner should begin to use "shorthand" recording methods, particularly for commonly occurring expressions. The abbreviations should not be too extensive or too difficult for someone else to decipher, however, since another psychologist may wish to look over the protocol at a future time. Some commonly used abbreviations are shown in Table 2-1.

Table 2-1   Commonly Used Abbreviations

ll = looks like	bec = because
DK = don't know	et = everything
bf = butterfly	wd = word
cd = could	r = are
w = with	c = see
st = something	u = you
so = someone	

Evaluating Children

Some special considerations are made in the administration procedures when the subject is a child. In the literature on this subject, however, substantial disagreement has existed on exactly what should be altered in the administration of the Rorschach with child subjects. On the one hand, Klopfer, Fox, and Troup (1956) state: "In our clinical experience, we have never encountered the need to depart from the standard administrative procedure, except to gear the language to the level of the child's comprehension" (p. 14).

On the other hand, there are those who advocate specific modifications with child subjects—for example, use of a trial blot before the regular series (Hertz, 1936), avoiding the recording of reaction time (Halpern, 1953), use of an immediate inquiry (Francis-Williams, 1968; Halpern, 1960), and greater emphasis on establishing rapport, even to the extent of having the small child subject sit on the examiner's lap (Halpern, 1953).

Our experience has shown that the Rorschach technique should not be administered to subjects under the age of 5 (though a very mature 4-year-old might still be a subject). It is also recommended that the examiner be even more concerned about establishing rapport and encouraging the child than would be the case with an adult subject. Thus, as always with the Rorschach technique, the goal should be seen as the garnering of important information about the subject. One should not strive for a barren and counterproductive "standardization" that essentially produces a Rorschach record of little or no clinical use. This is particularly the case with young children.

We do not use a sample inkblot, but when using the traditional administration and scoring technique for children aged 5–8, we do recommend immediate inquiry for determinants, et cetera, after each inkblot rather than in a separate Inquiry phase. We typically do not have very young children sit on our laps, but we try to relate to them in as warm, encouraging, and flexible a manner as possible (e.g., taking a break, if necessary, during the administration). Generally, we are more willing to compromise standardization in favor of rapport with very young and with immature children.

THE RORSCHACH BLOTS

As noted in Chapter 1, Hermann Rorschach's initial experimentation was done with 15 inkblots, but he was only able to have his work printed by agreeing to limit the test to 10. The printer reduced Rorschach's blots in size, altered their colors, and, through defects in printing, also introduced varieties of shading not intended by the author (Ellenberger, 1954). These altered and imperfect reproductions of Rorschach's plates constitute what are known today throughout the world as the Rorschach test.

Rorschach students should acquaint themselves with the stimulus value of the 10 blots, since in the process of interpreting a protocol, the examiner must constantly seek to disentangle the stimulus-determined parts of the protocol from parts that represent dynamic projections of the subject's personality. As Zubin (1956) notes: "Some responses reflect more heavily the stimulus properties; others reflect these to a lesser degree, and the latter are called 'projective'" (p. 183).

The 10 blots of the Rorschach technique are divided into the five achromatic or black-and-white cards (Cards I, IV, V, VI, and VII) and the five chromatic or colored cards (Cards II, III, VIII, IX, and X). Of the chromatic series, Cards II and III are printed in black and red; Cards VIII, IX, and X are printed in a variety of bright colors.

The Ten Blots

Card I

The research literature dealing with responses to Card I generally supports the common-sense clinical view that the subject is presented with a stressful new situation. It has been our observation that in response to the first Rorschach blot, the subject often reveals a great deal about his or her personality. It is, so to speak, the subject's first chance to tell you who he or she is.

The literature also supports the notion that Card I is perceived quite negatively and has a negative stimulus value that is second only to Card IV. Negatively toned responses to Card I must, therefore, be interpreted with a great deal of caution. Responses such as "a rather ugly bat" or "a sinister-looking moth" may simply be appropriate reactions to the stimulus properties of Card I.

Card II

In general, the literature suggests that this blot tends to be upsetting to certain classes of subjects, the chromatic color being largely responsible. Females tend to report dislike of Card II in particular, perhaps, as suggested by Hershenson (1949), due to an association with menstrual blood. Some research also indicates more reactions of dislike to this blot among unstable rather than stable subjects.

Clinicians generally cite Card II as sexually evocative (with a penis area near the top and a vaginal area beneath). This was corroborated in a study by Pascal, Roesch, Devine, and Suttell (1950) in which Card II was found to be the second most evocative blot for sexual responses.

Card III

Many clinicians place great stock in responses to Card III as an indication of social interaction patterns. Thus, if popular human figures are seen on this blot, are they described as engaged in a cooperative action, a battle, et cetera? Unfortunately, no convincing empirical data relevant to this assertion about Card III have been presented.

Clinicians have also stated that the absence of human association on this card should be considered pathological (e.g., R. Allen, 1966). Data presented by Hammer (1966), however, indicate that a surprisingly large number of normal subjects do not report seeing people on this blot (23% of normal females, 27% of normal males).

The sexes of the figures perceived on this blot have also been of interest to clinicians. The simplest (and unfortunately, a very persistent) interpretation in this regard is to see the sex of the figure as indicative of the sexual identification of the subject. Thus, a male subject who sees female figures might be viewed as having a feminine sexual identification. Given the large percentages of subjects reported by Ames (1975) who perceived figures of the opposite sex on Card III, such simplistic interpretation of sexual identification is clearly unwarranted.

In our experience, the gender characteristics of Card III do constitute highly useful clinical material. This is especially true in cases where the subject is perplexed and disturbed over the possible sex of the figures, and is either unable to reach a decision or describes the figures as having both male and female sexual parts. Such responses often indicate confused sexual identification.

Card IV

Many clinicians believe that Card IV tends to elicit feelings toward the father; this blot has often been referred to as the "father card." Empirical studies on this point have yielded equivocal results, suggesting that such an interpretation of Card IV responses may be incorrect.

The problem is compounded by the clear and consistent negative image of Card IV. This blot elicits fewer positive responses than any of the other blots. Such negatively toned responses as "a large ugly animal" or "a frightening gorilla" may thus be appropriate responses to the stimulus characteristics of the blot rather than a reflection of underlying dynamic trends. This leads to the frequent potential error noted by Zimmerman, Lambert, and Class (1966): "The strongly negative quality typically ascribed to [Card] IV suggest[s] an implicit bias . . . which might lead a naive examiner to find all his subjects obsessed with . . . negative attitudes toward authority" (p. 259).

It is our belief that Card IV can help elicit attitudes toward authority figures (whether male or female), but such interpretations should not be made without sufficient evidence, particularly regarding negative feelings toward male authority figures. Clinicians should also keep in mind that attitudes toward the father and authority in general may be projected on any of the blots.

Card V

This blot has been referred to as the "reality card" because of the ease with which it elicits the popular winged object. It is thought to be an easy card for the subject, relatively undisturbing, and to provide a breathing space after the disturbing character of the earlier cards. The research literature generally supports these views, indicating, for example, that this blot is the easiest on which to obtain a high form-level response. The blot has also been shown to draw the least number of sexual responses from subjects.

Some clinicians have suggested pathological implications for a failure to see the popular flying animal, but a study by Molish (1951) did not find this to differentiate between normal, neurotic, and schizophrenic groups. This type of interpretation must therefore be considered doubtful.

Card VI

This blot has been referred to as the "sex card" because of the phallic symbol at the top and a vaginal symbol below. Pascal et al. (1950) found that Card VI was the blot most frequently responded to with sexual percepts.

On the whole, the general empirical evidence on blot stimulus character-istics indicates that Card VI is sexually suggestive, particularly of male sexu-ality, and that it tends to elicit negative reactions. However, blanket inter-pretations should not be made on the assumption that this card is the so-called sex card. The clinician should be aware that information relevant to sexual functioning can be brought forth by other blots. Furthermore, it must be recognized that it is difficult for subjects to see clear percepts on Card VI, which also affects subjects' responses to this blot.

Card VII

Card VII traditionally has been regarded by clinicians as the reverse of Card IV; subjects are thought to respond positively to the blot and concepts appro-priate to a mother-child relationship are thought to be involved. Thus, Card VII has been referred to as the "mother card."

Research data indicate that Card VII often elicits a positive response from subjects, but the evidence of this card's particular ability to evoke attitudes toward the mother is not encouraging. Card VII is also one of the most difficult blots in terms of producing responses of good form-level.

Clinicians should be aware that attitudes toward the mother can be projected onto any card and should be wary of categorically interpreting Card VII responses in terms of the mother without sufficient evidence. In view of the predominantly female gender of sexual responses to this card, it also seems likely that some subjects can be expected to react to the female genitals perceived on the blot.

Card VIII

Clinicians have generally asserted that Card VIII can be considered a mild stimulus, given the soft pastel coloring and the ease of discerning animals at the side. Other interpretations include the suggestion that failure to perceive the popular animals should be considered indicative of serious disturbance and the suggestion that the type of animal seen should be considered an expression of certain ego qualities.

The empirical data definitely suggest that Card VIII is one of the most preferred blots and that the colors add to the generally positive response. Normal subjects have been shown to give the popular animal response more frequently than schizophrenics (Molish, 1951). There are as yet no data relevant to the "ego qualities" hypothesis as to the type of animal seen.

It is suggested that clinicians refrain from interpreting the very popular animals (bears, rodents) that are often seen in response to the blot in the absence of evidence that the specific animal has some dynamic meaning for the subject. It is also advisable that clinicians investigate the subject's associations to the specific types of animals seen, because although the choice of animal may indeed have dynamic significance, the meaning may be idiosyncratic to the subject (see Chapter 10).

Card IX

Both the clinical and the research literature on this blot agree that Card IX has an unstructured quality that makes it difficult to discern percepts. This blot is consequently the most frequently rejected, has the slowest reaction time of the 10 blots, and is the most difficult on which to produce percepts of good form-level. This blot also usually elicits a positive response, which is augmented by the color of the blot. However, neurotic subjects generally respond less positively to this blot than do normal subjects. As noted by Klopfer and Davidson (1962), this blot elicits a great variety of responses, thus adding to its value in the Rorschach series.

Card X

Card X is a complex blot and somewhat disorganized. The coloring yields a positive response from subjects, but the lack of cohesiveness often elicits a negative reaction. Card X has been judged the second most difficult blot on which to distinguish percepts. It also has one of the slowest reaction times and is second only to Card IX in terms of the difficulty of producing high form-level responses.

In our experience and in the opinions of Alcock (1963) and Halpern (1953), key dynamic responses are often elicited on Card X because it is the last in the series. "The note on which the subject is willing to let the matter rest is of great importance, frequently representing a composite picture of his problems and conflict" (Halpern, 1953, p. 52). On Card X the subject has his or her last opportunity to tell the examiner who he or she is.

OVERVIEW

Each of the 10 Rorschach blots is a distinct stimulus that influences responses. In the process of interpretation, the examiner must strive to untangle the stimulus elements from the dynamic elements in each subject's responses, as well as possible interactions between the two. In interpreting Rorschach protocols, the following general guidelines are suggested: The examiner should be most reluctant to accord dynamic meaning to responses that are in keeping with the stimulus qualities of the blots and should conversely give greater weight to responses that seem out of step with the blot stimulus characteristics.

The examiner should be warned against making blanket assumptions regarding Card IV as the "father card," Card VI as the "sex card," Card VII as the "mother card," and so on. Because the dynamic referents of many Rorschach responses are unclear, it would be of great practical help to the Rorschach clinician if such assumptions could be made. However, the research data do not generally support such assumptions about card meaning. The clinician faced with obscure responses and symbols in the patient's record would do better to clarify the dynamic meaning of the responses through the techniques presented in Chapter 11.

3

Defining the Response and Scoring for Location

Fundamentally, the Rorschach may be regarded as both a standardized interview and as a behavioral sample of the subject's perceptual operations in a situation using standardized but comparatively unstructured stimuli. Once such information about the subject is obtained, the examiner is confronted with the task of classifying and organizing these data so that they will lend themselves to meaningful personality interpretation. The assumption implicit with the Rorschach is that the subject's associations to the blots are very much like his or her typical perceptions outside of the examination situation. The ambiguity of the inkblots, however, makes it far more difficult for subjects to draw upon conventional response patterns and well-practiced behaviors. Thus, a great deal is revealed about the subject's adaptive maneuvers and aspects of his or her personality that is frequently disguised in the ordinary course of everyday living.

The Rorschach scoring process is basically an attempt to provide a summary of the subject's performance; it utilizes a kind of symbolic shorthand that enables various components of perception and association and their interrelationships to be quantified. The sets of scoring rules developed for the Rorschach provide a commonly understood communication network for Rorschach workers and also facilitate the comparison of a particular subject's protocol with Rorschach data available for a broad spectrum of groups identified on the basis of numerous criteria. Scoring can, therefore, be seen as an important step in making the subject's productions more manageable for evaluation.

THE SCORING CATEGORIES—AN OVERVIEW

The approach to scoring used here is essentially that of Klopfer and his associates. Based on the clinical, research, and teaching experience of the present authors, however, the Klopfer system has been modified where it was felt to be too complex and/or somewhat arbitrary.

Every Rorschach percept is scored from five different standpoints. First, the location score encompasses where the percept was seen and how much of the blot was incorporated in the concept.

A second element scored, called *determinants*, entails a consideration of the qualities of the inkblot that determine how the percept was seen. Determinants are classed as form, movement, color, and shading.

The third category is scoring each response for one of a wide range of content possibilities that reflect the subject matter of the percept.

The fourth score assigned is for *form-level*, which taps the accuracy of the percept in terms of congruence between shape of the blot area chosen and the configuration of the concept seen. Put another way, form-level assesses whether a reasonable "fit" exists between the inkblot and the response.

The fifth and last scoring category involves the degree of conventionality of the percept. If a percept is very commonly seen, it is labeled a *popular*. If, on the other hand, it occurs no more than once in 100 records, it is designated *original*. It should be noted that the great majority of responses are neither popular nor original.

THE SCORABLE RESPONSE

Before embarking on a formal scoring procedure, it must be ascertained what can be legitimately scored. This is not always an easy matter because a response, per se, may not be sufficiently differentiated from a comment or remark. This may be particularly apparent in the case of young children and, to a lesser degree, in adults with limited verbal ability. As far as possible, all verbalizations should be recorded regardless of whether they are judged to be a remark or, subsequently, a legitimate response. An emotionally charged comment appended to a scorable percept can sometimes be far more revealing than the percept as such, especially if the latter turns out to be a vague, poorly defined concept.

A *response* is a separate, discrete idea or concept given in association to a clearly delineated portion of the blot or to the entire inkblot. It is sometimes necessary to question the subject quite directly with respect to whether the association was intended as a remark or a response. If the subject states it was meant as a response and an elaboration or further explanation is offered, then it is generally scored as a response.

One of the most difficult aspects of traditional Rorschach scoring is the differentiation between a *specification* and a *separate response*. In general, one should be guided by two principles in distinguishing a specification from a response: (1) the tightness or looseness with which the total concept is described (the more tightly bound the concept, the less likely the scorer should be to assign more than one response to it) and (2) whether or not elements of the concept can be and commonly are seen by themselves. Examples are given in the following three verbalizations:

Card II:	It looks like two people with hats on their heads.
Card III:	I see two men pulling apart a crab.
Card X:	An underwater sea scene—crabs up here, sea urchins, and seahorses.

The verbalization to Card II is a tightly organized response; furthermore, the hat, while not an uncommon response to the top red area, is really a specification of the head of the figure seen. Thus, only one response would be scored for Card II. The Card III verbalization, however, while still fairly tightly organized, contains an element (the crab) very often perceived as a separate response by subjects. Thus, two responses would be scored on Card III. The verbalization to Card X is clearly four separate responses, since the concept is both loosely organized and contains elements often perceived as separate responses. (The sets of responses to both Cards III and X should be bracketed, as described later.)

Klopfer proposes two broad scoring categories of responses: main and additional. In our experience, however, the distinction between these two classifications is often rather confusing. Consequently, this aspect of Klopfer scoring has been revised under the present scoring system: *Main responses* are only those percepts given spontaneously during the initial phase of the administration or in what is termed the *performance proper. The additional* scoring category is reserved entirely for new concepts given during the Inquiry phase, or for associations offered during the performance proper and then rejected in the course of the inquiry. Clarifications, elaborations, or further ideas elicited during the Inquiry phase to percepts already reported during the spontaneous Association phase are still included under main responses and are scored through the use of multiple determinants.

In the Klopfer system a main response receives only one location, form-level, determinant, content, and popularity-originality score. By contrast, in our approach a percept can be scored for several location, determinant, and content categories that are not differentiated on the basis of being primary or secondary. As will be discussed in the section on tabulation, eliminating the notion of single main determinant scoring clearly results in a far more inclusive and meaningful scoring system. It also obviates the need for applying arbitrary rules of precedence when making a main determinant assignment. For example, if a subject responded to the center red area of Card III as "a beautiful butterfly in flight" and went on to explain in the course of the inquiry that it appeared to look like a butterfly because of the attractive color and the graceful movement of its wings, it would be necessary under the Klopfer main-additional scoring system to decide whether movement or color was the main determinant. The other determinant, though perhaps of very nearly equal importance to the percept, would be designated as an additional and would not figure in the computations of any of the ratios and percentages.

LOCATION

Although it seems a simple matter to have the subject indicate where in the particular inkblot he or she saw the percept, this is often not the case. A number of subjects are defensively evasive and exceedingly vague in their percepts. The reverse is true also—some subjects are inordinately precise and insist on excluding many minute sections of the blots from their associations. A location sheet of the 10 blots reproduced in miniature is certainly a great help in fixing the boundaries of the blot areas used in the percept. However, many subjects, when asked to outline their percepts on a location sheet, do not invest a great deal in this assignment and are only perfunctory in their performance.

Because certain types of responses recur over and over again in particular blot areas, it is extremely helpful in scoring if the examiner takes the time initially to become familiar with the specific blot areas and responses ordinarily found in such areas. One way this can be achieved is by utilizing a comprehensive breakdown of areas such as that compiled by Hertz (1970) in her book *Frequency Tables for Scoring Rorschach Responses*. Students who study the Hertz card diagrams and frequency tables (with a set of the Rorschach plates in front of them to see the percepts more clearly) will feel far more at ease and confident in their location scoring.

As previously mentioned, *location* refers to the part of the blot that was utilized in the formation of the percept. Essentially, location responses may be divided into wholes and various categories of detail responses.

Whole Responses, W, W̵

In the category of whole responses, scored W, the entire blot is used with the exception of the white space; or it is obvious that the subject fully intended to use the whole blot but may have accidentally omitted a small area. Examples of whole responses are as follows:

Card I:	It resembles a bat. The whole thing. It has its wings spread.
Card VI (upside down):	The entire dark area looks like two Russian dancers with cossack hats.

In cut-off whole, or W̵, percepts, the subject uses minimally two-thirds of the blot and indicates that his or her intent was to use as much of the blot as possible with the conceivable exception of some comparatively small areas. Examples of W̵ responses include:

Card V:	This is a moth but these (side extensions) don't belong.
Card VI:	Looks like a bearskin rug but the very top is not part of it.

Usual Detail Responses: D and d

When a comparatively large section of the blot is used for the subject's concept and is readily delineated by space, color, or shading from the remainder of the blot, it is scored a large usual detail, D. A substantially smaller area that is just as easily demarcated in the blot is labeled a small usual detail with a d scoring. Designating these locations as "usual" conveys that they are the more obvious and frequently used portions of the blots. A list of these large and small usual details areas for each Rorschach card with the various areas actually outlined on miniature inkblots is reproduced from Klopfer, Ainsworth, Klopfer, and Holt (1954), with their permission. It should also be noted that simple combinations of D and d areas would also be scored respectively as D or d; for example, "a pig" seen on the bottom two-thirds of one side of Card VII would be scored D. The large and small usual detail areas of the 10 inkblots are reproduced on the following pages.

Card I

Large Usual Details

D_1 Entire center with or without lighter gray in lower portion.

D_2 Entire side.

D_3 Lower center without lighter gray.

D_4 Entire lower center.

D_5 Upper side.

D_6 Upper third of center.

Small Usual Details

d_1 Upper outer projections.

d_2 Lower side.

d_3 Upper, inner, claw-like extensions.

d_4 Uppermost projections.

d_5 Upper innermost details.

d_6 Bottom projection.

d_7 Small knob-like extension at lower side.

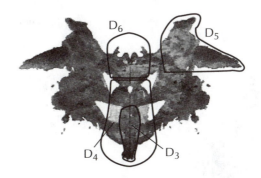

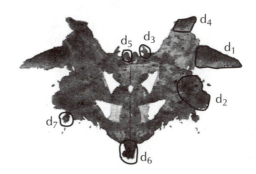

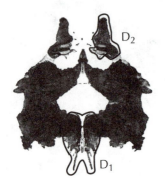

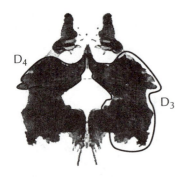

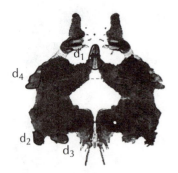

Card II

Large Usual Details

D_1 Lower red with or without black-red mixture.

D_2 Upper red.

D_3 Entire side black.

D_4 Upper portion of black.

Small Usual Details

d_1 Upper center.

d_2 Bottom outer projection.

d_3 Bottom projection adjacent to preceding *d*.

d_4 Upper side projection.

Card III

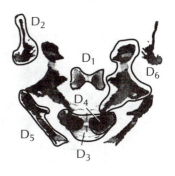

Large Usual Details

D_1 Inner red.

D_2 Outer red with or without tail-like extension.

D_3 Entire lower center.

D_4 Lower center black.

D_5 Lower side black.

D_6 Upper side black, head and upper part of body of usual figure.

D_7 Middle side black.

D_8 One of the two human figures.

D_9 Lower center light gray.

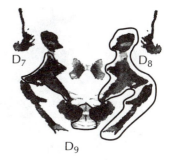

Small Usual Details

d_1 Bottom side portion with or without lower part of leg.

d_2 Top side black.

d_3 Side black lateral protrusion, usually upside down.

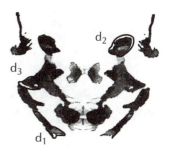

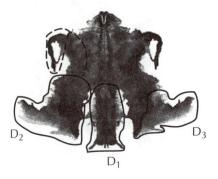

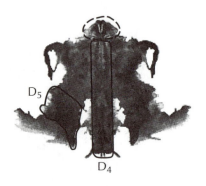

Card IV

Large Usual Details

D_1 Lower center.

D_2 Lower side black and gray, some-
       times including upper side portion.

D_3 Lower side light gray.

D_4 Entire vertical dark center.

D_5 Inner dark side detail.

Small Usual Details

d_1 Upper side extensions, sometimes
       with small adjacent portion.

d_2 Uppermost portion, sometimes
       including adjacent shaded portion.

d_3 Outermost lower side extension.

d_4 Lowermost portion of lower center
       detail.

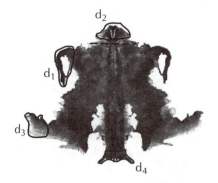

Card V

Large Usual Details

D_1 Entire side with or without light gray extensions.

D_2 Center vertical portion.

Small Usual Details

d_1 Bottom center.

d_2 Side extension sometimes with adjacent thin extensions.

d_3 Top center, with or without uppermost protrusions.

d_4 Contour of upper side detail.

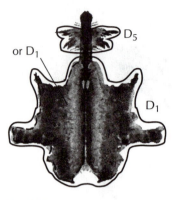

Card VI

Large Usual Details

D_1 Entire lower portion or half of lower portion.

D_2 Entire upper portion, sometimes including light gray uppermost portion of lower detail.

D_3 Upper black portion only of center column, sometimes without slightly shaded outer portion.

D_4 Entire dark vertical center.

D_5 Lighter part only of upper portion.

Small Usual Details

d_1 Uppermost detail with or without "whiskers."

d_2 Lower lateral extensions.

d_3 Two inner light gray ovals.

d_4 Bottom inner projections.

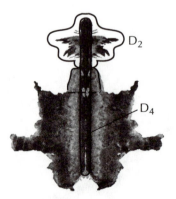

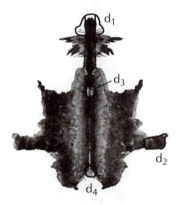

msp-85

Card VII

Large Usual Details

D_1 Entire bottom portion, sometimes each half separately.

D_2 Middle third.

D_3 Upper third, with or without uppermost projection.

D_4 Upper two-thirds.

Small Usual Details

d_1 Dark center bottom detail.

d_2 Top projections.

d_3 Light gray projections on upper inner corner of top third.

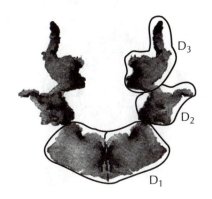

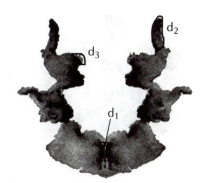

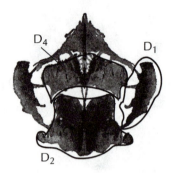

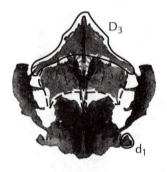

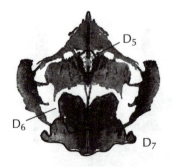

Card VIII

Large Usual Details

D_1 Side pink.

D_2 Lower pink and orange.

D_3 Top gray portion with or without center line, sometimes including rib-like figure and/or blue portion.

D_4 Middle blue portion.

D_5 Rib-like figure in upper center.

D_6 Bottom pink alone.

D_7 Bottom orange alone.

Small Usual Details

d_1 Lateral extensions of bottom orange.

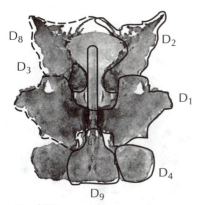

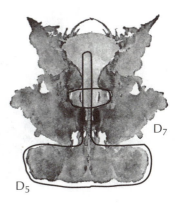

Card IX

Large Usual Details

D$_1$ Green portion.

D$_2$ Orange portion.

D$_3$ Small inner portion at junction of green and orange.

D$_4$ Lateral pink.

D$_5$ Entire pink portion plus center line, card inverted.

D$_6$ Entire pink or either half.

D$_7$ Center portion between lateral greens.

D$_8$ Center gray portion with or without D7.

D$_9$ Inner pink portion.

Small Usual Details

d$_1$ All or most of upper inner orange projections.

d$_2$ Eye-like portion in middle including green and white slits.

d$_3$ Arch-like light orange at top center.

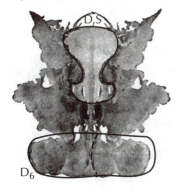

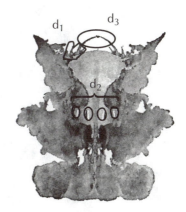

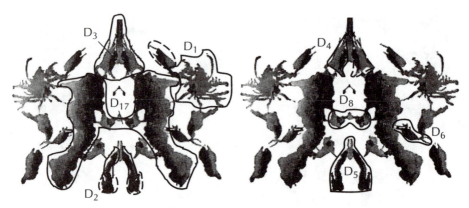

Card X

Large Usual Details

D_1 Outer blue, sometimes with outer green.

D_2 Inner green, dark portions only.

D_3 Entire gray portion at top.

D_4 Gray "animals" at top without inner gray column.

D_5 Entire inner green.

D_6 Outer gray-brown figures.

D_7 Light portion between inner greens.

D_8 Inner blue.

D_9 Pink portion separately.

D_{10} Inner yellow.

D_{11} Outer orange.

D_{12} Inner orange.

D_{13} Outer upper green.

D_{14} Gray column at top without gray "animals" beside it..

D_{15} Outer yellow.

D_{16} Pink with entire top gray, card inverted.

D_{17} Pink with inner blue.

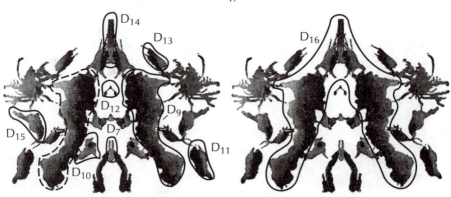

Unusual Details: (Dd) dd, de, di, and dr

In contrast to the usual details, the *unusual details* are those percepts that cannot be classified as whole, usual details, or space responses. The symbol Dd is used to subsume all the types of percepts falling into this scoring category. It should be noted, however, that Dd is never employed to score an individual response. As the name implies, the unusual detail is not a commonplace area and occurs significantly less frequently than the usual detail.

The dd, or tiny detail response, alludes to percepts that occur in very small areas. The de detail denotes the use of only the contour or the very edge of the blot. If any other portion of the blot is used, the scoring is dd. The di, or inside detail, represents areas that are entirely within the inkblot and not easily differentiated by any of the obvious blot characteristics. The dr, or rare detail, refers to unusual locations that do not fall into any of the other usual or unusual scoring categories. These percepts often contain arbitrary subdivisions and/or omissions of a section of a very distinct blot area. They can be as small as the dd response or approach a W in size and can involve unusual combinations of usual detail percepts. Examples of the four types of unusual details and their locations are shown in Figure 3-1.

White Space Responses: S

A *white space* scoring depicts concepts that use the white area within a blot or surrounding it. It is essentially a reversal of figure and ground. Examples of white space responses are:

Card II:	The white in the center looks like a space ship.
Card VII (upside down):	The middle reminds me of a bust of George Washington.

White space can be combined with any of the other location scorings. For example:

Card I:	A jack-o-lantern. These (the white spaces) are the eyes and the mouth. W (S)
Card I:	This is a huge ocean and these (little dots) are tiny islands. S (dd)

For tabulation purposes there is really no difference between a response scored S (dd) or one scored dd (S). However, the parenthetical notation is useful to indicate whether the figure or ground seems primary in a particular response; the location area that seems secondary is put in the parentheses.

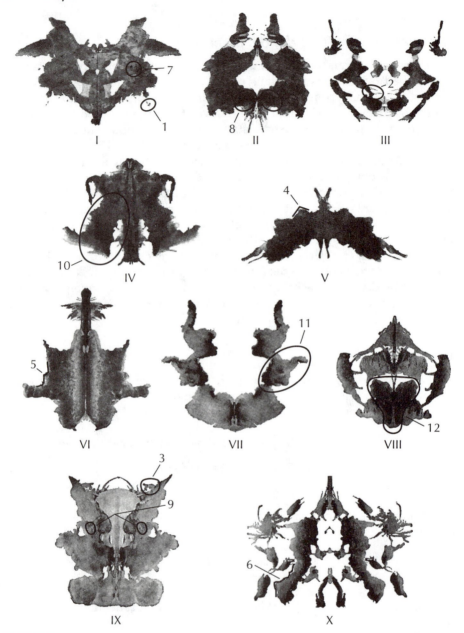

FIGURE 3-1   Examples of Unusual Detail (Dd). *Tiny detail (dd):* 1. Card I: A musical note; 2. Card III: Birds' beaks—they look sharp; 3. Card IX: A boot. *Edge detail (de):* 4. Card V: An outline of a mountain; 5. Card VI: a man's profile; 6. Card X: A coastline. *Inner detail (di):* 7. Card I: A target with the bull's-eye; 8. Card II: Kidney; 9. Card IX: Eyes. *Rare detail (dr):* 10. Card IV: a chess piece—probably a pawn; 11. Card VII: A fish burying its nose into a mound of seaweed; 12. Card VIII: An animal face.

Bracketing of Locations

In some situations, two or more separate responses may be related to one another. In such instances, the two or more location areas are bracketed. More specifically, bracketing of location scorings is often indicated when a subject first offers a detail response and then endeavors to include the remainder of the blot. This is typically done in somewhat indefinite fashion, for example:

Card VIII: Two animals of prey. The rest of the card could be woods, rocks, and water—hunting grounds.

These responses would be scored:

$$\left\{\begin{array}{l} D \\ W \end{array}\right.$$

The bracketing indicates the relationship between these two responses.

The subject may also begin with a number of distinct detail responses on a particular card and then endeavor to integrate the details by giving a casually organized whole percept. For example:

Card X: Crabs, seahorses, and coral. The whole thing must be an underwater scene.

These responses would be scored:

$$\left\{\begin{array}{l} D \\ D \\ D \\ W \end{array}\right.$$

▲ 4

Scoring Determinants

As previously mentioned, determinant scores reflect the properties of the inkblot that contribute to the percept. The four principal categories are form, movement, color, and shading. There may be one or a combination of determinants that are utilized in a particular response (see Chapter 2 for the inquiry technique to elicit determinants). In the case of multiple determinants, the one most important to the percept is listed first. Where it is impossible to ascertain the principal determinant, merely for convenience's sake the order of notation is: human movement, animal movement, color, and, lastly, shading. As indicated before, *all* determinants occurring in a multiple scoring are subsequently tabulated and appear in the various ratios.

Practically speaking, multiple scoring ordinarily means a double determinant. Occasionally it may be necessary to have a triple determinant. Beyond three determinants, however, it is likely that the scoring process is best served by breaking the ostensible single percept into several separate responses that then can be bracketed to reflect their interrelationship. If the Rorschach scorer errs, it should be in the direction of parsimony rather than in the direction of overscoring.

FORM RESPONSES: F

When only the outline of the blot determines the response, the score given is F. This scoring is, in a sense, a scoring by exclusion; that is, when movement, color, or shading are not elicited as determinants, leaving only the shape, F is scored. Form responses may have exceedingly vague contours, such as a map of an unspecified region or a rock. On the other hand, they may have a very definite shape, as, for example:

Card I (D4):	The Liberty Bell.
Card IV (D2):	Big boots.

As is the case for movement, color, and shading, F is not limited to any particular location area, but may be scored for percepts entailing any of the locations covered in Chapter 3.

MOVEMENT: M, FM, Fm, mF, m

While form, color, and shading are present in various inkblots for subjects to utilize in their concepts if they so desire, it is obvious that incorporating movement into a response requires a subject to project some form of action or life. There are three principal types of movement percepts: human movement, animal movement, and inanimate movement. Human movement, M, is the appropriate scoring when the response indicates human-like activity, expression, or posture. An M scoring may involve a whole human or a portion of a human figure in some form of action. The action may be very minimal, such as a facial expression. Furthermore, caricatures, statues, or animals that appear to be in human-like action are also scored M. It is most important to recognize that implicit in all M percepts is a form-dominant element, whether it be well delineated or extremely vague. It is never correct, therefore, to score F separately from M for a given percept. Examples of various types of M responses are as follows:

Card III (W):	The whole thing reminds me of two people carrying something.
Card IV (W):	A giant, you can only see his huge shoes and legs, sitting on a stump.
Card VII (upper two-thirds):	Comic strip little old ladies glowering at each other.
Card II (Black area):	Two bears in love, kissing one another.

Paralleling human movement, FM is scored whenever animal-like action is present in a response. Such percepts may involve a whole or parts of an animal and drawings or caricatures of animals. Animals in human-like activity receive an M scoring, but when animals are actually trained to perform like humans, such as a trained chimpanzee riding a bicycle, the appropriate scoring is FM rather than M. As was the case with M, form is also implied in FM responses and is never scored separately. Illustrations of FM percepts are:

Card I (W):   All of it looks like a bat, it has wings spread and seems to be flying.

Card VIII (W):   It reminds me of a fancy ornament, with the two sides resembling stalking leopards.

Card V (d₂):   The open jaws of a crocodile ready to receive its food.

Card II (D₂):   Two trained seals in a balancing act.

The inanimate movement category subsumes responses that convey the notion of natural or mechanical forces at work, forces that may at times be abstract or symbolic. In contrast to M and FM, inanimate movement has three subcategories, which are used to differentiate between distinct form percepts, those that are semidefinite, and those that are entirely vague or indefinite. The Fm type of movement scoring is appropriate when there is a clear-cut, recognizable shape. Two responses of this kind are:

Card VI (D₂):   A rocket blasting off.

Card VII (D₄):   Flags blowing in the wind.

The mF scoring is used when there is some evidence of form but it has a vague, ambiguous quality. Exemplifying this kind of percept are:

Card VII (W):   Several boulders dangerously balanced on one another, ready to tumble.

Card X (W):   A brilliant display of exploding fireworks of all different kinds.

The last type of inanimate movement score, m, is reserved for percepts where there is a complete absence of form, as in the following:

Card V (W):   It reminds me of deterioration—something coming apart.

Card IX (W):   Chaos and turmoil, a head-on clash of the good and evil forces.

COLOR RESPONSES

Chromatic Color Scores: FC, CF, C

As the name indicates, a response of this type reflects the use of blot colors in the subject's concept. Color percepts may be divided into chromatic and achromatic categories. In the former, such colors as red, green, brown, and orange are integrated into the concept. Achromatic color responses, on the other hand, entail the use of black, gray, and white as colors.

There is a further subdivision of chromatic color responses into natural and arbitrary color percepts. The natural color classification signifies the use of a color ordinarily associated with the percept being described, in its usual state. Essentially, this means that there is no incongruity between the color chosen and the object or creature as it is generally seen. By contrast, the arbitrary use of color indicates a forced quality or what might be termed the use of color in a colorless way—that is, the particular color chosen for the concept is irrelevant and any other color woud be equally appropriate.

There are, in turn, three kinds of natural chromatic color scores. The first, FC, is employed when a color component is combined with a definite and well-recognized shape and, additionally, the color is in consonance with the concept. Samples of this type of percept are:

Card III (D_1):   A very pretty red bow.

Card X (D_{13}):   The green color and the shape suggest grasshoppers.

The same scoring criteria apply to a CF scoring as to FC, with the exception that in the former, the contours are less definite—that is, the percept is less form-controlled. For example:

Card II (D_1):   They resemble blood stains.

Card IX (D_6):   These look very much like scoops of strawberry ice cream.

The third subclassification of natural chromatic color response is reserved for pure color concepts where form is entirely absent and only color is used in the determination of the percept. The symbol C is employed to convey the presence of pure color. An example is:

Card VIII (D_4):   The blue is water.

It would not be justified, however, to score the above type of response C if it occurred only once in the record; if it occurred only once, one should assign it a CF scoring. However, if the subject perseverated the concept water in association to the blue areas on Cards IX and X as well as VIII, and the response in each instance was without visible shape and any kind of relationship to other portions of the blot, then C would be the appropriate scoring.

There are several other variations of C response scoring. The first of these is color naming, using the symbol C_n to reflect that the subject simply enumerated the various hues in the card. Color naming should not be scored loosely and must meet several strict criteria, foremost of which is that the subject must state unequivocally that he or she is making a response rather than offering a comment or a remark about the card. In addition, there must be no other more adequate color responses in subsequent responses to that inkblot. A second variation is called color description, C_{des}; this is used when the subject goes somewhat beyond color naming and endeavors to describe certain qualities of the colors. An example of C_{des} would be labeling the colors "a delicate blending of pastels that merge with one another."

The category of arbitrary color responses essentially is used for colors employed in an artificial or colorless manner, perhaps merely to demarcate various blot areas. An arbitrary use of color occurs most frequently in anatomical and map percepts. When the form is distinct and recognizable, the scoring is F/C. Examples of F/C are:

Card VIII (W): The organs of the human body: the ribs and the lungs and the intestines. It might be a colored medical chart in an anatomy book.

Card IX (D_6): Pink frogs even though there are no frogs that color.

The C/F scoring category is reserved for the arbitrary use of color in a percept with less definite shape. Examples of such percepts are:

Card IX (W): A map with a different color for each country. They don't look like any countries in particular.

Card X (D_9): Pink clouds, though you never see clouds quite that color.

Achromatic Color Scores: FC', C'F, C'

The achromatic scores are the exact counterparts of the chromatic scoring categories but, as mentioned before, are used only when black, gray or white are the colors included in the formation of the concept. Once again, the three subdivisions of this scoring category are on a continuum of distinctness of form. The FC' responses are scored when form is most definite and easily recognized. Illustrations of FC' scoring are:

Card V (W):   The whole thing looks like a huge black bat.

Card VII   They look like two little gray poodles.
(upper two-thirds):

C'F, the intermediate achromatic scoring subcategory, reflects the presence of some form dimension, but of a secondary and vague or very variable type. The following are C'F responses:

Card VI (center   The contrasting gray and black colors make it look
gray and black   like a forbidding crater somewhere on the moon.
areas):

Card VIII (white   Mounds of white snow.
area immediately
above lower pink):

As in the instance of chromatic color, C' is scored for achromatic color without any designation of form whatsoever. Such responses are:

Card IV (W):   A black stormy sky.

Card VII (the   The white of day and the black of night.
whole card plus the
center white area):

Color Symbolism: FC_{sym}, CF_{sym}, C_{sym}

The symbolic scoring categories are used when the colors in the subject's concept represent symbols of some sort. Once again, the model of the continuum of structured or definite form to unstructured or indefinite form is employed. The FC_{sym} scoring is appropriate when the color is used symbolically in conjunction with a clearly delineated object. Examples of such responses are:

Card X (D_{10}):   A cowardly lion. The yellow signifies cowardice.

Card VIII (D_6, card   Baby girls in pink outfits, the pink symbolizes that
held sideways):   they are girls.

The CF_{sym} percepts are those in which some degree of form, albeit indistinct, is present and, once again, the color is used symbolically. The following percepts are scored CF_{sym}:

| Card X (W): | An abstract painting composed of many different colors and shapes intertwining with one another, symbolizing the complexity of life. |
| Card X (D_5): | A peculiarly shaped green object, probably a fertility symbol. |

C_{sym} is scored when color is employed to convey an abstract idea, with form totally omitted from the percept. Two examples of color symbolism responses are:

| Card II (D_1): | The red part stands for passion. |
| Card VIII (D_4): | I don't know what this is other than symbolizing a blue mood. |

It should be noted here that the various achromatic scoring categories, namely FC', C'F, and C', can be appended with a symbolic notation in order to indicate the symbolic use of white, gray, and black in a percept, just as color symbolism is scored. Symbolic achromatic responses, however, tend to be considerably less frequent than the chromatic variety.

SHADING RESPONSES: c, K, k

Shading responses are scored when the subject uses the nuances of shading of achromatic or chromatic inkblot areas in the formation of the percept. There are essentially three broad classifications of shading scores: surface and texture; three-dimensional or depth scores either as distance or diffusion; and lastly, a three-dimensional conception projected on a two-dimensional plane. The notion of definiteness of form applies to all shading responses just as it does to all color concepts. Again, there is a three-fold subdivision based on whether the form of the percept is definite and distinct, vague or variable, or entirely without shape.

Surface or Texture Responses: Fc, cF, c

An Fc is scored when the shading aspects of the blot are employed to describe a certain surface impression such as roughness or a carved effect, and the form is definite. A scoring of Fc is also appropriate when an object has an indefinite shape, but the subject uses shading nuances to indicate a very finely differentiated texture effect, as in a piece of very silky material.

Some examples of Fc scoring are:

Card IV (W):	A bearskin with a thick and furry appearance.
Card VI (D3):	An artistically carved, highly polished bedpost.
Card VII (D1):	Granite-like rock that has been worn smooth and is very pleasant to the touch.
Card VIII (D4):	Some pieces of silky-like material with an interesting design woven into it.

In comparison to Fc, where the form may be quite definite, cF is scored when a shading component is used in a percept having indefinite shape and in which the surface impression itself is not highly differentiated. The following are cF type responses:

| Card IV (W): | A piece of meat wrapped up in cellophane. |
| Card VI (W, top and side extensions cut off): | Just a piece of fur of some sort. |

A c or pure texture response is a percept where shape is entirely ignored, and shading is used in an essentially undifferentiated manner. Examples of c responses are:

| Card VII (W): | All of it looks so soft, just like cotton. |
| Card I (W): | The whole thing gives a slimy spongy feeling— something you wouldn't want to touch unless you had to. |

Distance and Diffusion Scores: FK, KF, K

The scoring FK is given for all vista percepts when shading is used to describe distance between several objects or between two parts of the same percept. Illustrations of FK scoring are:

| Card II (the dark areas and the white space): | A landscape with woods and hills, a castle in the distance set near the shore of a lake. |
| Card III (D3): | A three-dimensional view of the pelvis—you can see the front bones and the back bones. |

Contrasted with a definite form implicit in an FK scoring, KF is utilized when the outline of the percept is unclear and the impression is given of space-filling diffusion. Examples are:

Card VII (W):	Clouds of different shapes.
Card IX (D$_8$):	It looks like water coming out in a very fine spray, almost a mist.

When there is no visible form and the concepts denote space-filling diffusion, the scoring is K. Fog or room-encompassing darkness on any of the cards would qualify for a K scoring.

Three-Dimensional Space Projected on a Two-Dimensional Plane: Fk, kF, k

This category of shading score is used for x-rays and topographical maps. Once again, the definiteness of the form determines whether Fk, kF, or k is appropriately scored. When the x-ray is of a specific part of the body or the topographical map is of a particular country or region, then Fk is scored in preference to kF. Pure k is rarely scored, as both maps and x-rays have some element of form. If the subject's statement itself is vague, such as "it gives an x-ray–like impression," this would be scored k.

MULTIPLE DETERMINANTS

A subject may utilize more than one determinant in developing a percept. There are many commonplace double-determinant combinations, and occasionally a triple determinant is warranted. When it appears as if more than three determinants are required, however, it is very likely that several responses are actually involved, each of which should be scored separately. Examples of multiple-determinant scoring are:

Card II (D$_3$):	Two bears, they look furry, black bears (D Fc·FC').
Card II (W):	Reminds me of two witches dangling. They have their hands and legs up. They're wearing black coats and pointed red hats (W M·FC·FC').
Card III (D$_2$):	Bright red blood dripping down (D CF·mF).
Card III (black areas):	Two cannibals over a big pot. The black makes me say cannibals. The bottom part is the pot with some gray smoke coming from it (D M·FC'·KF).
Card VIII (D$_4$):	A bluish mist with dim forms in it (D CF·KF).
Card X (D$_8$):	Two bluebirds flying toward each other (D FM ·FC).

▲ 5

Scoring Populars,
Form-Level, and the
Simple Content
Categories

SCORING FOR CONTENT

Content refers to the nature of what is actually seen by the subject in contrast to the perceptual processes involved. Basically, content is concerned with the associations the subject offers to the inkblot material and not with the aspects of the blot (form, movement, color, and shading) that determine what was seen. There is literally no end to the number of possible scoring categories for content. Generally speaking, however, the majority of associations fall within the three major categories of humans, animals, and objects. When a response appears to defy classification into one of the more usual content scoring categories, then a special category may be added. Such special categories may be especially significant in a Rorschach record if the particular content is perseverated. For example, if the subject gives the response "reminds me of death" to a number of the cards, it would be most important and significant to have this reflected in a content scoring category.

Human Content: H, Hd, (H), (Hd)

There are fundamentally four types of human content scoring. The first type covers content pertaining to the perception of a whole human figure or a major part of it. The symbol designated for this type of human content is H. An example of a concept scored H is:

Card III:	Two people carrying something.

A second type of human content scoring possible is human detail, Hd. This category is reserved for percepts involving a portion of the human figure. Illustrative of this kind of content is:

Card II (upper center, small usual detail):	Two hands pressed together as if in the act of prayer.

It should be noted that the Hd scoring is restricted to body parts that are associated with living human beings rather than anatomical concepts.

The third subcategory under human content is (H), indicating that the human figure is removed from reality to some degree—a piece of sculpture, a caricature, or, conceivably, a mythological figure. A typical (H) response scoring is:

Card IX (orange portions):	Two witches casting a spell.

There is also (Hd) scoring that conveys that only a portion of a caricature drawing or imaginary human figure is involved in the percept. Exemplifying this kind of response is:

Card X (upper third of pink areas):	Just the heads of two little elves.

Animal Scoring: A, Ad, (A), (Ad)

The symbol A is scored for percepts depicting a whole or almost complete animal figure. For example:

Card X (lower green):	Two caterpillars.

Again, consistent with the human detail scoring, Ad is the content category used when only a part of an animal is perceived. A response of this type is:

| Card IV (lower center small usual detail): | A bull's head with big horns. |

There is also an (A) scoring for animal-like monsters, mythological animals, and caricatures or sculptures of animal figures. This symbol is also used when the concept of the animal is unrealistic because it is humanized. A good example of (A) scoring is:

| Card V: | A strange rabbit in some kind of costume. From the way it is standing on its toes, it might be in a ballet. |

Parts of animals that are unrealistic representations are scored (Ad), such as:

| Card I (side large details): | Heads of dragons with their mouths wide open. |

Object Scores: Obj, H_{obj}, A_{obj}

Another type of content category scoring pertains to various types of objects. The symbol Obj is used for a response that involves a man-made object, for example:

| Card II (upper red): | A pair of red socks. |

There are also human objects, H_{obj}, and animal objects, A_{obj}, content scoring classifications. The former is used specifically for objects very intimately related to humans. An example is:

| Card X (central portion of inner blue): | A skillfully shaped false tooth that a dentist is probably getting ready to put into someone's mouth. |

The scoring A_{obj} is appropriate when a part of an animal's body is being used ornamentally, or possibly, practically. The following illustrates A_{obj} content:

| Card VI: | A fur rug. |

| Card X (small center orange area): | A wishbone from a chicken. |

Other Content Categories: At, A_{at}, Sex, N, Geo, Pl, Art, Abs

As noted before, there are an almost unlimited number of possible content categories. Some that occur with reasonable frequency include anatomy, At, which is scored for an anatomical treatment of parts of the human body. An At scoring would be given for:

Card VIII (upper center dark area and extensions emanating from it):	Human spinal column and some ribs diagrammed in a medical book.

There is also an animal anatomy scoring, A_{at}, for sections of an animal seen anatomically, such as in an anatomy chart.

Any percept pertaining to sexual organs or sexual activity receives the scoring Sex. This includes anatomical responses where there is a clear intent to convey some aspect of sexual functioning. Clear-cut examples of Sex content responses are:

Card VI (upper extension):	A penis.
Card VII (lower center darker area):	A vagina.

Whenever a natural landscape is seen involving such features of nature as rivers, forests, mountains, and, conceivably, a sunset, the scoring is N, nature. However, rivers, lakes, and islands not seen as part of a landscape are scored geography, Geo, as are topographical features explicitly seen as a portion of a map or scientific representation. Plants and flowers receive the scoring Pl.

The symbol Art is utilized for paintings, designs, or various drawings in which no specific content is identified. If a subject, for example, describes Card X as "modern art," the appropriate scoring would be Art. Lastly, the symbol Abs, standing for abstract, denotes a percept where once again there is no specific content and what is being conveyed is merely an idea. The content category abstract would be used for a percept such as:

Card II:	Just a feeling of forces of various kinds acting on one another.

Other content categories that occur with some frequency include X-ray, Oral, Food, Anal, Map, Clouds, Smoke, Geometry, Architecture, Alphabet,

Clothing, Botany, Landscape, Water, Aggression, Explosion, Blood, Fire, Ice, Music, Science, Religion, Eyes, and Mask responses. As noted previously, however, the content categories mentioned in this chapter are not designed to be all-inclusive, and content scorings may be assigned to responses that do not fall easily into the above categories.

POPULAR AND ORIGINAL RESPONSES

The popularity-originality aspect of content scoring is basically concerned with frequency of occurrence of particular responses to specific blot areas. The symbol P denotes a commonplace percept, that is, one that occurs with a high degree of frequency. Unfortunately, there has been no real agreement on what constitutes a "frequent" response. Some Rorschach workers state that a popular response is a percept found in 1 in 3 records, while others feel that 1 in 10 is sufficiently frequent to warrant the label popular. There are also problems of the same sort with respect to an O or original response, although here there is somewhat more agreement that an original designation should not be used for responses that occur more often than 1 in 100 records. Most responses found in a given record are, of course, neither original nor popular, but rather fall somewhere between the extremes of being very ordinary or highly unique.

It is recommended that the popular scoring be restricted to percepts found in Beck's list of populars, which is reproduced in Table 5-1. We view the Beck populars as preferable to those presented by Klopfer, both because of the more specific statistical criteria he used in setting up the populars and because of the greater possible range of his scores.

Original percepts are somewhat difficult to score even for the most experienced Rorschach worker and are virtually impossible to identify by a Rorschach student. Responses that seem very different and creative for the neophyte Rorschach scorer may in fact be found in Rorschach protocols with some frequency. Hertz (1970) labels various original responses in her tables, and these tables can be used to provide some basis for scoring originality. It should be pointed out, however, that, in our opinion, Hertz is overly liberal in characterizing a percept as original and, therefore, her tables can serve as no more than a general guide. Original responses can have a minus designation, implying that the percept is bizarre or incongruent with the configuration of a particular inkblot.

FORM-LEVEL SCORING

Form-level describes how well the percept given by the subject conforms to the inkblot outline. Several systems have been developed for scoring form

TABLE 5-1   Beck's Popular Responses

Card I:	Bat, moth, or butterfly (W). Human form (D_3 and D_1)(might be child or woman, either whole or incomplete).
Card II:	Two humans (W). Butterfly or moth (D_1). Bear or dog (D_3).
Card III:	Two humans or representations of humans (D_8 and D_3). Butterfly, bow tie, ribbon, or variations of these (D_1).
Card IV:	Animal skin, hide, pelt, or rug, or human dressed in animal skin coat, or a massive, furry animal(W). Human foot or shoe (D_3). Boot or human leg (D_2).
Card V:	Bat, moth, or butterfly (W). Animal or human leg, with muscle element involved (upper half of d_2).
Card VI:	Animal skin, hide, pelt, or rug: (W) or (D_1).
Card VII:	Human heads, faces, women's heads (D_3) or whole human (W).
Card VIII:	Animals (D_1). However, if a specific animal is named, bears, rodents, beavers, muskrats, squirrels, and cats (lions, tigers, etc.), they are considered popular. Skeletal forms (D_5). Ribs are essential. Tree or a bush (D_3).
Card IX:	Head, face of a human, or a named person such as Winston Churchill (D_4).*
Card X:	Crab, lobster, or spider (D_1). Dog or special breed of dog (D_{10}). Rabbit's head or variations (bunny's head, etc.—D_7).

*This response is scored as a popular, regardless of the position of the card. If the subject turns Card IX and sees a human head, a popular is scored. All of the other 19 popular forms are scored P only if the card is held in the upright position.
Adapted from Beck, S. J., Beck, A. G., Levitt, E. E., and Molish, H. B. *Rorschach's test. I: Basic Processes.* New York: Grune & Stratton, 1961.

quality, including one by Klopfer et al. (1954), that endeavor to rate form on a numerical scale. For various reasons, these approaches have proved somewhat unsatisfactory, and assessing form quality with confidence and reliability remains a frustratingly elusive aspect of Rorschach scoring.

The approach described here tries to obviate some of the complexities of dealing with form quality, and, if anything, it may err in the direction of being too simplistic. In the present system, form quality is scored in two categories: + for good or average form, and – for poor form. Several components are considered in the judgment of form quality. The first, accuracy, is indicative of the degree of agreement between the configurations of the inkblots and the concepts offered by the subject. Accuracy relates to the definiteness with which the subject describes the percept. For example, a subject can give a precisely outlined response of two people on Card III, identifying the head, torso extremities, and other details of the figures. By contrast, a subject can also elect to limit responses to those having fairly indefinite or varied shapes, such as rocks or flowers. If the subject gives fairly well-delineated percepts to areas of the inkblots that match the percept, then, obviously, adequate form is present. If a distinctly shaped concept is at variance with a section of the blot chosen, then poor form quality is clearly the case.

Single-determinant concepts with an indefinite or semidefinite form are the most difficult to score because the inkblots, per se, are not really structured to comply with any single concept. In most cases, therefore, responses that are only quasidefinite, having a somewhat amorphous quality, cannot be readily scored poor form. Sometimes, however, a vaguely defined percept is located in a fairly distinct blot area that is strictly at variance with the concept and, in these instances, a minus form-level scoring is indicated. An example of the latter would be:

Card III: The whole thing looks like some kind of fish.

Another consideration in evaluating form-level is the degree of elaboration involved in the subject's percept. In some instances there is virtually no attempt to delineate the response in detail, and in other instances a great effort is made to point out various parts that make the percept much clearer. Amplifications and elaborations can be redundant or, in less frequent instances, can bring in details that, in effect, spoil the concept and give it a minus form quality. An example of the last type of elaborating process is the following:

Card V: A bat with its wings spread in flight. It is shaped just like a bat, but I see these things coming out of the wings as lizards' mouths.

An organizational component also enters into the assessment of form quality. Some subjects omit certain of the blot areas or bring them into loose relationship with other areas, whereas other subjects can develop much more meaningful interrelationships between various blot parts. As in the case of elaboration discussed above, organizational efforts can be seriously flawed and largely undermine a response that initially had good form. An example of this:

Card X: An underwater scene with various kinds of fish swimming around. The pink in the center are big pieces of coral that the blue fish in the middle are towing in the water.

Rather than relying strictly on one's own judgment to determine the consonance between the concept and the inkblot with respect to form, it is suggested that Hertz's frequency tables be used as a reference supplemented by the form quality tables found in Exner's text (1974). A very large number of percepts and their locations are included in these two sets of tables, and each response is designated as good or poor form.

With respect to the Hertz tables, it is our experience that some of the minus scorings are, in fact, rather average form quality and therefore should be properly classed as plus responses. Thus, her minus form-level scorings should be treated somewhat circumspectly. On the other hand, one can have confidence that any percept she scores as having good form has indeed complied with the criteria for adequate form-level and should always receive a plus scoring.

▲6

Tabulation and Quantitative Interpretation

TABULATION OF SCORES AND COMPUTATION OF PERCENTAGES AND RATIOS

The tabulation process and the subsequent computation of percentages and ratios are essentially an effort to summarize the subject's Rorschach performance and to analyze it from a number of standpoints. While there are some commercial forms available to facilitate this process, the student can do just as well by using some blank sheets of paper and carefully following the procedures outlined here.

The initial step in tabulation is to collect the Rorschach responses from all 10 cards and make up a scoring summary sheet (see sample summary sheets in Chapter 16). The summary sheet consists of listing the reaction time and total time for each of the 10 cards, plus the scoring for every response. In addition to noting the location, determinant, and content scoring and denoting, where appropriate, whether the percept is a plus or minus form-level and a popular or original, a one- or several-word description of the response should be included. Rather than thumbing through numerous Rorschach response forms, the clinician then works entirely with the single summary sheet, which gives an overview of the performance, shows the sequence of responses, and, most importantly, reduces the possibility of errors in tabulating. One note of caution might be sounded here: Clinicians who score the

TABLE 6-1   Rorschach Technique: Tabulation Sheet

Location	Determinants		Content	
W	F	FC′	H	Aggression
W(S)			(H)	Alphabet
W̶	M	C′F	Hd	Anal
	FM	C′	(Hd)	Architecture
D				Blood
D(S)	Fm	FC	A	Botany
	mF	F/C	(A)	Clothing
d	m		Ad	Clouds
d(S)		CF	(Ad)	Explosion
	Fk	C/F		Eyes
dd	kF		Obj	Fire
de	k	C_{des}	H_{Obj}	Food
Dd ⟨ di		C_{sym}	Aobj	Ice
dr	FK	C		Landscape
(S) with any	KF	C_n	At	Map
of above	K		A_{at}	Masks
		Multiple		Music
	Fc	Determinants	Sex	Oral
S	cF		N	Religion
S(D)	c		Geo	Science
S(d)			Pl	Smoke
S (with any			Art	Water
Dd category			Abs	X-ray
responses				
				Multiple Content

Number of responses (R) _____   Consider additionals separately

Rejections: Cards _____   Not more than 20 possible—Beck's list

Number of P_____

Number of O_____

Average R/T chromatic: Sum of reaction times to Cards II, III, VIII, IX, X + 5

Average R/T achromatic: Sum of reaction times to Cards I, IV, V, VI, VII + 5

F% _____   Number of pure F + R × 100

F+% _____   Treat multiple determinant as a unit. Consider only form-dominant responses (M, FM, Fm, Fk, FK, F, Fc, FC′, F/C and FC) in the calculation of F+%. If a part of a multiple determin- ant is not form-dominant, then the multiple-determinant response is omitted entirely from the F+% computation. Multiple determinants that are partially poor form are treated as if the whole

TABLE 6-1 *Continued*

	percept is –. Total number of + single and + multiple-determinant responses in which form is dominant should be divided by the sum of + and – form-dominant responses × 100.
A%_____	Sum of A, (A), Ad, and (Ad) + R × 100
H%_____	Sum of H, (H), Hd, and (Hd) + R × 100
Any other content percent that seems significant	10% or more
W:M_____	W includes W(S), W̶, and W̶(S) but omits DW
Sum C_____	Sum of color responses weighted as follows:

$$1/2\text{—FC} \quad 1\text{—CF} \quad 1\text{-}1/2\text{—C}$$
$$\phantom{1/2\text{—FC} \quad 1\text{—CF} \quad 1\text{-}1/2\text{—}} C_{des}$$
$$F/C \quad\quad C/F \quad\quad C_{sym}$$
$$ C_{n}$$

M: sum C_____	
m:c_____	m includes FM, Fm, mF, and m c includes Fc, cF, c, FC', c'F, C'
VIII–X%	Total number of responses to Cards VIII, IX, and X + R × 100
FK + F + Fc%_____	Sum of FK, F, and Fc + R × 100. Should be equal to or larger than F%
(H + A):(Hd + AD)_____	Includes H, (H), A, (A), Hd, (Hd), Ad, and (Ad) but not H_{obj} or A_{obj}

Apperception: W_____%   D_____%   d_____%   Dd and S (pure S)_____%

Determine Use of Areas from Following Table[1]

W		D		d		Dd and S	
((W))	10%	((D))	30%				
(W)	11–20	(D)	31–45	(d)	5%		
W	21–30	D	46–55	d	6–15	Dd S	10%
W̲	31–45	D̲	56–65	d̲	16–25	D̲d̲ S̲	11–15
W̳	46–60	D̳	66–80	d̳	26–35	D̳d̳ S̳	16–20
W̳̳	≥ 61	D̳̳	≥ 80	d̳̳	≥36	D̳̳d̳̳ S̳̳	≥21

[1]The third line indicates the usual percentages for the four location areas. The number of parentheses next to the location symbol reflects the degree to which the percentage is *below* average. The number of lines beneath the symbol represents the degree to which percentage is *above* average.

Rorschach during the inquiry are well advised, before proceeding with the summary sheet, to review the responses in more reflective and leisurely fashion to make certain that the scoring is indeed correct.

Once the clinician is confident of the scoring, the percepts are tallied in the various categories on a sheet as shown in Table 6-1.

Several features of this tabulation sheet might be pointed out. First, any location, determinant, or content subclassification that does not occur in a particular record need not be listed on the tabulation sheet: For example, if Fc were missing from a protocol, then it would be omitted from the tabulation sheet.

Second, multiple determinants and multiple content are treated as a unit when listing and, in the case of determinants, when figuring F + %. For other tabulations, however, each part is considered separately.

Minus scores are added to the plus scores for the same symbol with a bracketed number next to the total to indicate the number that were minus. Additional responses that appeared during the inquiry are represented by plus signs and listed next to the appropriate symbol in brackets, but do not count in the total. Some examples of minus and additional scoring notations are:

1. Six responses scored FM, of which three were minus and two were additional, would be listed FM = 4 (–3) (+2).
2. Three responses scored Fc, all of which were minus, would be noted as Fc = 3 (–3).
3. Four responses scored CF, all additional, would be tabulated as CF = (+4).
4. Five responses scored M, no minuses, no additionals, would be entered as simple M = 5.

After the tabulations are completed, percentages and ratios are computed as indicated.

QUANTITATIVE INTERPRETATION

Analysis of percentages and ratios of the sundry Rorschach scoring categories can be exceedingly useful. One should be aware, however, that the empirical evidence for the validity of the meaning of various location and determinant categories and percentages and ratios utilizing these components of the Rorschach is short of compelling. On the other hand, there are many less formal clinical studies in consensual agreement with regard to what various quantitative aspects of the record mean. The most judicious posture that a Rorschach worker can assume in dealing with quantitative material, therefore, is to treat these interpretations as working hypotheses subject to corroboration or rejection based on other sources of information about the subject. These other data pertaining to the individual being evaluated might include qualitative aspects of the Rorschach observations of behavior, performance on other tests in the battery, and anamnestic data regarding such variables as age, sex, socioeconomic background, and other relevant historical factors.

The Rorschach worker should never attach an inordinate degree of significance to a single percentage or ratio, but rather should look for interrelationships between variables and endeavor to determine whether a meaningful configuration exists. Furthermore, while 1 of the 10 cards may have traumatic impact for a subject, the subject's performance on all 10 must be carefully considered, with the sequencing of responses within each card and for the set of cards, per se, receiving special attention. Only by searching for patterns of personality factors by scrutinizing a variety of results and behavioral and background features can the clinician arrive at a genuinely revealing picture.

There is material on the tabulation sheet that does not enter directly into the calculation of various percentages and ratios. This includes the additional responses. In making interpretations, the Rorschach worker should carefully review additionals, for they may either confirm or dilute certain interpretations that were made on the basis of the more formal record. A protocol composed of a relatively small number of primarily stereotyped responses would be interpreted quite differently if the subject also had given a number of fairly imaginative additional responses in the Inquiry phase of testing. One must also carefully examine the quality of various location and determinant scorings as well as consider the percentages and ratios. Two subjects may have the same W%, but a very different interpretation would be in order if one of them adhered to vague, poorly defined W's and the other gave whole responses that were very well integrated and highly creative. Both animal and human movement in particular lend themselves to much latitude in quality.

What are presented in the following pages of this chapter are general and comparatively elementary interpretive guidelines. For a more in-depth consideration of the interpretation of quantitative aspects of the Rorschach, the worker should consult more advanced texts. Among those that can be especially recommended as compatible with the approach of this book are Klopfer et al. (1954), Schachtel (1966), and, specifically for diagnostic assistance, Schafer (1948). As stated before, when assigning interpretative meanings to various Rorschach location, determinant, or content areas, one is dealing with material that is essentially hypothetical and, therefore, requires corroboration from as many other sources as possible, particularly those of a psychodynamic nature (see later chapters).

Location Scores

The location areas basically reflect the intellectual approach the subject uses in dealing with various situations. The average range of scores for the different types of location areas are W, 20–30%; D, 45–50%; d, 5–15%; and Dd and S, < 10% (see Chapter 7 for more detailed normative data). The use of percentages adjusts for the total number of responses given by a subject.

While each of the location, determinant, and content scorings will be treated separately, it cannot be overemphasized that Rorschach ratios and percentages should be treated configurationally, and that one particular aspect of the scoring profile should not be considered in isolation, uninfluenced by other elements of the subject's performance.

In general, W responses are thought to relate to organizational ability. Before making any assumptions about W's, however, it is necessary to assess their quality; that is, are they good or poor form. The whole responses that reflect good form might suggest strong conceptualization and a capacity to deal with the abstract. On the other hand, W's of a very mundane or even poor quality could possibly derive from the intellectual operations of an individual who has high aspirations for him- or herself without the ability to achieve them. It may be posited that a low W percentage may be consistent with minimal organizational drive and disinterest in seeking interrelationships between diverse aspects of experience. As will be discussed under movement, the number of W's should also be examined within the framework of the number of M's the subject produces. The presence of cutoff W's may indicate critical proclivities that can have constructive components or be compulsively disruptive.

The D and d percentages, when they occur in the average range, can best be interpreted as appropriate, common-sense, and practical application of intelligence probably resulting in a successful coping style with the environmental demands of everyday living. When there is an exaggerated number of the two types of usual details, it may be hypothesized that the subject feels somewhat anxious, insecure, and possibly inadequate and, as a consequence, limits Rorschach responses to the mundane and stereotyped, avoiding anything that is not obvious. More than 15 percent of d is sometimes found in a carping, highly pedantical individual. A low percentage of D's usually results in an inordinate number of W's, which then have to be examined for quality and interpreted in keeping with the suggestions made above.

The scoring category of Dd and S may not be present in a particular record, and no special significance should be attached to its absence. When Dd's do occur, many interpretations are possible, ranging from an imaginative responsiveness to one's surroundings, to a hyperalert, obsessive interaction with the environment. More specifically, the Dd percept is most germane for interpreting compulsive or obsessive thinking. A number of de responses may be compatible with an anxious individual who resists engaging the environment and maintains the majority of relationships on a superficial, noninvolving level.

Responses scored di are also reflective of anxiety and some concern with social relationships. The dr percept may be most reflective of a great deal of sensitivity and perceptiveness, but may also occur with autistic thinking. An inordinate number of S concepts are found in personalities with strong negativistic and oppositional tendencies. When space responses are coupled with good whole responses, they may indicate inner strength and an appropriate capacity to assert oneself.

Determinant Scorings

Form Scores

The percentages of pure form responses normally range from 30% to 50%. If the percentage is greater than 50, considerable rigidity and constriction may be present. In essence, the higher the F%, the more conventional and unspontaneous the subject. By contrast, an F% less than 30 is found in compulsive individuals who readily personalize situations. The production of large numbers of pure F's requires the least degree of energy and investment on the part of the subject. Thus, a record abounding in F's may be consistent with a defensively evasive individual. On the other hand, a person with very limited emotional and intellectual resources may also produce such a record. It is especially necessary to interpret the F% in light of the presence of other form-dominant responses such as M, FC, and Fc that, when occurring in any numbers, may reveal substantial personality assets, counterbalancing either a high or low number of F's.

Movement Scores

Movement (including human movement, animal movement, and inanimate movement) generally relates to an individual's ideational activity, empathy, maturity, capacity for delayed gratification, and living with oneself.

M, or human movement, is probably the most critical of all determinants found in a Rorschach protocol. It must be remembered that the M response entails a projective process, namely, ascribing movement to an inkblot. It also involves the very complex and demanding task of describing human attributes. Thus, M clearly relates to imagination and elements of identification and empathy with other people. An average number of M's in a record would be around three, with a person offering this number likely to be reasonably intelligent, well integrated, and fairly creative, with potential for maintaining successful social relationships.

In contrast to M, FM (animal movement) reflects the less mature aspects of personality that are not under the same degree of conscious control and may be manifested in difficulties in controlling immediate gratification of impulse life. At the same time, some FM should be present, as such responses represent a source of energy and vitality and are, in fact, a precursor of M percepts. This latter is especially true in young children, where a record with a number of FM responses would be regarded positively and, with the maturing process, it would be conjectured that many of the FM's would be translated into M types of movement.

The inanimate-type movement percept (encompassing Fm, mF, and m) is generally associated with unpleasant feelings indicative of repressed conflicts and tension. Two or more m responses may indicate that the individual is experiencing marked stress and sees his or her situation as growing progressively more out of control. In that m indicates that the individual is aware of threatening feelings, an absence of m type responses, when the individual is in an obvious conflict situation, has very negative implications. In a normal record the proportion of the various types of movement responses should be about two M's, one FM, and one-half m.

The W to M ratio is very important in the quantitative interpretation. The ratio of two W's to one M is considered optimal, and the interpretation that is suggested is that aspiration level and ability are commensurate. When the W to M ratio exceeds four to one, then it is hypothesized that aspiration has moved beyond available resources and is too high. On the other hand, when the W's are less than twice the number of human movement responses, then it is ordinarily posited that the individual is narcissistically preoccupied with his or her daydreams and fantasies and has not found suitable channels for his or her creative potentials. Movement is also intricately bound up with various types of color responses.

Color Scores

The assumption made about color responses (both chromatic and achromatic) is that they reveal much of how the subject deals with and responds to environmental stimuli, which, in turn, taps the nature of interactions with other people. Color responses may be regarded as located on a continuum, with C on one end of the scale indicative of wild emotionality and impulsivity and FC, at the other end, consistent with responsiveness and consideration for others. The FC color response may be best described as exemplifying emotional control, that is, the capacity to react to affectively charged situations in a socially appropriate manner as would a well-adjusted person. When the FC has an arbitrary component such as in the F/C scoring, it is posited that this outer show of responsiveness is superficial and forced, and that genuine feelings are not really involved.

The CF response, which is intermediate between FC and C, reflects some measure of control but lacks the integration of the FC percept. On the one hand, CF types of responses reflect a degree of uninhibitedness and spontaneity but, when too numerous, some lapse in control. The C/F response, like the F/C, represents a studied attempt to be spontaneously responsive.

The pure C percept, which is entirely without form, suggests an affective explosiveness in which the individual is at the mercy of his or her emotions and cannot exercise any control over them. Color naming (C_n), color descriptions (C_{des}), and color symbolism (C_{sym}) all, in varying degrees, represent some effort to impose restraints over raw feelings, generally with rather poor success. The record of a reasonably well-adjusted person should contain two or three times as many FC's and CF's and no pure C responses.

The M to sum C ratio is highly significant and pivotal in assessing the individual's personality. Essentially, this ratio focuses on the balance between the subject's inner life and his or her capacity to deal with external stimulation. It may be viewed simplistically as tapping an introversion-extroversion dimension. Generally speaking, it is hypothesized that there should be two or three times as many M's as sum C and that the sum of M and sum C should be at least three. If the record contains too little M, then one may be dealing with the self-centered, infantile personality. By the same token, if there is too much M, then the individual may be overly withdrawn and too immersed in fantasy living. When the sum of M and sum of C is less than three, the subject very likely is constricted in his or her life and reacts in an inhibited, rigid, colorless, and repressed fashion. When the sum of M and sum C is greater than seven, a very rich and versatile life may be suggested.

The M to sum C ratio should always be contrasted with the m to c ratio, the latter being the more basic tendencies of the individual that are not fully accepted. When these two ratios are in the same direction, this underlines the M to sum C interpretation. When these ratios are at variance with one another, some conflict may exist between behavioral patterns and inner needs.

The percentage of responses to the last three cards is also interpreted as revealing some aspects of the individual's affective life. The expectation is that 30–40% of the responses in a particular Rorschach record will be given to these three color cards. The degree of affective responsiveness to these cards in terms of number of responses is conjectured to be less under the individual's con- scious control than the way in which color as such is used in various percepts.

Achromatic color percepts are seen as dilute or toned-down chromatic percepts and merely an extension of the subject's responsiveness to color. When C' type responses of a grey or black variety dominate a protocol, however, it may be surmised that some depressive features are present. C' responses that involve white space may indicate negativism and aggressiveness. In both instances there is evidence of withdrawal and some unresponsiveness to the environment.

Shading Scores

All shading responses may be interpreted as having an anxiety component within the context of affectional needs and modes of gratifying them. When Fc is the type of texture response that predominates in a record, it may be hypothesized that one is dealing primarily with an unaggressive, ingratiatingly passive person who is sensitively aware of the feelings of others. While this person may have almost infantile cravings for closeness to others, social interactions are likely to be controlled and quite tactful. In contrast to Fc, cF and c probably represent varying degrees of far more primitive, undifferentiated dependency needs. These affectional yearnings may well be on an essentially physical contact level. The pure c response in particular may occur in individuals who are markedly infantile in their emotional demands.

The FK kind of response, in contrast to the surface, tactual types of c responses, implies distance and perspective. An FK percept is hypothesized to mean dealing with one's anxiety by engaging in introspection in an effort to understand the nature of the anxiety rather than merely seeking outside sources of support. Thus, FK may be interpreted as reflective of insight and a positive sign of adjustment. The KF and K types of percept are also three-dimensional, but lack form and are far more disruptive in nature than FK. They may be regarded as indicating that the individual has not been able to develop adequate defenses for dealing with anxiety, which, consequently, is free-floating. The Fk, kF, and k percepts that translate three-dimensional space into two dimensions such as x-rays imply that the subject is attempting to use intellectualization in handling anxiety. The Fk type of response is consistent with at least some measure of intellectual control, whereas kF and k reveal that intellectualization is not working very successfully in containing anxiety.

As noted earlier, the m to c ratio is used in conjunction with M to C to determine if the person's behavioral patterns are consistent with his or her basic personality.

The FK + F + Fc% is referred to as the extended F% and is basically a measure of refined control. It is hypothesized that the percentage reflects the way tact and insight modify the individual's basic rigidity. Optimally, FK + Fc should be 25–75% of pure F. When it is less than 25%, long-standing repressive types of defenses may be disrupting the expression of affectional needs. If FK + Fc is more than 75%, the individual may be driven by cravings for affection and may operate in a hypersensitive and mostly dependent manner in his or her transactions with others.

Content Scores

Content scores, per se, are manifestations of the diversity and range of the subject's interest. A broad range of associations to the blot material is usually suggestive of good intelligence, whereas a very limited number of content categories may be indicative of limited intellectual ability and reveal something of the subject's defensive operations.

Animal content should be around 55% at most and preferably might be no more than 20%. A high percentage of human responses is consistent with an interest in other people. Of greater dynamic significance than percentages of human and animal percepts is how people or animals are described in the percept—that is, the nature of their activity and outstanding characteristics.

Both Hd and Ad may indicate anxiety and a wary cautiousness. There normally should be twice the number of H and A responses as Hd and Ad responses. If H + A is less than 50% Hd + Ad, the subject may be experiencing considerable anxiety.

Anatomy percepts are generally interpreted as excessive interest in parts of the body, which may be hypochondriacal. Anatomy responses are also interpreted as reflective of intellectual types of defenses.

Among the other content categories that might be mentioned are sexual percepts indicative of sexual or erotic preoccupations, and blood, which may relate to aggressiveness and hostility expressed either inwardly or outwardly. A number of object responses would be consistent with abstract ability and/or a disinterest in people. Eye concepts of various sorts are particularly significant and may suggest that the subject feels under critical surveillance and is quite self-conscious. An almost paranoid stance toward the environment may sometimes be indicated.

Content will be discussed much more exhaustively in the latter sections of this text, but it should be pointed out here that a fixed interpretation for specific associations to the cards can be grossly incorrect. It behooves the examiner to look at the Rorschach record in a more comprehensive and penetrating fashion to discern meaningful personality patterns for the specific individual being evaluated.

Populars and Originals

It would be expected that the average record would have seven or so populars or near populars, indicating a capacity to think in a conventional, conforming fashion. Too many populars might be interpreted as overly stereotyped thinking, possibly due to a limited intellect; the subject may also be very anxiety-ridden and cling to the most obvious. Originals of good quality can be compatible with high-level intellectual ability and capacity for creative thinking. On the other hand, originals of minus form-level might point to defective reality appreciation.

Form-Level

The F+% deals with how well the individual's reality controls are functioning within the framework of accuracy of perception, or the goodness of fit between the inkblot and the response. When there are a number of responses in which the percept is at variance with the configuration of the blot resulting in –'s, then the F+% is lowered, suggesting defective reality appreciation. The F+% should normally be in the 80–90% range. When it is 70–80%, it may be hypothesized that the reality sense is weakened and the person is adjusting on the borderline level. Below 70% would be compatible with markedly vitiated logical controls or possibly someone of seriously impaired intelligence. When the F+% rises above 90% and gets into the 95–100% range, then one is likely to be dealing with a rigid, highly perfectionistic person.

Miscellaneous Aspects of the Scoring Profile

The examination of the total number of percepts given to Rorschach cards may reveal much about the person's intellectual abilities. The average adult would give anywhere from 20–40 responses. A record with below 20 responses suggests a constricted personality or a person who has limited cognitive abilities at his or her disposal. A large number of responses may be obtained from a very imaginative subject. However, if the responses are composed largely of small detail-type percepts, this may indicate compulsivity. A reaction time to chromatic cards that is far more rapid than that to achromatic cards may be present in the record of an individual who is highly stimulated by his or her emotions. When the reaction time to the black and white cards is more rapid, the person may be emotionally blocked and defending against the expression of his or her feelings.

Sequence Analysis

The Rorschach worker must examine the summary sheet carefully, looking at the reaction times and the number and kind of percepts given to each of the 10 cards taken in sequence. A sudden shift to notably poorer form quality or a reduction in the number of responses may suggest that the particular card is stimulating some very negative associations, undermining the individual's reality testing and productivity. Knowing which types of concepts occur frequently on a particular card is helpful in carrying out sequence analysis. If a subject gave fairly popular responses through seven of the cards and then, on Card VIII, became quite idiosyncratic in his or her associations, it might be conjectured that the card had special emotional impact. Additional responses are important in the process of sequence analysis and often give valuable clues as to the nature of the individual's controls and his or her desire to inhibit or censor certain associational material.

The related topic of content sequence analysis will be discussed in Chapter 12.

▲ 7

Normative Data

Normative data relevant to the Rorschach are often sparse, dated, and understandable only in reference to a particular school of scoring. Nonetheless, the examiner who wishes to use the technique in a nomothetic manner will require a normative basis for his or her inferences. The following sources of data may prove useful in this connection since they are understandable in terms of a Klopfer-based system.

A comprehensive set of norms for children was presented by Ames, Métraux, Rodell, and Walker (1974). These authors worked with Rorschach records of 650 children, aged 2–10 years, of "mostly highly educated parents" (Ames et al., 1974, p. xiii). These records were supplemented by the addition of 900 protocols of various levels of socioeconomic status. Levitt and Truumaa (1972) surveyed 162 sources that provided normative data on the Rorschach records of children and adolescents. Using strict criteria for the inclusion of data, these authors reduced the studies to 15 investigations, including the normative studies of the Ames group. Although Levitt and Truumaa distinguished between the records of subjects of average and above-average intelligence, they did not take into account the variables of race and socioeconomic status.

Norms for adolescents were also provided by Ames, Métraux, and Walker (1971) in a study of 700 children aged 10–16. The Levitt and Truumaa volume (1972) likewise deals with normative data on adolescents. Comprehensive norms for elderly individuals were prepared by Ames, Métraux, Rodell, and Walker (1973) using 200 subjects over age 70. Ames et al. (1974) also reported expectancies for adult subjects.

Exner (1986a)[1] has provided the largest and most contemporary set of norms for Rorschach perceptual data. His data base includes 600 adult non-patients and 1,580 normal children and adolescents from 5 to 16 years old. He also provides data from several large clinical samples. We have summarized some of the data from Exner's normal subjects here because they frequently differ from the norms and rules of thumb developed using Klopfer's method. In particular, a number of scores (or "codes," as Exner calls them) appear more frequently in Comprehensive System records than in records collected using Klopfer's method. It is not possible to know, with certainty, the source(s) of these differences. (We doubt very much that they are simply the result of changes in the way people respond to Rorschach stimuli over the years.) One factor strikes us as most plausibly accounting for many of the differences. While we have no hard data on this point, it is our strong impression that responses scored via the Comprehensive System are more likely to receive multiple determinants and multiple contents than are responses scored by Klopfer's method.

LOCATION SCORES

W%

Ames et al. (1974) report that W% remains fairly steady from age 2 through age 10, hovering around 50. However, their findings also indicate that W% increases with decreasing socioeconomic status. The inner city sample consisting primarily of black children obtained W%s in the 70s.

In the summarized Levitt and Truumaa data, W% for subjects of average intelligence dropped gradually from 51 at age 5 to approximately 22 at age 16. Among the bright subjects, a drop was also seen, from approximately 53% at age 5 to approximately 44% at age 16. According to Ames et al. (1974), there is a general expectancy of between 20 and 30% of W's for normal adults.

Among elderly subjects, Ames et al. (1973) determined W% as being 36 among normal elderly subjects, 43 among presenile elderly, and 46 among senile elderly subjects. Thus, a gradual increase in W% is reported as the subject moves toward senescence.

After a high of 64% for 5 year olds, W% in Exner's (1986a) sample of normal children and adolescents[2] remained fairly steady between age 6 (47%)

---

[1]We have elected to present data for the 1986 Comprehensive System norms because Exner (1991) excluded all records with fewer than 14 responses prior to tabulating the most recent Comprehensive System norms. The normative data on Klopfer's approach includes such brief records.

[2]For ease of exposition we will henceforth refer to Exner's children and adolescents collectively as "children," using specific ages to make important distinctions.

and age 16 (43%). This pattern is similar to that for Levitt and Truumaa's bright children. Exner's normal adults gave more W's (39%) than individuals tested using the Klopfer method. These patterns of W's may have been due to secular trends in education. The Comprehensive System data were collected more recently than the Klopfer samples and, as a result, the adults assessed were apparently better educated (cf. Exner, 1991). Perhaps the children's education was better because it was more recent. As previously noted, the tendency to give W's is related to intellectual capacity.

D%

Ames et al. (1974) indicate that D%, for their sample of 2–10-year-olds, ranged from 33 to 48, with an average close to 40. Increased use of D% was seen after 6 years, with a peak at 9 years. Levitt and Truumaa (1972) note a gradual decline of D% from 47 at age 5 to approximately 41% at age 16 for their bright subjects. Ames et al. (1971) found that the mean D% for their adolescent subjects ranged from a low of 41 at 10 years to a high of 47 at 14 years.

Ames et al. (1974) report an expectancy of between 50% and 70% of D's among adults. In their study of elderly subjects, Ames et al. (1973) noted D% of 47%, 47%, and 45% for their normal, presenile, and senile subjects, respectively.

D% increased about 17% between the ages of 5 (43%) and 15 (60%) (Exner, 1986a). This pattern was similar to that found by Ames and her coworkers using Klopfer's method. There was a noticeable dip at age 16 (52%). Normal adults averaged 61%, placing them in the middle of the expected range for adults tested by Klopfer's method.

Dd%

In the Ames (1974) study, Dd% is perceived to increase gradually from age 2 to age 6, at which point it reaches 15 percent. It is then reported to drop back to 8% at age 10. Much smaller Dd%s are indicated by Ames et al. in their inner city sample, ranging from 4% at age 5 to a maximum of 8% at age 6.

For their adolescent subjects aged 10–16 years, Ames et al. (1971) found the mean Dd% to be 8%. Ames et al. (1974) note the expected occurrence of Dd to be approximately 10% for adult subjects. With respect to elderly subjects, Ames et al. (1973) report mean Dd%s of 15%, 9%, and 8% for normal, presenile, and senile elderly subjects, respectively.

In contrast to the findings of Ames et al. (1974), Dd% was rather steady in Exner's (1986a) samples. Dd% fluctuated only between 7% and 10% in Exner's normal children, except for two notable dips to 3% (ages 5 and 9). Exner's normal adults produced about the same proportion of Dd's (8%) as individuals tested using Klopfer's method.

DETERMINANTS

Form

For child subjects, Ames et al. (1974) indicate mean F% above 50 for all ages in their sample. The F% determinant is reported to be at its highest at age 2 years (90%), declining steadily to a low point of 52% at age 7. It is then reported to rise to a mean of 63% at 10 years. It should be noted that, in general, Ames et al. (1974) have also found that F% was higher among their inner city subjects than among their other subjects, ranging between 76% at age 9 to 91% at age 5½. Among adolescent subjects, Ames et al. (1971) report mean F% falling very close to 62% at every age except 16 years, when it drops to 56%.

Ames et al. (1974) indicate an expectancy for F% of 50 or less in adult records. Among elderly subjects, Ames et al. (1973) indicate F%s of 65%, 56%, and 57% for their subjects aged 70, 80, and 90, respectively.

Exner's (1986a) normal children displayed a different pattern of pure form responses than children tested using Klopfer's method. F% dropped fairly steadily from age 5 (57%) to age 10 (40%), rising precipitously at age 11 (50%). F% stayed near 50% from age 12 to age 16. F% in Exner's normal adults (35%) was also toward the low end of the expectations for adults developed using Klopfer's method.

Human Movement (M)

According to Ames et al. (1974), the average number of M responses increases with age in an almost steady progression from 2 to 10 years. M is reported as being an average of only 0.1 responses at age 2, reaching a maximum of 1.7 responses at age 10. M responses among the inner city sample are considerably fewer, reaching a maximum mean of only 0.7 by age 10.

In their summarized data, Levitt and Truumaa (1972) note a steady increase in M responses from a mean of 0.45 at age 5 for their average subjects to a mean of 2.36 at age 16. For their bright subjects, an average of 1.2 M responses is seen at age 5, gradually increasing to 2.77 by age 16.

Ames et al. (1974) have indicated a general expectancy of two or three M responses in the average adult record. Ames et al. (1973) also observe that a person with superior intelligence might be expected to give 5 or more M responses in a record. Among their normal, presenile, and senile elderly subjects, Ames et al. (1973) have found mean M responses of 3.3, 1.6, and 0.2, respectively.

Subjects in Exner's (1986a) norm samples tended to give slightly more M's than subjects tested using Klopfer's method. Five-year-olds averaged nearly 1 M, the average rising fairly steadily to over 3 at age 16. Exner's normal adults also averaged over 4 M's, as opposed to the 2 or 3 expected by Klopfer. The differences in intellectual capacity among samples described in the discussion of W% may also help account for these differences in M.

Animal Movement (FM)

Ames et al. (1974) report a progression of 0.1 FM responses at 2 years to 1.9 FM responses at 7 years. In general, FM responses increase with age. Like the M response pattern, FM responses among inner city subjects are found to be fewer. Mean FM responses among inner city subjects were reported by these investigators to range up to only 1.0 at age 9.

Levitt and Truumaa indicate that FM responses for their average and bright groups combined increased from 1.59 at age 5 to a maximum of 2.81 by age 12, decreased slightly thereafter, and reached an average of 2.41 by age 16. Among their adolescent subjects, Ames et al. (1971) indicate a range of 2.0 to 2.5 FM responses, with the exception of age 15, at which a mean of 1.6 is recorded.

Among adult subjects, Ames et al. (1974) note an expectancy of 1 to 2 FM responses in a record. Among their elderly subjects, Ames et al. (1973) indicate mean FM responses of 2.7, 2.0, and 0.3 in the normal, presenile, and senile elderly subjects, respectively.

Child subjects examined using the Comprehensive System method tended to give substantially more FM's (3 to 3.5) than individuals examined via Klopfer's approach (Exner, 1986a). Modal adults gave 4 FM's, at least twice the rate expected using Klopfer's method.

Inanimate Movement (m)

Ames et al. (1974) found that m responses do not exceed 0.2 throughout the preschool period, but are seen as increasing after age 5 up to a peak of 0.8 at age 7, thereafter dropping back to about 0.5. Among their inner city subjects, m responses occurred even less frequently, ranging from none at age 5 up to only a maximum average of 0.2 at various ages thereafter.

In the Levitt and Truumaa (1972) summary data, an increase in m responses with age is seen in both the average and the bright groups. For the average subjects, mean m responses increased from 0.26 at age 5 to 0.62 by age 16. In the bright subjects, mean m responses increased from 0.44 at age 5 to 0.89 by age 16. Ames et al. (1971) likewise report an increase in m responses as one enters the teenage years.

Ames et al. (1973) reported a decrease in m responses with increasing age among their elderly subjects. At 70 years, a mean m of 0.33 was found, decreasing to 0.28 among their 80-year-old subjects, and to 0.15 among their 90-year-old subjects.

It should be noted that the m responses referred to above include the Fm, mF, and m categories taken together.

The pattern of m responses among Exner's (1986a) child subjects was similar to that found by Ames et al. (1974). Inanimate movement was never common, peaking at .59 at age 8. Exner's adult subjects were far more prone to give m's than were his child examinees, averaging over 1 animal movement response per record.

Color Responses

Ames et al. (1974) reported a gradual increase in CF responses among children, from near zero at 2 years, to an average of approximately 0.5 from 2½ to 4 years, and to about 1.3 from age 4½ through 7 years. A slow decrease is reported thereafter. Pure C responses show less of a change with development but do slowly increase to a peak at 7 years. Ames et al. described FC responses as never frequent in childhood, but showing an increasing trend, from virtual absence at 2 years to highs of 0.7 at ages 7 and 9. The inner city sample of Ames shows clearly less responsiveness to color in all three categories (FC, CF, and C).

The Levitt and Truumaa (1972) combined data indicate a gradual decrease for C responses, from an average of 0.37 at age 5 to 0.03 responses by age 16. For the CF category the trend is also a decreasing one, from an average of 1.16 at age 5 to an average of 0.62 by age 13. Between ages 13 and 16, there is a slight increase in the mean number of CF responses (reaching 0.76 by age 16). In the data on adolescents presented by Ames et al. (1971), mean FC responses show little change with age—averaging 0.3 at age 10 and 0.5 by age 16. Little change in mean CF responses is likewise reported by Ames et al., until age 16, at which time a sudden spurt in this type of response is seen (a mean of 1.2 of such responses at age 16). C responses show no particular trend with age in the Ames data on adolescents. The mean number of C responses is 0.2 at age 10 and 0.1 at age 16.

The expectancy of color responses for adult subjects, as noted by Ames et al. (1974), is about 3.0 FC responses, and perhaps one CF response per record. Among the elderly subjects in the Ames et al. study (1973), mean FC responses of 0.38, 0.37, and 0.54 were found for the 70-year-old subjects, the 80-year-old subjects, and the 90-year-old subjects, respectively. Mean CF responses of 0.69, 0.52, and 0.54 were found for the same three groups, respectively.

Exner's (1986a) subjects gave about 2 to 2.5 CF's compared to about 1 for subjects tested using Klopfer's method. Pure color responses were common in the records of Exner's subjects only before age 8. The average thereafter was less than 0.5, falling fairly steadily to adulthood. As with Klopfer's approach, the typical adult examined using the Comprehensive System method gave no C's. FC's were more common among Exner's subjects than among those tested using Klopfer's method. Youngsters less than 7 years old averaged less than 1 FC, those between 7 and 10 gave 1.5 FC's, and other children gave about 2.

Adults also gave nearly 4 FC's compared to the 3 that Klopfer-based data lead us to expect.

CONTENT

Human Responses

Ames et al. (1974) report a slow but steady increase in H% from age 2 (average = 3) to age 10 (average = 16). However, this age trend appears to be very much a function of the high socioeconomic status of these children. The age trends in H% were more obscure in children from working-class backgrounds, and they were actually reversed among inner city children, dropping from 22% at age 5 to 5% at age 8, and increasing again to 12% by age 10. One might question whether a white examiner testing a black child may have been a determining factor in the inner city age trend. In the summarized Levitt and Truumaa data (1972), no age trends in H% were found in children of average intelligence. (H% of 11.2 would be expected at all the ages.) In children of above-average intelligence, H% was noted to increase with age, from 10.3% at age 5 to 18% at age 10.

Ames et al. (1971) reported a relative stabilization of H% for adolescent boys and girls combined. When the sexes were considered separately, they found that the boys dropped from a high of 19.5% at age 10 to 13.9% at age 15 (16.1% at age 16). On the other hand, girls passed from 18.2% at age 10 to 21.9% at age 15 (20.1% at age 16).

Levitt and Truumaa (1972) found no relation between age and H% among adolescents of average intelligence; 11.2% was expected. They did find that the increase in H% leveled off with age among adolescents of above-average intelligence; it leveled off at about 20% in the teenage years.

In summarizing normative data on adults, Ames et al. (1974) state that the general expectancy is of 10–15% for H%. Levitt and Truumaa (1972) also report an expectancy of 10–20% in adults, the more intelligent subjects being in the upper part of the range.

Among elderly subjects, Ames et al. (1973) measured H% at 24%, 17%, and 5% in normal, presenile, and senile subjects, respectively. H% also increased with age among the elderly, from 16 at age 70 to 18 at age 80 and 24 at age 90. This increase with age was also found in the longitudinal data.

Exner's (1986a) data for "pure H"—those instances in which human content is *primary* in a percept—is similar to the data collected using Klopfer's method. H% rose slowly and fairly steadily in children, from 7% at age 5 to 14% at age 16. The typical adult gave 10% pure H's and 17% H's when *secondary* contents were included, bracketing the range of Klopfer-based expectations.

Animal Responses (A)

Ames et al. (1974) found that A% described a fairly steady pattern from age 2 through 10. It varied irregularly from a low of 41% to a high of 56. A% was also found to vary with socioeconomic status, being higher in the lower social classes. (Among inner city children, average A% was as high as 71% at age 8.) Levitt and Truumaa (1972) reported little relationship between age and A% among children of either average or above-average intelligence (A% was nearly 50 in these children). Interestingly, these authors did not find that A% varied with intelligence.

Ames et al. (1971) report that A% remained relatively stable in the adolescent years, again accounting for approximately half the test responses. The data of Levitt and Truumaa (1972) are consistent with the Ames data. Ames et al. (1974) suggest an expectancy of 35–50% for A% in the adult years. Among elderly subjects, Ames et al. (1973) measured A% to be 46%, 55%, and 40% for normal, presenile, and senile subjects, respectively. There was a slight increase with age, from 52% at age 70 to 53% at age 80 and 56% at age 90. This tendency of A% to increase slightly with age among the elderly was confirmed by longitudinal findings.

A% decreased irregularly from 48% in Exner's (1986a) 6-year-olds to 38% in his 16-year-olds. Adults A% was 42, placing them squarely in the middle of the Klopfer-based expected range. These figures should be lower, given our earlier suggestion that Exner's subjects may have had better intellectual tools than those studied via Klopfer's method.

Anatomy Responses (At)

Ames et al. (1974) found an average of less than 1 anatomic response per record through all the childhood age groups except age 9, where the mean was 1.2. "Anatomy responses . . . come inconspicuously at 8, 9, and 10 years, approximating about one response per child at each of these ages. A few girls at 10 years give *only* anatomic responses" (Ames et al., 1974, p. 82). Unfortunately, socioeconomic variables were not considered with respect to the At response. Levitt and Truumaa (1972) report a similar finding of less than 1.0 At responses at all ages.

In the adolescent period anatomic responses remained fairly static, averaging below 1.0 response per record except at age 14, where the mean was 1.21 (Ames et al., 1971). Levitt and Truumaa (1972) report means below 1.0 for all the adolescent ages.

Among elderly subjects a decided increase in anatomy percepts was found with progressive senility; the average responses per record were 0.5, 1.4, and 8.4 for normal, presenile, and senile subjects respectively (Ames et al., 1973). In fact, anatomic responses were the most common responses in the records of senile subjects. In contrast, At% decreased with age, from 12 at age 70 to 10 at age 80 and 0 at age 90. This decrease is confirmed by the longitudinal data of Ames et al. (1973). These authors also report that At% increased with decreased socioeconomic status, from 8.16% to 15.79%. The institutionalized elderly were also found to have higher At% than the noninstitutionalized subjects—17.63 versus 6.38.

Exner (1986a) did not report At responses. In 1991 he reported that the average number of At's for children under 10 years old was less than 0.5, rising to 1.14 at age 12 and dropping thereafter to .41 at age 16. The At rate for adults was virtually identical to that for 16-year-olds.

POPULAR RESPONSES

The responses scored popular in the Ames collection of normative studies were specifically chosen using statistical criteria from the responses of the normative samples. The actual frequencies and percentages thus obtained are, therefore, likely to be of little value to the psychologist who uses other lists of populars. However, the general trends found are worth noting. Ames et al. (1974) found that P% doubled from age 2 to age 10. Levitt and Truumaa (1972) also found a substantial increase with age during childhood. Subjects from lower socioeconomic backgrounds in the Ames investigation were generally higher in P% than subjects from the higher social classes. P stayed relatively constant through the adolescent years according to the Ames data (Ames et al., 1971), though Levitt and Truumaa found a slight increase with age. Among the elderly the popular score was found to drop from the normal to the presenile to the senile subjects (Ames et al., 1973). P% does not seem to be related to socioeconomic status among the elderly.

Noninstitutionalized subjects gave significantly more popular responses than did the institutionalized.

Despite using a different list of populars, Exner (1986a) found that his adults, like those tested via the Klopfer method, gave between 6 and 7 populars. P% fluctuated little in Exner's data, remaining in the 26% to 30% range for the most part.

RESPONSE TOTAL (R)

Ames et al. (1974) report that for their child subjects, total R showed a tendency to increase during childhood, from a mean of 9.6 at 2 years to 18.6 at 9 years. It should be noted that R was found to be smaller among children from lower socioeconomic backgrounds. Thus, while 9-year-old children from the higher socioeconomic backgrounds displayed a mean of 18.6 total responses, subjects from the inner city displayed a mean of 10 responses. Levitt and Truumaa (1972) indicate that R has a slight tendency to increase, from an average of 15.6 at age 5 to 20.8 by age 16. These statistics represent their average and bright groups combined. In the Ames et al. data (1971) on adolescents, similar statistics are presented. Ames et al. also note that for the adolescent group, girls typically give a larger number of responses than do boys.

In the Ames et al. data (1973) on elderly subjects, a steady decrease in number of responses with increased deterioration of the subject is noted. Normal subjects gave a mean of 26 responses, preseniles a mean of 16, while seniles gave a mean of only 13 responses. Female subjects tended to give more responses than the male subjects. A consistent drop with age was also seen— subjects in their 70s gave a mean of 19.52 responses, those in their 80s a mean of 15.27 responses, and those in their 90s a mean of 14.98 responses.

Exner's (1986a) data on total responses were quite consistent with those collected using Klopfer's methods. R rose from 15.3 at age 5 to 19.6 at age 8, fluctuating between 19.6 and 21.6 thereafter through age 16. Exner's adults averaged 22.6 responses, toward the low end of the expectations generated by Klopfer's method.

▲ 8

Pathological
Verbalizations

The examinee's general verbalizations during the procedure can be used as an indicator of pathological verbalization, which is particularly characteristic of, though not confined to, schizophrenic illness. Hermann Rorschach (1921/1942) first noted the occurrence of such responses in the records of individuals suffering from schizophrenia and "mental defectives." Other early Rorschachers (Levy & Beck, 1934; Piotrowski, 1937) also noted the clinical significance of certain pathological verbalizations.

As explained by Rapaport et al. (1946), this application of the Rorschach is an extension of the long-practiced psychiatric technique of using verbal interview behavior to elicit peculiarities of schizophrenic thought and speech (e.g., Bleuler, 1911/1950). The Rorschach technique was seen by Rapaport as a vehicle that is even more sensitive than the psychiatric interview to this type of thinking. Indeed, some psychiatric authorities came to accept such evidence as the most definitive evidence of schizophrenic illness (e.g., Knight, 1954).

Many persons who would have been diagnosed as suffering from schizophrenia at the time pioneers like Rapaport et al. (1946) were investigating pathological verbalizations are termed Bipolar, Manic according to modern diagnostic criteria such as those in the *DSM-III-R*. Consequently, patients currently diagnosed Bipolar, Manic tend to give many of responses described in this chapter, especially the responses we will term "fluid" and those high in "personal meaning" (cf. Grossman, Harrow, & Sands, 1986; Harrow, Grossman, Silverstein, Meltzer, & Kettering, 1986; Marengo & Harrow, 1985). As first suggested by Rorschach, individuals with other cognitive deficits not attributable to schizophrenia also tend to give some of the responses described in this chapter. Mentally deficient individuals and those suffering from organic brain dysfunction are especially likely to give those responses we will describe as "rigid" and infused with "objective meaning" (cf. Exner, 1986a; Goldfried et al., 1971, ch. 11; Swartz, 1970).

Rapaport was the first Rorschacher to put forward an extensive categorization of pathological verbalizations (Rapaport et al., 1946). Later writers have pointed out a number of problems with Rapaport's categories, including scoring unreliability, overlap, conceptual confusion, and contradictory definitions (cf. Schuldberg & Boster, 1985). Nevertheless, all subsequent efforts to measure deviant thinking via the Rorschach have built on the pioneering efforts of Rapaport. We shall therefore use his work as a point of departure for this chapter. We have elected to present in detail five of his categories that have been studied by most researchers working in this area (e.g., Exner, 1986a; Johnston & Holzman, 1979) and are mentioned in most clinical treatises about pathological verbalizations (e.g., Lerner, 1991): Fabulized Combinations, Confabulations, Contaminations, Autistic Logic, and Perseveration. We have added a further seven categories useful in marking the dimensions of pathological verbalization identified by Schuldberg and Boster (1985): Fabulized responses, Incongruous Combinations, Relationship verbalizations, Incoherence, Self-References, Confusion, and Vague responses.

We will first present Rapaport's ideas about the general mental processes underlying pathological verbalizations. Then we will describe Schuldberg and Boster's (1985) empirical refinements of Rapaport's work that provide the scheme used to organize the remainder of the chapter. Next we will define the different types of pathological verbalizations and provide specific examples of them. The final section of the chapter details the clinical observations and research findings on the meaning of the pathological verbalizations.

GENERAL THEORY

Recognizing that the examinee's verbalizations in the Rorschach situation must be judged in relation to the stimulation provided by the inkblots, Rapaport used the concept of loss or increase of "distance" from the perceptual reality of the blots to develop his system for defining pathological verbalizations. He described the reality of the Rorschach situation as follows:

> Normal subjects will understand the testing situation and the test instructions to mean that they are to give responses for which sufficient justification may be found in the perceptual qualities of the inkblot; that they must give responses which are completely acceptable to everyday conventional logic; and that, just as they should not

give responses which they cannot confirm by reference to the inkblot, so they should not give responses which are so dominated by the perceptual configurations of the inkblot that they are no longer subject to critical control, and thus become absurdly combined or absurdly integrated. (Rapaport et al., 1946, p. 329)

Given this context, a pathological increase of distance occurs when the examinee's response shows little regard for the perceptual properties of the blot or when a good response is unjustifiably embellished. A pathological decrease of distance occurs when, on the other hand, an examinee takes the reality of a blot too seriously, endowing it with "real" affective or logical properties.

Schuldberg and Boster (1985) used multivariate statistical techniques to reanalyze some of Rapaport et al.'s (1946) data. Based on this reanalysis they suggested that Rapaport's concept of distance from the blot be recast as two independent dimensions. Their first dimension was marked at one end by responses infused with "personal meaning" supplied by the examinee, that is, meaning that was not justified by the stimulus properties of the blots. The other end of that dimension was marked by responses that represented an examinee's attempt to treat the blot as if it possessed a concrete reality—an "objective meaning"—of its own. Schuldberg and Boster interpreted their second dimension as reflecting the examinee's attentional set(s). At one end of this second continuum are responses reflecting mental rigidity, that is, difficulty breaking a mental set to create new ideas. Responses at the other end of the second dimension indicate excessive fluidity, that is, an inability to maintain a stable, task-relevant cognitive set.

Many other schemes are available to organize the literature on pathological verbalizations (cf., Johnston & Holzman, 1979). Indeed, the abundance of theories in this area strikes us as a serious problem. Most tend to be employed by their originators and a handful of dedicated followers; none appears to have a wide following. Hence, as you will see below, empirical results have not been as cumulative as one would hope. We have adopted Schuldberg and Boster's dimensions as the primary organizing scheme for the remainder of this chapter for two reasons. First, they organize many types of responses parsimoniously. Second, Schuldberg and Boster (1985) have offered a cogent discussion of the relationships between their dimensions and other theories.

DEFINITIONS AND EXAMPLES

Fluid Responses

The following four types of responses are "classic": long studied and widely used by clinicians. They also mark the pole of Schuldberg and Boster's second dimension that is characterized by an overly fluid cognitive set.

Fabulized responses (Fab) have undue affective elaboration or specificity, indicating an increase in psychological distance from the stimulus provided by the blot. Feelings, motives, or other qualities are ascribed to the percept despite the fact that the blot reveals nothing that would account for the elaboration. Examples of excessive affective elaboration include:

Card I (W):	A happy dog's face.
Card II (both D3 and white space):	A lake surrounded by dangerous rocks.
Card VIII (both D1):	Two ferocious-looking wolves.

The following are examples of *Fab* responses characterized by overspecificity:

Card III (both D8):	Two people . . . could be Adam and Eve.
Card VIII (both D1):	Two chipmunks . . . could be Chip and Dale.
Card IX (D3):	The Wicked Witch of the West.

According to Rapaport, *Fabulized combinations (Fabcom)* involve an implausible relationship between two or more percepts. The combination is usually based on spatial contiguity rather than on a logical relationship. Such responses reflect a loss of distance: overly concrete acceptance of the combination "because it is there." He included in this category both responses in which an implausible relationship is posited between two or more objects identified in different portions of the blot and responses involving implausible relationships within a single portion of a blot. Later investigators have thought it wise to distinguish between these two types of *Fabcoms* (e.g., Exner, 1986a; Solovay et al., 1986). Some subcategorize these responses within *Fabcom* (e.g., Lerner, Sugarman, & Barbour, 1985). In the Comprehensive System, on the other hand, responses of the second type "involving the condensation of blot details or images that are inappropriate[ly] merged into a single object" (Exner, 1986a, p. 163) are referred to as Incongruous Combinations *(Incom)*.[1]

Incom responses include:

Card II (D3, d1):	A bear with an anteater's nose.
Card III (D8):	A man with a duck's head.
Card V:	A butterfly with his hands out.

[1]It is important to note that Johnston and Holzman (1979) defined *Incom* more broadly than did Exner (1986a). Johnston and Holzman included inappropriate activity (e.g., a beetle crying) in their definition of *Incom*, whereas such responses do not appear to be coded in the Comprehensive System. They also define transparencies (e.g., a man sitting here . . . you can see his heart pumping) as *Incoms*, whereas Exner codes them as *Fabcoms*. Readers should be aware that this area is rife with these kinds of definitional inconsistencies.

The following are examples of *Fabcom* (as defined by Exner, 1986a) responses:

Card VIII (D1, D2):　　Two beavers dancing on an ice cream cone.

Card X (D1, D13):　　A crab grabbing a rat's tail.

Card X (D4, D14):　　Two ants fighting over a baseball.

Confabulations (Confab) have been defined differently by different authors. The term was originally introduced by Rorschach, who used it to subsume a number of the pathological verbalizations described here. Rapaport defined Confabulations as a more pathological variant of *Fab* responses. He scored *Confab* when a response was so embellished with fantasy and affective elaboration that the reality of the procedural situation seemed to have been completely lost. These responses reflect a pathological increase of distance from the blot. For example:

Card IV (W):　　A big, ugly menacing man stomping around. He's coming to get me.

Card VI (D4):　　The light streak in here reminds me of the wide and powerfully flowing Mississippi River.

Card IX (D8)　　The light bulb is—I think it's manmade. And the pink is down here and it gives energy for the light bulb.

Terminology is especially confusing when it comes to Confabulations. The Comprehensive System includes a code for Confabulation, but it is defined differently from Rapaport's *Confabs*. In the Comprehensive System *Confab* is scored only in the rare instances when a subject attends only to a detail area of the blot but generalizes a response from that detail to a larger area, for example, "this part looks like a nose cone—it must be a rocket" (Exner, 1986a). For the sake of theoretical and interpretive consistency with the remainder of the pathological verbalizations described in this chapter, we are going to employ Rapaport's definition of *Confab*. We are, also however, going to report data from the Comprehensive System. Meloy and Singer (1991) have pointed out that the Comprehensive System Deviant Response *(DR)* is virtually identical to Rapaport's *Confab*. The *DR* is slightly more expansive, including both circumstantial responses and inappropriate phrases (Exner, 1986a).

Rigid Responses

The next two types of percepts are the conceptual opposite of those just described. They mark the pole of Schuldberg and Boster's second dimension characterized by an inability to shift mental sets.

Perseveration (Persev) occurs when the examinee clings to one specific content across several inkblots even when it does not fit the contours of the blot. According to Rapaport, *Relationship verbalizations (Rel)* occur when the examinee constructs relationships between parts of the same blot or percepts on different blots. Examples of the first type of *Rel* response include:

| Card II: | I don't know what this is (W except D1), but it appears to have grown out of this (D1). |
| Card III: | Two people (both D8) . . . they seem to have evolved out of this (D9). |

Hard data are not available, but it is our strong impression that the second type of *Rel* response is much more common than the first. For example:

| Card VIII (both D1): | These could be the cubs of that other bear (Card IV, W). |
| Card IX (both D2): | These could be witches at a Halloween party, like the jack-o-lantern (Card I, W). |

Examinees have even gone so far as to construct a story that progresses through all ten blots.

Personal Meaning Responses

The next two types of responses best define the "personal meaning" pole of Schuldberg and Boster's first dimension, *Incoherence (In coh)* and *Self-Reference (SRef)*.

Incoh responses use the percept simply as a "starting point for personal associations" (Rapaport et al., 1946, p. 353); the response is impossible for the examiner to understand in any context. For example:

Card II:	Tears go up in the air. Blood and break their neck. You know, reject.
Card V:	I don't know what I think of a beaver, might be because it swims.
Card X:	This looks like an underwater scene. The blue is like the sweatshirt I have on. The red is like my brother's shirt. This is a mess, the fish are all swirling around like they're in battle.

SRef responses were defined by Rapaport et al. (1946) as "verbalizations [that] convey the subject's feeling that the card or the inquiry has some special reference to him. In the true self-reference, all awareness of the impersonal reality of the card is lost" (p. 359). Examples include:

Card II (both D3):	Doggy heads (Show me the noses) Now you imply I am too nosey!
Card IV (W):	An insect crawling toward me.
Card IV (middle of d2):	Looks like the lips of a vagina . . . I look something like that myself.

Rapaport and colleagues (1946) went on to say that "[Self-reference responses] must be carefully differentiated from . . . reminiscences" (p. 359). Exner (1986a) agrees, interpreting Rapaport's "reminiscences" as an indication of defensiveness rather than an indication of deviant thinking. Reminiscences are coded as Personalized responses in the Comprehensive System (cf. Exner, 1986a). Examples of Personalized responses, presented here for purposes of contrast, to clarify the scoring of *SRef*, include:

Card III (D1):	It looks like a butterfly . . . I see them all the time in my yard.
Card IX (D2):	A flower . . . my wife grows them.
Card VIII (both D1):	Two bears—like I saw in the circus.
Card X (D3):	A spike for bills . . . I have one on my desk.

"Objective Meaning" Responses

The following two types of responses define the conceptual opposite of the responses just described. These responses are given by examinees who try to interpret the blot stimuli too literally.

Confusion (Conf) is characterized by the examinee's feeling "that his response *is* and yet *cannot* be . . . reveals in his attitude a definite perplexity about this contradiction" (Rapaport et al., 1946, p. 352). Here are some examples:

Card III (D2, D3):	It's a bear . . . no, if it were a cut on his head the blood certainly wouldn't be standing up; it would be dripping down.

| Card VIII (W): | These two animals look like squirrels. No, they are rats—or maybe even racoons. They are climbing this tree. |
| Card X (D1): | This looks like some type of insect, you know, like under the sea—some type of—no not under the sea—some type of crab, yeah, under the sea. |

Schuldberg and Boster (1985) did not include *Vague (Vague)* responses in their study. However, *Vague* responses appear to us to be good markers of this dimension because they are an "almost" response in which the subject fails to commit him- or herself to a definite form. Examples include:

Card I (WS):	I can almost get a witch's face, but I can't quite make it out.
Card V (d2, D1):	I can almost get a crab from this . . . I'm not sure . . . these might be wings.
Card VI (W):	This could be a skin tacked up on the wall . . . I can't quite get it, but it is there some place.

Mixed Responses

We call the following two types of responses "mixed" because they represent a mixture of Schuldberg and Boster's dimensions. *Contaminations (Contam)* fall almost squarely at the intersection of the two dimensions. *Autistic Logic (Alog)* responses fall about halfway between the intersection of the two dimensions and the personal meaning end of the first dimension. *Alogs* also fall about halfway between the intersection and the fluid end of the second dimension.

Contam responses involve a loss of distance from the reality of the blot that causes the fusion of two or more discrete impressions into a single response that clearly violates reality. Often a neologism is used to refer to the fused response. For example:

Card III (D1):	It has the shape of a bow tie and the color of a butterfly so it must be a buttertie.
Card III (WS):	This is blood here at the top and down here at the bottom. This is an atoll with water in the middle. It's a bloody atoll.
Card V (W):	A rabbit-bat.

Alog is strained reasoning used to justify a response. The reasoning is often given with an air of certainty even though it bears little relationship to conventional forms of logic. Such reasoning is often based on the position of the percept within the blot, indicating a loss of psychological distance from the reality of the blot. Instances of such strained reasoning are manifest when the examinee says things such as:

Card II (D1):	It must be the South Pole. (Why?) Because it's at the bottom of the picture.
Card III (both D6):	A man and a woman. (Why?) Because they are together.
Card VIII (D1):	These are small rats. (Why?) Because they are only a small part of the picture.

Less frequently, a pathological increase in distance may also be manifest in Autistic Logic. For example:

Card X (W):	An orchestral score, a fashionable audience. (Why?) The tones of the instruments.

RESEARCH AND CLINICAL FINDINGS

Fluid Responses

Fabulized responses are the least pathological of the pathological verbalizations as viewed by Rapaport, with all subsequent workers following suit. Watkins and Stauffacher (1952) developed a useful quantitative index of pathological thinking by weighting a number of Rapaport's categories. In that scheme, called the Delta Index, *Fab* responses received the lowest possible weighting (.25 out of 1.00). Overspecific *Fab* responses receive the same weight in the Thought Disorder Index (TDI), a contemporary elaboration and refinement of the Delta Index (Johnston & Holzman, 1979; Solovay et al., 1986). The Comprehensive System index of deviant thinking, WSUM6, omitted this category altogether, presumably because it was felt to be insufficiently pathological (Exner, 1986a).[2] Studying the Holtzman inkblot technique (HIT), Cod-

---

[2]We are discussing the various types of pathological verbalization separately because recent research has suggested that composite measures such as the Delta Index, TDI, and WSUM6 obscure important differences among groups that are revealed by some of the individual response types (e.g., Edell, 1987).

kind (1966) found that persons high on a measure of the acceptance of and use of imagery gave more *Fab* responses than did those who rejected imagery. Clinical experience, as well, suggests that *Fab* responses are frequently given by introspective, sensitive individuals who enjoy playing with language. Normal individuals are aware of the liberties they are taking with reality in giving *Fab* responses. Therefore, the presence of some *Fab* responses is not proof of psychopathology. Unfortunately, no normative data are available for *Fab*. Experience suggests that most normals give, at most, one or two *Fab* responses.

Research with clinical samples provides support for the contention that *Fab* responses are not as pathological as the other responses discussed in this chapter. Rapaport et al. (1946) found "a high incidence of, and special emphasis upon, fabulized responses is characteristic for those clinical groups in which ideation is quantitatively and qualitatively rich, though not irrealistic to the point of clearly psychotic thinking" (p. 337). We reanalyzed their data in order to confirm their interpretation. We found that 14 of Rapaport et al.'s 65 schizophrenic subjects (19%) gave at least one *Fab*, as did 9 of their 33 preschizophrenic patients (probably Schizoid, Borderline, or Schizotypal in modern parlance) (27%), and 9 of their 52 neurotic patients (17%). On the other hand, only 3 of Rapaport et al.'s 43 depressed subjects (7%) and 4 of their 54 state police officer controls (7%) gave *Fab* responses. The mean *(M)* number of Fabulized responses given by Rapaport et al.'s subjects were, respectively, .3, 1.3, .23, .07, and .07. These data are not easily reconciled with the findings of Swartz (1970), who, studying the HIT, found *Fab* responses more common among those with depression and normals than among individuals suffering from schizophrenia or mental retardation. This inconsistency does, however, support the contention that *Fab* responses are qualitatively different from the other responses discussed in this chapter. They do not appear to index problems with reasoning. Rather, they appear to result from a mild breakdown in defenses that permits the expression of fantasy and affect. These breakthroughs *embellish* the examinee's responses with *associations* not suggested by the reality of the blots, but do not *distort* them in ways at variance with the real stimulus value of the blots (cf. Quinlan, Harrow, Tucker, & Carlson, 1972).

Recall that *Incongruous Combinations* in the Comprehensive System correspond to the Rapaport *Fabcoms* that involve only one portion of the blot. *Incoms* are weighted .25 (out of 1.00) in the TDI and 2 (out of 7) in the WSUM6. The psychological process underlying *Incoms* (and *Fabcoms*) is thought to differ from that underlying *Fab* responses. Whereas *Fabs* are thought to reflect associative elaborations, *Incoms* reflect problems in reasoning. Specifically, *Incoms* (and *Fabcoms*) involve a condensation of perceptions and ideas in a way that disregards the usual conceptual boundaries between ideas and objects (cf. Quinlan & Harrow, 1974).

Nonpatient adults sampled by Exner (1986a) gave as many as five *Incoms*, but the modal nonpatient gave none.[3] The typical child between the ages of 5 and 15 gives one *Incom*, the mean score falling off steadily with advancing age until it becomes adult-like at age 16. Exner's (1986a) inpatients suffering from schizophrenia ($N = 320$) were more likely to give *Incoms* than were nonpatients ($N = 600$), depressed inpatients ($N = 210$), or outpatients manifesting "character problems" ($N = 200$) including legal problems and substance abuse (66% versus 43%, 55%, and 49%, respectively). The schizophrenic inpatients were not, however, appreciably more likely to give *Incoms* than were a group of 160 "preschizophrenics" (individuals diagnosed with Borderline or Schizotypal Personality Disorders) (Exner, 1986b). On average, those suffering from schizophrenia gave more *Incoms* than did normals, those who were depressed, those manifesting "character problems," or the sample of "preschizophrenic" subjects (1.51 versus .54, .91, .98, and 1.23, respectively). However, since the standard deviations for all these distributions are larger than the means, there is much overlap among the different samples. In a small study, Lerner et al. (1985) found that their schizophrenic subjects ($N = 19$) gave an average of .74 *Incoms* and neurotic outpatients averaged .60, while the rate for their "preschizophrenics" (patients with Borderline Personality Disorders; $N = 15$) was 1.22. All these data strongly support the contention that *Incom* responses represent very mild degrees of deviant thinking. Certainly, the presence of *Incoms* in a record does not, in itself, provide definitive evidence of psychotic thinking.

The foregoing interpretation is supported by the findings of Johnston and Holzman (1979), using their broad definition of *Incom*. They found Incongruous Combinations most common among their 21 nonpsychotic subjects (52%), next most common among their 97 normal controls and normal parents of subjects (30%), and least common among their 69 schizophrenic patients (20%). This also appears to be true for children. Nineteen boys aged 5 to 13 diagnosed with Separation Anxiety Disorder (SAD) produced significantly more *Incoms* ($M = 1.68$) than 14 normal controls ($M = .57$) (Goddard & Tuber, 1989). Finally, Tuber and Coates (1989) reported that twenty-six 5- to 12-year-old boys with Gender Identity Disorder (GID) had a higher median number of Incongruous Combinations than did 18 normal controls.

Fabulized combinations are thought to be a step up the pathology ladder from *Fab* and *Incom* responses (cf. Meloy & Singer, 1991). *Fabcom* responses (as defined by Rapaport) are weighted .25 in the Delta Index if the examinee recognizes their fanciful nature and .50 if the examinee does not. In the systems that segregate *Incoms*, *Fabcoms* are weighted .50 (TDI) and 4 (WSUM6). They

---

[3]We have elected to present data from the 1986 Comprehensive System norms because Exner (1991) excluded all records with fewer than 14 responses prior to tabulating the most recent Comprehensive System norms. The normative data on Klopfer's approach includes such brief records.

are rare among normals. Exner (1986a) found that while a nonpatient adult examinee may give as many as four *Fabcoms,* the modal nonpatient gives none. He found that very young children (i.e., ages 5 through 7) give fewer *Fabcoms* than do 8-year-olds.[4] This may be because they lack the cognitive or verbal development to give a response as complex, albeit pathological, as a *Fabcom.* Among nonpatient children, 8-year-olds give the most *Fabcoms:* an average of one per record. *Fabcoms* drop off after age 8 to the near-adult average of .31 among 16-year-olds.

Exner (1986a, 1986b) found that schizophrenic inpatients are far more likely to give *Fabcoms* than are nonpatients, depressed inpatients, outpatients with character problems, and preschizophrenic subjects (78% vs. 12%, 37%, 37%, and 43%, respectively). The mean for schizophrenic patients is also considerably higher than the mean for normals, depressed patients, individuals with character problems, and preschizophrenic persons (1.59 vs. .18, .54, .54, and .70, respectively). Lerner et al. (1985) did not replicate this pattern of findings. They found that their schizophrenic subjects gave an average of .74 *Fabcoms* and neurotic outpatients averaged .60, while the rate for their preschizophrenic patients was .81.

Studies using Rapaport's broad definition of *Fabcom* reveal a pattern similar to that found by Lerner et al. (1985) and add to it. Rapaport et al.'s (1946) data yielded lower absolute rates of *Fabcoms.* Although only 14% of Rapaport et al.'s individuals with schizophrenia gave these responses, this rate was still much higher than in their groups of depressed patients (4%), neurotics (6%), and controls (2%). However, *Fabcoms* were most common among Rapaport et al.'s preschizophrenics (33%). The means for these groups were .14, .04, .06, .02, and .4.[5] Wilson (1985) found that his small ($N = 29$) group of schizophrenic subjects gave an average of 1.10 *Fabcoms* and patients suffering from Major Depression (N = 26) averaged 1.34, while the rate for his preschizophrenics (individuals diagnosed with Borderline or Schizotypal Personality Disorders; N = 26) was 2.42. Likewise, Singer and Larson (1981) found their small sample of preschizophrenic patients (individuals diagnosed with Borderline Personality Disorder; $N = 25$) gave significantly more *Fabcoms* than schizophrenic subjects ($N = 44$), neurotic patients ($N = 25$), or normal controls ($N = 20$).

The foregoing data are consistent with Hill's (1972) comment, based on her experience with the narrower, Comprehensive System–like HIT definition of *Fabcom,* that:

---

[4]Exner's (1986a) samples of normal children included approximately 100 children at each age level.

[5]It is impossible to know why Rapaport et al.'s (1946) mean scores are almost always lower than those of more contemporary researchers. Therefore, we urge the reader to attend to the *patterns* of mean scores presented in this chapter rather than their absolute values.

In a nonpsychotic population, [*Fabcom*] is often found in the records of obsessive-compulsive individuals. The [*Fabcom*] response reveals their passive relativistic feeling that any combination of things is possible. The world around them does not appear meaningfully integrated or amenable to integration. Such ideation suggests a pathological tendency and may reveal a preschizophrenic condition in which thinking is based on fantasy and autism, replacing an adherence to objective reality in everyday situations. (p. 123)

The data are also consistent with Blatt and Ritzler's (1974) hypothesis—operating from the twin perspectives of cognitive developmental theory and psychoanalytic object relations theory—that *Fabcoms* imply a general, albeit mild, laxness of self/other and fantasy/reality boundaries. This interpretation of the meaning of Fabulized Combinations has received further support in three additional studies that used Blatt and Ritzler's hypothesis as a point of departure. Levin (1990) found that 77% of female college students who suffered frequent nightmares gave *Fabcoms* ($M = 1.87$) compared with 53% of controls ($M = .83$) (both $Ns = 30$). Goddard and Tuber's (1989) boys with SAD produced significantly more *Fabcoms* ($M = 1.63$) than did their normal controls ($M = .89$). Finally, Tuber and Coates (1989) reported that their boys with GID had a higher median number of Fabulized Combinations than did the normal controls.

Confabulations, as defined by Rapaport et al. (1946), are considered another step up the pathology ladder from *Fabcoms*. They receive a weight of .50 in the Delta Index if they involve "extreme affect loading or specificity" and 1.00 if they reflect "farfetched elaboration." In the TDI, Confabulations include Rapaport *Confabs* plus the rather rare responses Rapaport designated *DW* and *DrW*; they are weighted .75 (Johnston & Holzman, 1979). Similar responses in the Comprehensive System (*DR's*) (cf. Meloy & Singer, 1991) are weighted 3 in the WSUM6. *Confabs* reflect overgeneralized reasoning wherein conclusions are drawn on the basis of minimal evidence (Weiner, 1966). Lerner et al. (1985) suggested that Confabulations are a Rorschach manifestation of displacement.

Exner (1986a) found that while a nonpatient adult examinee gave as many as four *Confabs*, the modal nonpatient gave none. He found that the number of subjects giving *Confabs* dropped steadily with age: 97% of 5-year-olds give *Confabs* ($M = 1.61$), while only 9% of 16-year-olds did so. There was a precipitous drop in the propensity to give *Confabs* between the ages of 9 (75%; $M = .99$) to 10 (44%; $M = .49$).

Blatt and Ritzler (1974) suggested that *Confabs* reflect problems in maintaining boundaries between internal and external (i.e., fantasy and reality). They believe that the inability to maintain this boundary is one of the roots of schizophrenia. However, empirical data have not consistently supported the link between *Confabs* and schizophrenia. Exner (1986a, 1986b) found that depressed inpatients were far more likely to give *Confabs* than were pre-schizophrenic subjects, nonpatients, outpatients with character problems, and schizophrenic inpatients (87% vs. 18%, 34%, 41%, and 46%, respectively). On the other hand, the mean for depressed patients was only half as high as that for schizophrenic patients (.63 vs. 1.21). The mean for schizophrenic patients was also considerably higher than the mean for preschizophrenic subjects, nonpatients, and outpatients with character problems (.45, .51, and .90, respectively). Wilson (1985) found that his schizophrenic subjects gave an average of 1.69 *Confabs*, while the rate for preschizophrenic individuals was almost twice that (2.88), and the average for 26 patients suffering from Major Depression was .61. On the other hand, Lerner et al. (1985) found that their schizophrenic and preschizophrenic subjects had nearly identical means (1.53 and 1.66, respectively); even their neurotic outpatients averaged .47 *Confabs*. Similarly, Rapaport et al. (1946) found that their schizophrenic subjects gave about as many *Confabs* (27%; $M = .5$) as did his preschizophrenic subjects (21%; $M = .4$). However, *Confabs* were rare among the depressed subjects (2%) and neurotic patients (2%), and absent from the records of their control subjects. Using a definition of *Confab* that included the rather rare responses that Rapaport called *DW* and *DrW*, 36% of Johnston and Holzman's (1979) schizophrenic patients gave Confabulations, as did 22% of the parents of schizophrenics, but 24% of their nonpsychotic subjects also gave *Confabs*. Confabulations were much less common (7%), but by no means unheard of, among their other normal subjects (controls and other parents).

Levin (1990) found that his frequent nightmare sufferers gave *Confabs* more frequently (17%; $M = .47$) than did his controls (3%; $M = .07$). On average, Goddard and Tuber's (1989) SAD boys produced more than four times more Confabulations ($M = 2.37$) than did the controls ($M = .57$). Tuber and Coates's (1989) subjects with GID gave a higher median number of *Confabs* than did their controls.

The inconsistency of the data on *Confab* counsels caution in its use. The presence of *Confabs* certainly suggests the presence of psychopathology and, perhaps, the degree of pathology. The presence of a Confabulation response certainly does not indicate a psychotic degree of psychopathology, however.

Schuldberg and Boster (1985) suggested that the fluid responses correspond "to the flamboyant and fluid test behavior (characterized by fabulized combinations) of a group of patients . . . referred to as borderline . . . schizotypal personality disorder . . . [or] preschizophrenics. . . . It is also likely that expansive manic subjects would score high on this dimension of verbal style" (p. 211). This interpretation, which is supported by the foregoing data, suggests that schizophrenic patients scoring high on this dimension are likely to be characterized by positive symptoms of the disorder, such as hallucinations and delusions. This contention is firmly supported in a further look at Johnston and Holzman's (1979) data. Their 49 recently hospitalized schizophrenic subjects were much more likely to give *Incoms, Fabcoms,* and *Confabs* (27%, 41%, and 45%, respectively) than were their 20 chronic/deteriorated patients (5%, 25%, and 15%). Rapaport et al.'s (1946) data are modestly supportive only in the case of Confabulations (55% vs. 46%); this may be a function of their very small ($N = 13$) sample of chronic/deteriorated patients. This hypothesis regarding positive symptoms is particularly likely to hold if responses infused with personal meaning are also present (cf. Schuldberg and Boster, 1985).

Rigid Responses

Perseveration is not included in the WSUM6, probably because Exner feels it indexes cognitive rigidity and dysfunction that is qualitatively different from the thought disorder indexed by *Incoms, Fabcoms, Alogs,* and *Contams* (cf. Exner, 1986a, pp. 362–363). *Persev* responses receive a weight of .25 in the TDI. Like *Fab* responses, Perseverations appear to result from an associational disturbance—in this case a paucity of appropriate associational connections owing to an inability to shift cognitive sets (Johnston & Holzman, 1979).

Unlike most of the responses discussed in this chapter, Exner's (1986a) definition of *Persev* is broader than Rapaport's (1946). Hence, *Persev* responses were relatively common in most of Exner's samples. Among his normal children the rate fluctuated irregularly from 48% ($M = .89$) at age 5 to 13% at age 11 ($M = .21$). Only 5% of Exner's (1986a) normal adults gave a *Persev*. The rate of *Persevs* in Exner's (1986b) preschizophrenic patients was about the same: 7% ($M = .08$). The rate was higher in his schizophrenic and depressed patients (about 15%; $M = .17$), and much higher among his outpatient subjects with character problems (24%; $M = .25$).

Like studies using the relatively broad Comprehensive System definition of *Persev*, studies using Rapaport's narrower definition suggest that these responses are related to the presence of, and perhaps to the severity of, psychopathology, but not to type of psychopathology. Rapaport and colleagues (1946) found *Persev* responses most common among their schizophrenic (13%) and preschizophrenic subjects (15%). They were far less common among their depressed subjects (5%), neurotic patients (0), and controls (2%). Johnston and Holzman (1979) found higher rates of *Persev* responses in the records of their schizophrenic (26%) and nonpsychotic subjects (24%) than among their normals (controls and parents of subjects—6%).

Relationship responses are weighted either .25 or .50 in the Delta Index, depending on their severity. They are weighted .25 in the TDI. Available research suggests that the lower weighting is probably most appropriate. *Rel* responses were uncommon in Rapaport et al.'s (1946) study, but they discriminated among very different levels of disturbance. Nine percent of the schizophrenic subjects gave *Rels*, as opposed to 6% of preschizophrenic individuals, 2% of depressed patients, and none of the neurotic or control subjects. On the other hand, Johnston and Holzman's (1979) schizophrenic patients, non-psychotic subjects, and normals (controls or parents of patients) all gave *Rels* at approximately the same rate (11.5%, 9%, and 8%, respectively).

Schuldberg and Boster (1985) believe that both types of rigid responses, along with the objective meaning responses (see later section), are consistent with Goldstein's (1944) classic description of schizophrenic concreteness (cf. Harrow, Adler, & Hanf, 1974). Thus, these kinds of responses may be more common among individuals with affective blunting, social inadequacy, and other negative symptoms of schizophrenia than among schizophrenic individuals with more florid positive symptoms, such as hallucinations and delusions. This hypothesis is strongly supported by the fact that *Persev* responses were far more common among Johnston and Holzman's (1979) chronic/deteriorated schizophrenic patients (45%) than among their recently hospitalized sample (18%). The chronic/deteriorated sample also had the highest scores on Phillips' (1953) process/reactive scale (i.e., toward the process end), suggesting that Perseveration is also associated with a relatively poor prognosis. Rapaport et al. (1946) found Perseveration slightly more common among their small sample of chronic/deteriorated schizophrenic subjects (15%) than among their recently hospitalized patients (13%).

The support for these interpretations is less solid in the case of Relationship responses. *Rel* responses were more common among Rapaport et al.'s (1946) chronic/deteriorated schizophrenic subjects (23%) than among recently hospitalized patients (6%), but this relationship was reversed in Johnston and Holzman's (1979) data (5% vs. 14%). Clearly, *Rel* responses should be interpreted as suggesting negative symptoms and a relatively unfavorable prognosis only in the presence of additional indicators, including objective meaning responses.

Rigid responses may also be associated with other forms of pathology. Goldstein (1944) himself believed concrete thinking to be the symptom, *sine qua non*, of organic brain damage. Perseveration, in particular, is a well-known characteristic of the performance of many brain-injured persons on a variety of tasks, including the Rorschach (e.g., Evans & Marmorston, 1964; Neiger, Slemon, & Quirk, 1962). Our clinical experience also suggests that individuals of low general intelligence may also give rigid responses (cf. Harrow et al., 1974).

Personal Meaning Responses

Incoherence occurs as the result of the extreme eruption of personal themes, unrelated to the blot or to the situation, into an examinee's response. Thus, it is not surprising that it receives the maximum weight of 1.00 in both the Delta

Index and the TDI. Few empirical data are available on *Incoh,* but they consistently link *Incoh* responses with deteriorated schizophrenia. Johnston and Holzman (1979) found *Incoh* responses in the records of 30% of their chronic/deteriorated schizophrenic subjects, but in only 6% of their recently hospitalized schizophrenic subjects. These results were consistent with Rapaport et al.'s (1946) data. Thirty-eight percent of Rapaport et al.'s chronic/deteriorated schizophrenic subjects gave *Incoh* responses, compared to only 8% of the recently hospitalized subjects. None of the nonschizophrenic subjects in either study gave an *Incoh* response. Swartz (1970) obtained similar results in his study of the HIT. He found no Incoherence in the records of his normal or depressed subjects. He did find *Incoh* responses in the records of some of his mentally retarded subjects, in addition to his patients suffering from schizophrenia. Swartz noted that examinees who give *Incoh* responses are likely to give several, a finding supported by Rapaport's data. Thus, the empirical data clearly indicate that *Incoh* responses are most likely to be found in the records of individuals whose disorder is severe and difficult to treat (cf. Schuldberg & Boster, 1985).

Self-reference responses are scored under "loss of distance" in the TDI, that category receiving a weight of .25. Empirical data suggest that this weight may be too low. Self-reference responses are infrequent even in clinical samples, so dependable norms are not available. *SRef* responses occurred with such low frequency in Johnston and Holzman's (1979) studies that they did not report on them (apart from the TDI as a whole). Rapaport et al. (1946) found *Srefs* exclusively in his schizophrenic (21%) and preschizophrenic (6%) samples. Within his schizophrenic samples, Self-reference responses were far more common among his chronic/deteriorated subjects (31%) than among his recently hospitalized subjects (6.5%).

SRefs are more common among the 45 responses requested in the HIT; degrees of self-reference are scored quantitatively, along a 3-point scale. Even so, Swartz (1970) found *Srefs* in the HIT records of only 19% of his schizophrenic subjects. *Srefs* were not more common among his schizophrenic subjects than among his depressed subjects (20%), but were far more common in those two groups than among normal or mentally retarded individuals (5%). Jortner (1966) found that his schizophrenic subjects were especially likely to give bizarre *Sref* responses, strongly suggesting a breakdown in the sense of reality involving a loss of sense of the bodily self. Hozier (cited in Jortner, 1966) interpreted these responses consistently with Blatt and Ritzler's (1974) interpretation of *Fabcoms, Confabs,* and *Contams.* She believes these responses reflect a body that is not differentiated and bounded from everything that is "not body," leaving the individual with no frame of reference from which to distinguish events in the external world from purely internal, psychological events. The ultimate result of this lack of boundaries is depersonalization and self-preoccupation.

Owing to their infrequency and highly pathological implications, one needs to be careful in scoring personal meaning responses. It is especially important to distinguish Self-reference responses from the more benign Personalized responses scored in the Comprehensive System (see the previous section on scoring *Srefs*). The presence of a genuine *Incoh* in a record is a pathognomic sign indicating severe cognitive dysfunction that is probably psychotic in nature. Swartz's (1970) data indicate that *Srefs* are not uniquely associated with schizophrenia, but the empirical data indicate that persons giving either of the personal meaning responses are likely to be suffering from disorders that are severe and difficult to treat (cf. Schuldberg & Boster, 1985). The nature of the *Incoh* responses themselves suggests that, despite the fact that they are associated with chronicity and deterioration, they are likely to be associated with positive symptoms of schizophrenia such as hallucinations and delusions. This is probably also true of *Srefs*. This interpretation is especially likely to hold if a record also includes a number of fluid responses (cf. Schuldberg & Boster, 1985).

Objective Meaning Responses

Confusion is generated by the subject's effort to grapple with the "real" meaning of the inkblot. This approach to the test was described by Rorschach (1921/1942) as the examinee wanting to "recognize" the blots rather than treating the Rorschach task as one of "interpretation." *Confus* responses are weighted .50 in both the Delta Index and the TDI. Few empirical data are available on *Confus* responses, but those that are available indicate that those weights are probably too low. Johnston and Holzman (1979) found *Confus* responses much more common among their schizophrenic subjects (20%) and parents of schizophrenic patients (11%) than among their nonpsychotic patients (5%), controls (4%), and other parents (0). Rapaport et al.'s (1946) data are in good agreement with these results, in that *Confus* responses were found *only* among the schizophrenic subjects (9%). These results suggest that anyone giving a *Confus* response is likely to be suffering from a schizophrenic illness.

Vague responses were not included in Schuldberg and Boster's (1985) study, but they appear to us to index the objective meaning pole of Schuldberg and Boster's first dimension. They are weighted .25 in both the Delta Index and the TDI. *Vague* responses, per se, did not differentiate among the groups studied by Johnston and Holzman (1979). Seven percent of their schizophrenic patients—all recently hospitalized—gave *Vague* responses, but *Vague* responses were also given by 9% of their nonpsychotic subjects and 11.5% of their normal subjects (controls and subjects' parents). Obviously, *Vague* responses, in and of themselves, do not indicate the presence of psychopathology.

As previously noted, Schuldberg and Boster (1985) believe that both types of objective meaning responses, along with the rigid responses, are consistent with Goldstein's (1944) classic description of schizophrenic concreteness (cf. Harrow et al., 1974). *Confus* responses were more common among Johnston and Holzman's (1979) chronic/deteriorated schizophrenic patients (35%) than among their recently hospitalized sample (14%). These results suggest that *Confus* responses may be associated with a relatively poor prognosis. They also suggest that *Confus* responses may be more common among individuals with affective blunting, social inadequacy, and other negative symptoms of schizophrenia than among individuals with more florid positive symptoms, such as hallucinations and delusions. However, these interpretations are not supported by Rapaport et al.'s (1946) data. Confusion responses were less common among their tiny sample of chronic/deteriorated schizophrenic subjects (0) than among recently hospitalized patients (11%). Nor, as already noted, do Johnston and Holzman's data support this view of *Vague* responses. Thus, objective meaning responses should be interpreted as suggesting negative symptoms and a relatively poor prognosis only in the presence of other indicators, such as rigid responses.

Objective meaning responses may also be associated with other forms of pathology. Goldstein (1944) felt that individuals suffering from organic brain damage are characterized by concrete thinking. Both types of objective meaning responses are similar to Piotrowski's (1937) Perplexity response. Several studies have found Perplexity to be characteristic of persons suffering from organic brain dysfunction (e.g., Evans & Marmorston, 1964; Neiger et al, 1962). Individuals of low general intelligence may also give objective meaning responses (cf. Harrow et al., 1974).

Mixed Responses

Contaminations are rare, very pathological verbalizations that appear to reflect the psychodynamic mechanism of condensation. They receive the maximum weight of 1.00 in both the Delta Index and the TDI and the maximum weight of 7 in WSUM6. *Contam* responses are almost unheard of among normals, be they children or adults. Only 3 of Exner's (1986a) 600 nonpatient adults gave *Contams*. None of his 210 inpatients suffering from depression and 3 of 160 preschizophrenic patients (Exner, 1986b) gave *Contams*, while 7 of his 200 outpatient "character problems" did so. Four of his 1,580 nonpatient youngsters (three 5-year-olds and a 7-year-old) gave a single *Contam*. However, unlike *Confabs, Contam* responses are found with nontrivial frequency among schizophrenic patients. Fifty-nine of Exner's 320 schizophrenic inpatients (18%) gave at least one *Contam* (Exner, 1991). Others' results, though revealing the occasional nonschizophrenic subject with a Contam, are quite similar to Exner's.

Seventeen percent of Rapaport et al.'s (1946) schizophrenic patients gave *Contams*, as did 1% of their nonpsychotic subjects (preschizophrenic, depressed, and neurotic subjects) and 2% of controls. Johnston and Holzman (1979) found *Contams* in the records of 13% of their schizophrenic subjects and none of their nonpsychotic or normal control subjects. They also found *Contams* in the records of 4% of the parents of schizophrenic patients, none of the parents of nonpsychotic patients, and 3% of the parents of their normal controls. Wilson's (1985) schizophrenic subjects also gave far more *Contams* than did his preschizophrenic and depressed patients (1.59 vs. .38 and .12, respectively). Lerner and colleagues' (1985) results conformed to this same pattern of means: schizophrenic subjects = .74, preschizophrenics = .17, and neurotic patients = .07. Edell (1987) reported that 16.5% of his "early" schizophrenic subjects (N = 30) gave *Contams*, as did 1 of his 17 mixed Borderline/Schizotypal patients. Neither his Borderline (N = 51) nor Schizotypal patients (N = 14) nor his normal controls (N = 20) gave any Contamination responses.

Blatt and Ritzler (1974) have suggested that *Contams* reflect problems in maintaining boundaries between self and others. They believe that the inability to maintain this boundary—which develops early in infancy among normal individuals—is one of the roots of schizophrenia. Their theoretical perspective is supported by three studies in addition to those involving schizophrenic subjects. Four of Levin's (1990) nightmare sufferers gave *Contams*, while none of his controls gave any. *Contams* were rare in Goddard and Tuber's (1989) SAD boys and their controls, but the mean was slightly higher among the former (.37 vs. .14). Contaminations were undoubtedly also rare in Tuber and Coates's (1989) study, but they also found that their boys with GID gave a higher median number of *Contams* than did their controls.

One should be extremely careful in scoring a *Contam*. Unless there is reason to suspect a schizophrenic process, it is probably best to err on the side of assuming one has made an administration or scoring error. The presence of a genuine *Contam* in an adolescent or adult patient's record is a pathognomic sign indicating severe cognitive dysfunction that is probably psychotic. Empirically, the odds are very high that the individual giving a *Contam* is suffering from a schizophrenic illness (cf. Jortner, 1966; Swartz, 1970). As the "mixed" classification of Contaminations in Schuldberg and Boster's (1985) scheme suggests, the available data do not clearly indicate what kinds of symptoms those giving *Contams* can be expected to display. *Contams* are far more common among Rapaport et al.'s (1946) chronic/deteriorated schizophrenic subjects (46%) than among their recently hospitalized patients (11%). This trend reversed, albeit not strongly, in Johnston and Holzman's (1979) data (5% vs. 16%).

Autistic Logic was considered extremely pathological in the Delta Index, receiving a weight of 1.00. It is considered somewhat less pathological in the two more modern indexes of thinking problems, receiving a weight of .75 in the TDI and 5 in WSUM6 (in which it is termed "Inappropriate Logic"). *Alog* responses are quite common among children under age 9: 93% of Exner's (1986a) 5-year-olds gave *Alogs*, as did 72% of his 8-year-olds. The proportion of nonpatient children giving *Alog* responses dropped precipitously at age 9, going down to 38%. Whatever the reason for this sudden drop in *Alogs*, they certainly do not have the same pathological implications in young children that they do in older youngsters or adults. Indeed, only 54% of Exner's (1986a) adult schizophrenic inpatients gave *Alog* responses, and their mean score (.86) was essentially identical to the 8-year-olds' (.83). *Alog* responses were quite rare among Exner's nonpatient adults; while one nonpatient gave three *Alog* responses, only 7% of the nonpatients gave any. Outpatients with character problems, depressed inpatients, and preschizophenic patients gave *Alog* responses more frequently (14%, 17%, and 19%, respectively) than did nonpatients, but not nearly as frequently as did the schizophrenic patients.

The pattern of Johnston and Holzman's (1979) results was in general agreement with Exner's. Only 33% of their schizophrenic subjects gave *Alogs*, compared to 5% of their nonpsychotic subjects. However, 19% of the parents of schizophrenics gave *Alogs*, compared to 9% of their very small sample of parents of nonpsychotics and 3% of their normals (controls and their parents). *Alogs* were less common among Rapaport et al.'s (1946) schizophrenic subjects (20%; $M = .29$) than among Exner's, but *none* of their nonschizophrenic subjects gave an *Alog*.

As with Contaminations, one must be extremely careful in scoring *Alogs*. Unless there is reason to suspect a schizophrenic process, it is probably best to err on the side of assuming one has made an administration or scoring error. The presence of a genuine *Alog* in a record is strong presumptive evidence that the examinee is suffering from a psychotic disorder. As with Contaminations, however, the available data do not clearly indicate what kinds of symptoms those giving *Alogs* can be expected to display. Autistic Logic is slightly more common among Rapaport et al.'s (1946) chronic/deteriorated schizophrenic subjects (23%) than among their recently hospitalized patients (19%). This trend reversed in Johnston and Holzman's (1979) data (25% vs. 37%).

▲ 9

Introduction to Content Analysis

While Hermann Rorschach and many of his later followers in the United States have tended to deemphasize the importance of the content of Rorschach responses, clinicians have increasingly come to recognize that what the subject reports seeing in the blot constitutes very valuable data. Several studies (Potkay, 1971; Powers & Hamlin, 1957; Symonds, 1955) have demonstrated that clinicians rely heavily on content in arriving at conclusions about test subjects. Furthermore, the accumulated evidence on test validity is generally quite favorable for the various content scales that have been developed (Anastasi, 1976; Aronow & Reznikoff, 1976). In keeping with this increasing recognition of the pivotal importance of inkblot content, the present chapter will discuss the major approaches to such content interpretation.

NOMOTHETIC VERSUS IDIOGRAPHIC INTERPRETATION OF CONTENT

In general, we may distinguish between two primary approaches to Rorschach content interpretation. Consistent with Allport's delineation of the two major types of personality description (Allport, 1937, 1961), these two approaches might be dubbed the nomothetic versus the idiographic. As noted by Allport, the nomothetic approach to personality description contrasts a particular subject to a comparison group in terms of the degree to which a particular trait or characteristic is present. One is then able to state that a subject is above or below the mean of a particular comparison group for sets of specific traits, and how far away from the mean his or her score is.

A number of nomethetically based inkblot content scales have been put forward, including the Elizur scales of anxiety and hostility (Elizur, 1947), the "homosexual signs" scale (Wheeler, 1949), De Vos's scales of affective inference (De Vos, 1952), scales developed by Zubin and coworkers (Zubin, Eron, & Schumer, 1965), the Barrier and Penetration scales of Fisher and Cleveland (1958, 1968), the Endicott (1972) scales of depression and suspiciousness, and the Holt content scales of primary process and secondary process (Holt & Havel, 1960). The reader interested in the accumulated empirical evidence bearing on these nomothetic content scales is referred to the appropriate chapters in Aronow and Reznikoff (1976) and to Reznikoff et al. (1982).

In contrast to the nomothetic approach, the idiographic approach to personality description focuses not on those traits or characteristics that are conceptualized as common denominators of everyone's behavior, but, rather, on those aspects of the individual that are unique. A high degree of descriptive specificity thus characterizes the idiographic approach. When the clinician interprets the content of the subject's Rorschach responses from the idiographic perspective, the content is used to portray the subject's highly individual views of him- or herself and his or her environment.

An example of nomothetic versus idiographic content interpretation will help to clarify the distinction.

A 25-year-old male homosexual psychiatric outpatient reports the following percept on Card I of the Rorschach:

> Two witches—one on the right, one on the left—and a body in between them. The witches have their capes and hoods on. They're not seducing her or he—it's like a ritual—a sacrifice.

The patient's associations to this percept were as follows:

> On TV last night—I saw the actress who was in King Kong—that made me think of the girl being sacrificed. (What does this make you think of in your own life?) We all sacrifice—I'm sacrificing my own day just being here—and sometimes we sacrifice in the things we do at work. (What does a witch remind you of?) Evil and good. Most people think they're evil—but who's to say—maybe they do good, too.[1]

This response would be dealt with from a nomothetic content perspective by scoring it on various content scales—as to whether and to what extent it constituted a response indicating such traits as anxiety, hostility, dependency,

---

[1]The method by which such associations to Rorschach percepts are obtained is discussed in Chapter 11.

suspiciousness, et cetera. The subject's total scale scores might then be compared with those of other subjects in relevant "comparison groups."

In contrast, the idiographic approach to understanding this response would focus on such qualitative aspects of the response as the subject's transformation of the witch into someone who may do "good"—perhaps indicating the defense mechanism of denial. Another possible meaning for this particular subject might involve the question of whether he perceived his mother as seductive, and his need to deny it—"they're *not* seducing . . ."). Also notable is his subtle doubt as to the sex of the figure in the middle ("her or he"), perhaps indicating some confusion in sexual identity. Irritation is expressed in the patient's remark about "I'm sacrificing my own day just being here." In short, the content of the patient's response and his highly individual manner of verbalizing reveal much about his idiographic personality functioning.

Thus, the two primary modes of content interpretation, the nomothetic and the idiographic, produce different types of information about the test subject. The interpretive procedure also is quite different in each case. It could be argued that because the Rorschach technique requires the subject alone to provide the structure of the response, a great heterogeneity of content results, which allows for the expression of stylistic differences. One might, therefore, expect the responses produced to lend themselves most readily to an analysis of the subject's idiosyncratic views rather than a structured nomothetic assessment of the degree to which particular traits are present. In any event, there is as yet insufficient information on reliability, validity, and norms for the nomothetic content scales; they are not ready for clinical use at this time (Aronow & Reznikoff, 1976; Reznikoff et al., 1982). Their primary use, at present, is for research. The remaining clinical discussion of content will therefore deal entirely with the idiographic mode of content interpretation.

IDIOGRAPHIC CONTENT INTERPRETATION

The idiographic interpretation of the "witch" response summarized above serves to highlight the major aspects of idiographic interpretive technique:

1. Symbolism is central to idiographic content interpretation. Thus, the content of the response is often assumed to symbolize or stand for an aspect of the subject's life. The interpretation of Rorschach percepts is similar in this respect to the psychoanalytic interpretation of dreams—both types of interpretation assume that the material to be interpreted may be understood as an expression of the subject's emotional life. However, not all Rorschach percepts can be understood as symbolic expressions that relate to the subject's personality. Rather, the Rorschach response represents something of a blend of symbolic-emotional elements with an objective description of the blots. Thus, the Rorschach clinician must learn to identify those Rorschach responses that are likely to be particularly revealing of personality and to otherwise disentangle the projective from the nonprojective aspects of particular responses. (This is discussed further in the following chapter.)

2. Idiographic content interpretation often relies heavily on "stylistic analysis" of the subject's response, placing emphasis on verbalizations that may accompany the percept. Thus, in the response noted above, it is not only the content per se that is interpreted, but the subject's idiosyncratic way of expressing and modifying the percept, and also the subject's accompanying associations to the percept.

3. In most cases, conclusive interpretations about the idiographic meaning of particular Rorschach responses and verbalizations are difficult to reach. A particular aspect of the response, in other words, usually "suggests" a particular interpretation. Only if there is a confluence of data from several sources in the response record can the clinician be reasonably confident of the accuracy of interpretations.

INFORMATION PROVIDED BY IDIOGRAPHIC CONTENT INTERPRETATION

In a previous volume (Aronow & Reznikoff, 1976), we summarized our findings regarding the major types of information revealed by subjects in their inkblot responses. As with dreams, the self-concept is foremost; inkblot responses often serve as a mirror for the individual. How the subject sees him- or herself is often vividly displayed in the response, particularly with respect to negative or unresolved aspects of the self-concept. Important others in the subject's life and aspects of the environment that impinge on the subject are also often highlighted in Rorschach responses. We have found it useful to classify the types of information produced by Rorschach responses into five broad categories: self-concept; attitudes toward significant others in the environment; perceptions of the environment, both social and otherwise; major concerns; and ongoing conflicts.

Self-Concept

The following percept on Card VI, expressed by a 29-year-old depressed female outpatient with a chronic obesity problem, is an example of how self-concept may be revealed:

| Card VI: | A primitive alimentary canal. |
| Associations: | Makes me think of a worm—what a worm might have. (What does a worm bring to mind?) Loath- |

ing, disgust—and that makes me think of my own
self-hatred—incompetency—ineffectuality,
weakness.

In this response the patient reveals a very poor self-image and anger
directed at the self, connected with her primitive oral needs.

Attitudes Toward Significant Others

The following percept on Card VII was elicited from a 26-year-old male patient
hospitalized for depression and paranoid thinking. His response reveals
feelings he has about his mother and his environment.

Card VII:	It looks like two young ladies talking to each other.
Associations:	(What does that remind you of?) Nothing much— they have freedom of movement—they're moving their lips. (What does freedom of movement make you think of in your own life?) Anything that stifles movement—like my mother. It's hard for me to express myself with her.

This response expresses the subject's feeling of restriction at the hands of
his mother.

Perceptions of the Environment

This percept on Card I was reported by a 24-year-old female patient hospitalized after a suicide attempt. Her impression of her environment is revealing.

Card I:	It could also be an insect.
Associations:	Makes me think of being stung or bitten by an insect—nature is destructive. (What does that bring to mind?) You have to be careful in life—you have to protect yourself. God created a world which is dangerous.

In this response the patient reveals her view of her environment as
malevolent and destructive.

Major Concerns

Major concerns is a highly heterogeneous category that involves all manner
of external and internal stress with which the ego is attempting to cope. An

example is seen in the following response to Card VII by a 23-year-old woman hospitalized with complaints of temper outbursts and bizarre behavior:

Card VII:

It looks like two little children with ponytails—they're on top of pillows. It looks like they're mad at each other—they're up in the air—somebody threw them up—now they're floating down.

Associations:

It's like a decal-decoration for a baby's room—something I'd put on the end of the crib. I went to Woolworth one day, and saw decals like that—something for babies. (What does their being mad remind you of?) They're not exactly angry—just teasing each other. (What does being mad make you think of in your own life?) Nobody exactly was against me—nobody said I have a boyfriend and you don't, I got engaged and you didn't—except my mother—she says my boyfriend and I don't love each other just because we argue. Since I came into the hospital, she doesn't say it anymore—now she says, "your fiancé loves you very much."

In this response, and the accompanying associations in particular, the patient reveals a complex of feelings involving stress induced by her relationship with her boyfriend. Other themes touched on here include anger toward both her mother and her boyfriend, her desire for children, feelings of inferiority in relation to other women, and secondary gain aspects of her hospitalization.

Ongoing Conflicts

An example of ongoing conflicts is seen in the following response to Card IX by a bisexual male outpatient with complaints of free-floating anxiety:

Card IX: It looks like a king and a queen.
Associations: Reminds me of myself in a way—sometimes going one way sexually, sometimes the other—AC-DC.

This response highlights the subject's split in sexual identity, with some underlying grandiosity also suggested.

The symmetricality of the inkblots is particularly conducive to eliciting such a sense of division in subjects. When symmetrically identical parts of a blot are described as opposites on some pole, as in this response, a split in the subject's feelings about the self or something external to the self is usually indicated.

Use of Content Categories

The interested reader is referred to our earlier volume for further discussion and examples of these categories of response. The reader should be aware, however, that such categorization of responses, while didactically helpful, does some violence to a true understanding of the meaning of inkblot responses. A particular inkblot response typically combines elements that cut across these categories in a gestalt that is stylistically unique to each subject, reflecting the idiosyncratic way he or she views the self and the environment.

▲ 10

Guidelines to Valid Content Interpretation

Because of the requirement that the individual structure his or her own responses on the inkblot task, the Rorschach technique is able to provide qualitative information about the subject that nomothetically-based objective tests cannot possibly elicit. Idiographic content interpretation thus provides the clinician with very valuable information about subjects. At the same time, however, it must also be recognized that there are major hazards in this type of interpretation.

THE RORSCHACH PERCEPT VERSUS THE DREAM

As noted by Schafer (1954), the Rorschach percept must be considered distinctly inferior to the dream in terms of its interpretive potential. The inkblot response often represents a blend of the objective blot properties with projective elements. Considerable skill and experience are required to successfully disentangle these elements of the response. The dream, however, typically has no such objective stimulus in the real world. Furthermore, the narrative continuity and autobiographical specificity of the dream render it more suitable than the Rorschach percept for analysis. In addition, the associations obtained by the psychotherapist to the subject's dream provide further valuable data for purposes of interpretation; it is not standard practice, however, to garner associations to Rorschach percepts.[1]

It also must be recognized that the interpretive conte..t of inkblot administration often further reduces the power of such interpretation, as contrasted with the interpretation of dreams. The Rorschach examiner often has little prior information about the subject's background, personality, and idiosyncratic views of the world. The psychotherapist, in contrast, is intimately familiar with the patient whose dream is to be interpreted and is thus in a favorable position to interpret the patient's idiosyncratic use of the symbols. Additionally, the patient can and does correct wrong dream interpretations, whereas this is rarely the case in Rorschach interpretation.

In short, it is difficult to avoid Schafer's conclusion that "insofar as the Rorschach response expresses unconscious, infantile tendencies, it is ordinarily a guidepost to these tendencies and not a highly articulated map of the unconscious terrain" (Schafer, 1954, p. 96). As a less powerful tool than the dream, the Rorschach technique thus lends itself much more readily to wild symbolic analysis than does the dream. Too often, Rorschach content interpretation deteriorates into "wildly imaginative and highly subjective interpretations which have [served to render] . . . projective techniques more highly projective for the examiner than for the subject" (Anastasi, 1976, p. xi).

RULES FOR VALID CONTENT INTERPRETATION

Given this state of affairs, we have chosen to present a set of 16 guidelines to inkblot content interpretation that should help the clinician avoid wild analysis and maximize the accuracy of interpretations arrived at through the idiosyncratic interpretation of content.

The Conservative Interpretation

The Rorschach clinician must be very conservative in interpreting inkblot content; he or she should be aware of the instrument's inherent weaknesses. When in doubt as to whether a particular response should be interpreted, the clinician should prefer to err on the side of caution. While clinical sensitivity is clearly an important characteristic for the effective interpretation of content, the Ror- schacher must be wary of overconfidence that may lead to unjustified speculation; one must not go beyond the data in arriving at conclusions about subjects.

---

[1]Associative procedures that can be used with the Rorschach technique are discussed in Chapter 11.

The Doubtful Response

As noted by Hertzman and Pearce (1947), it is important for the Rorschacher to be willing to say that he or she does not know the meaning of doubtful responses. When the record consists largely of such responses, the psychologist must acknowledge in the psychological report that the psychodynamics of the subject are not clear (although the defensive style of the subject may be quite evident in the test responses). (See Schafer, 1954.)

Responses with Uncertain Referents

As also pointed out by Hertzman and Pearce (1947), the clinician must be particularly wary of interpreting responses whose referents are uncertain. Thus, if a male patient gives the following response to Card VII: "Two women who are crying—feeling sorry for themselves," it is by no means clear whether the patient is referring to himself or to other important figures in his life. While the dynamic inquiry technique presented in Chapter 11 can help to clarify the referents of doubtful responses, the clinician should refrain from interpreting such responses in the absence of clarifying material.

Misuse of "Fixed Meanings"

The Rorschacher should avoid interpretations based primarily on tables of "fixed meaning" for various content categories. As should be clear from our presentation thus far, the psychologist is often in doubt as to the dynamic meaning of many responses. The clinician might thus be tempted to resort to sources such as the "animal list" and associated ego qualities presented by Phillips and Smith (1953). Resorting to tables of fixed meaning for dynamic Rorschach interpretation is no more defensible than the use of "dream books" in the interpretation of dreams. Such categorized treatment of dynamic symbols ignores the highly idiosyncratic nature of symbol usage and is likely to lead to a very high degree of interpretative error.

Overreliance on Hypothetical Evocative Qualities

The clinician should avoid interpretations based primarily on assumed card meaning. Many authors have presented hypotheses with regard to particular evocative qualities of Rorschach blots. The most familiar such hypotheses are those that describe Card IV as the "father card," Card VI as the "sex card," and Card VII as the "mother card." The research literature on the subject reviewed in our earlier volume (Aronow & Reznikoff, 1976) concluded that the respective hypotheses regarding these cards must be considered doubtful. The clinician who assumes that responses to Card IV invariably reflect on the father, to Card VI on sexuality, and to Card VII on the mother is thus on very shaky ground.

Disentangling the Projective from the Nonprojective

The clinician must be able to disentangle the projective from the nonprojective aspects of the inkblot response. The subject's response may be regarded as a blend of objective description of and typical reaction to blot properties on the one hand, and projective elements from within the subject on the other. Extensive clinical experience is, of course, helpful in separating these two elements. A knowledge of common responses elicited by blots and blot areas can help in the teasing apart of the two elements. An awareness of how subjects typically respond to the blots is also useful in this regard.

As noted in Chapter 2, we suggest that one be most reluctant to interpret responses to blots that are in keeping with the blot stimulus properties. Negatively tinged responses to Cards I and IV, for example, should be interpreted with considerable caution since these blots are perceived by most subjects as very negative stimuli. If an emotionally negative response to Card I is obtained, one would thus require more evidence than usual that the response has projective elements and is not merely an appropriate emotional response to the blot stimulus properties.

Knowledge of General Psychodynamics

A firm grasp of general psychodynamics as well as defensive operations is very helpful to the psychologist engaging in the dynamic interpretations of content. In particular, training and experience in dream interpretation is highly beneficial to the Rorschach clinician. One's own personal analysis or psychotherapy is also likely to be useful in eliminating blind spots and increasing clinical sensitivity.

The Interpreter's Own "Blind Spots

The clinician should try to be sensitive to cumulative data on his or her own "blind spots" in interpretation. Thus, if a clinician finds him- or herself describing the dynamics of many diverse subjects in the same manner (a manner strikingly similar to the examiner's own dynamics), it is quite possible that the examiner is doing his or her own projecting in the interpretive situation. The opposite type of error (a blindness to certain aspects of psychodynamics) is more difficult for the examiner to discover.

Sequence Analysis

The sensitive clinician should interpret responses not as discrete entities but in reference to the surrounding responses. This aspect of inkblot interpretation, dubbed "sequence analysis" by early Rorschachers, is particularly valuable in dynamic Rorschach work. When a major conflictual theme in the subject's life manages to intrude into a Rorschach response, one often finds a fascinating "ebb and flow" of wish and defense, of ambivalent feelings, and of other related aspects of the subject's personality in the surrounding responses to the same blot and perhaps later in the protocol. Because of its great importance in projective interpretation, content sequence analysis will be discussed in more detail in Chapter 12.

Characteristics of Heavy Dynamic Loading

The skilled clinician should be aware of those characteristics that identify the response carrying a heavy dynamic loading, Mindess (1970), in particular, has written of the characteristics of revealing Rorschach responses, focusing on four such aspects: originality, emotional cathexis, imaginativeness, and repetition.

Originality
According to Mindess, the more unusual an idea is, the more justified one is in considering it symbolic. Thus, "a bat" seen on Card I is far less likely to be dynamically meaningful than a highly original response such as "the Greek winged victory, a statue of a woman representing freedom."

Emotional Cathexis
The more clearly imbued with emotion a response is, the more likely it is to be symbolic. Thus, seeing two people on the sides of Card I is less likely to be meaningful than seeing two people tearing a child apart.

Imaginativeness
The more the imagination of the subject is invoked by the percept, the more likely the percept is dynamically meaningful. Mindess presented an example of a highly imaginative response to Card IX: "Vapor shooting up into the air and in the background there are mountains, pure white, and golden gates, carved perfectly, and way back in the distance is a tower and that tower is the capitol of the world and it's so beautiful that it makes everything look bright" (Mindess, 1970, p. 85).

Repetition
Mindess has also suggested that a category of response repeated within the Rorschach record is more likely to be symbolically significant than a response that occurs only once.

The interested reader is referred to Mindess's (1970) article for a more detailed description of these response characteristics.

Confluence of Data

The examiner should look for a confluence of data before making statements about the subject. Major trends within the subject typically manifest themselves repeatedly in the battery. Sometimes, however, a particularly transparent response will suggest an important dynamic trend that is not confirmed elsewhere in the record. On such occasions it is usually appropriate to include such interpretations in the report but to also indicate their tentativeness. On the other hand, the examiner should also indicate those interpretations in which he or she has a good deal of confidence because evidence to support them occurs throughout the battery.

Quantitative Judgments Based on Idiographic Analysis

The Rorschacher should avoid quantitative judgments about subjects based on idiographic analysis. To the extent that the term *measurement* can be applied to idiographic interpretation, it is clearly a very primitive form of measurement, perhaps analogous to what Stevens (1951) has called a "nominal scale," with a one-to-one correspondence assumed to exist between the percepts and the relevant aspects of the subject's personality. This very primitive level of measurement implies that judgments of quantity (e.g., how anxious is the subject based on idiographic interpretation of content) cannot be expected from such data. It may be possible to make more sophisticated quantitative judgments based on nomothetic inkblot content scales, but the very limited reliability and normative data available on most of these scales make it inadvisable for the clinician to make such Rorschach-based quantitative judgments at this time.

At first blush, this rule would seem to contradict Schafer's (1954) dictum that the psychologist should seek to indicate the intensity of interpreted trends. Although the importance of specifying the degrees to which certain trends are present cannot be denied, such specification requires nomothetic scales with adequate psychometric foundations, notably lacking in the Rorschach technique. The clinician should thus form such quantitative judgments on the basis of appropriate nomothetic instruments.

Comprehensive History of the Subject

All else being constant, the greater the knowledge the examiner possesses about the background of the subject, the more effective will be the idiographic Rorschach interpretation. Given the highly idiosyncratic nature of symbol usage, the psychologist needs as intimate a knowledge of the subject as it is possible to acquire. Too often, examiners know little or nothing about the histories of the subjects, and sometimes even pride themselves on their ability to do "blind analysis." A high degree of interpretive error is likely to result from such analysis. We favor the taking of comprehensive histories from subjects as part of the assessment process.

Feedback from Others

The competent clinician should augment his or her clinical expertise by seeking feedback about the accuracy of observations from those in a position to render such judgments, most notably psychotherapists who have known the subjects over significant periods of time. Such feedback is likely to help identify the examiner's blind spots in interpretation.

Behavioral Data

The clinician must be alert to relevant behavior demonstrated during administration, behavior that may help the examiner arrive at a more meaningful interpretation of responses. Does the subject, for example, display signs of anxiety or agitation in the process of responding (voice breaking, occurrence of tics, profuse sweating, breaking of eye contact, shift of posture, etc.)? Does the subject give blatently sexual, morbid, gory, or bizarre responses with no sign of concern or emotional involvement? The clinician must regard him- or herself—during the Rorschach administration in particular—as an important clinical instrument for the detection and evaluation of such behavioral data that can help shed light on the dynamic constitution of the subject.

Subject as Partner

Finally, the Rorschach subject should be regarded by the examiner as a partner in the examination process rather than as a naive individual to be duped into revealing significant material. Leventhal et al. (1962) discussed the potential benefits of the "active handling of the patient-psychologist relationship" extensively (p. 77). Leventhal et al. have suggested an extensive prior interview in which the subject is encouraged to collaborate with the examiner to produce a useful record. The examiner may also wish to use this period for acquiring extensive historical material about the subject.

In our previous volume (Aronow & Reznikoff, 1976) we suggested that the patient may also be recruited as an active participant in the interpretative process by making major modifications in the Rorschach inquiry procedure. In our experience, patients typically know that the Rorschach technique is designed to reveal personality functioning. Once the initial response process is completed, they may then be asked to clarify the meaning of their percepts through an associative procedure and even by means of direct questioning. This modified clinical use of the Rorschach procedure will be discussed in Chapter 11.

▲ 11

Content-Oriented Administration Procedures

As noted in Chapter 10, dynamic interpretation of Rorschach responses obtained in the association phase of administration can be quite problematic, often leading to excursions into wild analysis. To help clarify the dynamic meaning of particular Rorschach responses and to counter the problem of wild analysis, a number of altered administration procedures have been proposed.

The earliest suggestion of modified procedure was put forward by Burt (1945). Burt chose to eliminate the standard inquiry procedure and to substitute an inquiry into the source of the percept in the subject's life experience. Unfortunately, Burt did not present the instructions used for his inquiry procedure, nor did he give the reader any idea of how such inquiry is to be conducted.

In contrast, Janis and Janis (1946/1965) presented a highly structured technique in which free associations to the Rorschach percepts are obtained. The Janis procedure involves standard instructions read to every subject and a procedure wherein chains of associations are obtained. Kessel, Harris, and Slagle (1969) also suggested the use of associations in clarifying the dynamic meaning of content.

Several authors have recommended other techniques for obtaining more dynamic information from the Rorschach technique. Appelbaum (1959/1965) suggested changing the atmosphere in which the procedure is administered, with the examiner indicating by his or her behavior that the formal session is over after the Rorschach is administered. The subject is then asked in an "informal" way to go through the cards again and to indicate if he or she sees anything else. Kornrich (1965) also suggested a "second run" through the blots to elicit new responses.

Halpern (1957/1965) advocates a procedure wherein the examiner, in a post-session, tries to validate his or her Rorschach-based hypotheses by directly questioning the subject about his or her personality. Leventhal et al. (1962) suggested an "active handling of the patient–psychologist relationship," with an extensive prior interview to establish a collaborative relationship with the examiner, and with the assessment itself turned into a combination of examination and interview procedure.

Arthur (1965) presented the only altered Rorschach procedure designed primarily for children. Arthur's technique is suitable for use with children who produce barren or constricted records. Arthur essentially asks her subjects questions that elicit thematic material. Thus, the subject is gradually required to construct a story around the percept.

Craddick (1975) proposed a procedure in which the subject is asked to select a card that best represents the self and "important others" in his or her life, as well as one that best represents the subject and the examiner. Reasons for the selections must be given.

Elitzur (1976) introduced an "imaginary story and self-interpretation" technique for use in Rorschach content analysis. Following the traditional inquiry, Elitzur has his subjects use each of the percepts as the main theme for an imaginary story. Subjects are then told that the stories should reflect what they are experiencing inwardly, and they are asked to identify with the characters of the story. The subjects' responses to the procedures are then interpreted from a gestalt perspective.

Cerney (1984) requests from the subject "One Last Response" on Card X. Cerney speculates that this extra procedure helps to identify those people who will respond well to the challenge of a psychotherapy situation. Jaffe (1988) similarly presented an altered procedure in which the subject is requested to produce a simple additional response from any of the 10 cards.

A more complete description of many of the procedures summarized here can be found in our previous book (Aronow & Reznikoff, 1976). None of these procedures has been adopted by clinicians to any great extent, in part because they typically involve additional time requirements. We have therefore developed what we call the Content Rorschach Technique, which substitutes a content-oriented inquiry for the traditional inquiry procedure, similar to what was initially suggested by Burt (1945).

THE CONTENT RORSCHACH TECHNIQUE

In the Content Rorschach Technique the Association phase of the Rorschach is first administered, using the standard instructions as presented in Chapter 2. After the subject has given response(s) to Card I, he or she is told, "Now I'd like you to show me where you saw these things on the blot. Where is the _____ you saw?" Locations are thus obtained with the help of a standard location sheet following each blot during this first phase of administration. This is done to ensure that the inquiry period may be devoted entirely to dynamic associations.

Following the completion of the first phase of testing with all 10 blots, subjects are then presented with the following instructions:

> There's one more part to this procedure. Sometimes what people see in the cards brings to mind something that they remember, either from recent times or from a long time ago, or makes them think of something. When I read back your responses to you, I'd like you to tell me the first thing that comes to mind.

After the subject's first association to these instructions, further associations may be elicited if the data warrant it. The subject may then be asked to associate to his or her associations, as in the Janis procedure; the subject may be asked to associate to a particular part of the percept, or the subject may be asked to respond to combinations of percepts, and the subject may even be asked to relate the percept to his or her own life. In other words, at this point the Rorschach is no longer a standard procedure; the examiner may direct the subject's verbalizations in any way that seems likely to lead to clinically meaningful information.

An example of the use of our inquiry technique will serve to further clarify its nature. A 23-year-old woman who was hospitalized following a suicide attempt gave the following response on Card III: "Two butlers preparing a meal." When Card III was reached in the second phase, the subject was read her response and was asked what it made her think of. She replied, "Just two butlers preparing pancakes or something." She was then asked what preparing pancackes reminded her of (since this was the new element she introduced in her association). She replied, "Now it reminds me of something very silly—my father and mother used to argue over who used to make the better pancakes." (What does that call to mind?) "It was a very silly fight—all you could do was laugh at them. My sister said my father's were better, so I always said my mother's were better."

In this chain of verbalizations, several dynamic elements are revealed, including parental conflict over oral supplies, denigration of the parents, a split of alliances in her childhood family, and rivalry with her sister.

The questioning technique that we have found to be most helpful has several characteristics:

1. The questions asked are open-ended—subjects are asked what something makes them think of, reminds them of, and so forth. There is as little focus as possible to these questions, thus maintaining the amorphous, projective nature of the task. We typically vary the wording of such questions so as to avoid sterotyped repetition: Thus, such phrases as, "What does _____ make you think of," "What does _____ call to mind," "What does that bring to mind" are used.

2. The examiner has great freedom in terms of choosing the direction in which he or she wants the procedure to continue. Thus, in the preceding example the examiner chose to respond to the new element (the pancakes) introduced in the patient's initial association. Some other possibilities might be to direct associations to a particular element (in the example, the examiner might have asked what butlers made the subject think of), or to link together more than one response for associative purposes (e.g., the subject might be asked what this response and another taken together called to mind).

3. If the subject does not tacitly acknowledge self-revealing aspects of his or her responses, we will for several responses ask the subject directly, "What might your seeing _____ in the inkblot reflect about your own life?" Such a questioning procedure leads many subjects to reveal important dynamic material in this part of the testing. When subjects do not respond to this questioning technique, the defensiveness and/or lack of psychological mindedness of the subject constitutes important clinical data.

4. At times, the subject's associations to inkblot responses lead to the subject speaking of important emotional subjects. At the examiner's discretion, the Rorschach administration may then be interrupted to pursue (by means of a direct interview) the emotional material that has been dredged up by means of the technique. Administration may then resume following the brief interview.

5. If the examiner is pressed for time, or if the subject is not responding with associations of clinical value, it is not necessary to obtain associations to all percepts in the record. Since the locations have already been ascertained in the first phase, scoring and tabulation are still possible.

When the Content Rorschach Technique is used in place of the traditional administration method, there are two major differences in scoring and tabulation. First, it is no longer possible to score the determinant category; also, the scoring of form-level is modified. Form-level must now be scored for all responses that can be said to have a definite form. Thus, a response on Card X, "a big hooray," would not be scored for form-level, nor would a response on Card VIII, "a chunk of meat," since a chunk of meat may have any shape at all. The Rorschach summary and tabulation sheets discussed in Chapter 7 may be used with the Content Rorschach Technique with the determinant column left blank on the summary sheets and the determinant totals and ratios omitted on the tabulation sheet. Protocols obtained by means of the Content Rorschach Technique are presented in Chapter 16 and elsewhere in this text.

▲12

Content Sequence Analysis

Many authors have written on the importance of structural sequence analysis in Rorschach interpretation, that is, viewing responses not in isolation, but in the context of, for example, the types of location areas and determinants occurring chronologically in the total record (e.g., Beck, Beck, Levitt, & Molish, 1961; Exner, 1974; Klopfer et al., 1954; also, see Chapter 7 in the present text). Such considerations also apply to content interpretation of the Rorschach record. Similarly, when seen from a content perspective, no response stands alone—all must be understood in the larger context of the complete record.

Because each person is unique, the chronological patterning of responses in each Rorschach record is likewise unique, and the variation in the sequence analysis that must be carried out is consequently enormous. Nonetheless, there are certain general sequence analysis issues that, though they may be manifested differently in diverse Rorschach records, do seem to have commonality as regards content sequence analysis in many protocols. In particular, we see five issues to which the Rorschach student should be alert.

REPETITION OF A THEME TO THE SAME INKBLOT

The repetition of a theme in responses to the *same* inkblot may imply that the theme is of some importance to the subject.

An example of this is seen in the following three responses to Card II by a 24-year-old woman who had been admitted to a psychiatric hospital because of a suicide attempt, and who subsequently had been diagnosed as paranoid schizophrenic.

II. 2" 1. Two old women having a coffee klatch.	II. 1. They have their cups raised—they're talking. (About what?) Gossiping. (Remind you of?) When I was a little girl—my mother was born in Germany—she and her friend would go into the kitchen, and talk in German—I'd never know what they would talk about. (Makes you think of?) Mixed feelings—glad she wasn't bothering me—but she wasn't there when I wanted to bother her.
II. 2. Two soldiers making a blood pact.	II. 2. This part could be a fur cape, the blood here—their hands are raised in a position where they could be making themselves blood brothers. (Make you think of?) It comes from what happened to me last week—when I felt that the man who hypnotized me made a blood pact with a group that called themelves the black scorpions—I don't know if it was real or in my head. (Remind you of?) Slitting my wrists—slitting the flesh in some way, letting blood.
II. 3. Two dogs looking out of the window, and seeing two people fighting outside. That's all.	II. 3. The two upper red things are people fighting. (Remind you of?) My sister and I watching my mother and her friend in the kitchen—feeling closed out. (Think of then?) Alienation—the window represents the fact they were speaking German.

In the first and third responses, we have a repetition of the theme of emotional distance and alienation from the mother. In the middle response, we find a reference to paranoid ideation and her recent suicide attempt. This might suggest a pivotal importance of this patient's experience of alienation and emotional distance in her childhood and a possible linkage to her subsequent emotional development and symptomatology.

REPETITION OF A THEME TO DIFFERENT INKBLOTS

The repetition of a theme in response to *different* inkblots might similarly imply that the theme is of importance to the subject. An example of such repetition of theme on different blots can be seen in the following responses of a 21-year-old male hospitalized because of a schizophrenic break.

I. It looks like a—
oh boy. It looks
like—oh boy. 38" 1.
It looks like two
people dancing.

I. 1. I first saw it as a coat—maybe two people locked together—maybe my mother and I locked together on an unconscious basis—two people, separate yet together.

II. 4" 1. It looks like
two lambs sucking
on some milk.

II. 1. Reminds me of my mother's operation—she had her breasts removed—and I felt very depressed, forlorn, and lost.

III. 3" 1. Two
people sitting
opposite each other.

III. 1. I saw a program once on someone who was throwing a violin. My mother is using the strings—of my own instrument. The smudge is how I'm carrying myself. Beauty isn't coming out of the music maker.

These responses largely speak for themselves in terms of the symbiotic, destructive relationship between this patient and his mother, and his intense hostility toward the mother. The extent to which similar associations suffuse his record points to the crucial nature of his relationship with his mother.

THE SHIFT BETWEEN WISH AND DEFENSE

The ebb and flow of the shift between wish and defense can often be seen in the sequencing of Rorschach response content. A good example of this is revealed in the following responses of a 35-year-old female psychiatric inpatient.

II. 6" 1. Two Folies
Bergère–type
women—they're all
made up—they're
putting their hands
together, with black
and red costumes—
they're sort of
dancing.

II. 1. I'm an entertainer—I like to be on stage—I'm basically an exhibitionist—I like to get attention.

II. 2. It looks like a
butterfly—but the
butterfly has two
sharp claws coming
out. It would be a
pretty butterfly,
except for the two
claws.

II. 2. I always loved butterflies—they're such delicate, pretty things. But this is a dangerous butterfly.

II. 3. There's also an
urn in the middle.
Now the two
women look like
they're half animal
and half women—
their feet look like
bears' feet. I don't
like them.

In this series of responses and associations one sees the shift from the decorative-passive feminine percept (Folies Bergère–type women), continued in the butterfly image, with the aggressive-hostile wishes then emerging to complicate the percept and the self-concept (dangerous butterfly with sharp claws). There is an attempt at recovery with a feminine-receptive percept (the urn), but the defensive recovery is unsuccessful, with the initial percept then complicated by the introduction of aggressive drive material (the Folies Bergère women now become half women and half animal, with the patient having an unpleasant reaction to this material).

ADEQUACY OF DEFENSES/DEFENSE OF REPRESSION

By viewing the sequence of the responses in terms of their content, one may see not only the shift between wish and defense, but also the general adequacy of the defenses, particularly with respect to the defense of repression. This is vividly seen in the responses to Card III of the same 21-year-old schizophrenic patient whose responses were reported above.

III. 3″ 1. Two peo
ple sitting opposite
each other.

III. 1. It seems scary—it looks like men facing each other, holding down women's heads in the water. I once had a roommate who I trusted—he misled me. My whole life could be reversing—it could be me killing my mother.

III. 2. Someone's
chest cavity—their
lungs.

III. 2. The breathing of life. It also makes me think of my mother's breasts being removed.

III. 3. Someone's
asshole.

III. 3. The pleasure of releasing myself, the sides look like buttocks, with the asshole here.

In this progression of three responses, one sees the deterioration of the defenses: The patient begins with fairly socialized and appropriate content (the popular human response), then goes to an internal anatomy response, and finally regresses to a primitive anal response as the defense of repression fails him.

SHIFTS IN FEELING TOWARD PERSONS AND TOPICS

By analyzing the sequence and general context of Rorschach responses, one can see shifts in subjects' feelings about a particular person or topic. An example of this is indicated in the following ordering of responses and associations of a 19-year-old female psychiatric outpatient with complaints of anxiety attacks.

IV. 7″ 1. A big grizzly bear—looking up at him from the ground.

IV. 1. It makes me think of my father—he's very tall and very domineering—it's like he's overpowering. (What does that bring to mind?) Anger at times—it's hard to fight back, although I'm start- ing to be able to tell him how I feel about things. He wanted me to go to Europe with him on a trip, but I realized that I didn't have to, and I told him so.

V. 15″ 1. It looks like some kind of a bug.

V. 1. It makes me think of something that bugs you. (What does that remind you of?) People being on your back about things. (What does that make you think of in your own life?) My boyfriend being on my back lots of times—usually about my moods. But, then, sometimes, he's very understanding.

V. 2. These are like animals—head and one foot of a horse. Like racing on a racetrack.

V. 2. My boyfriend and I went to the racetrack—I liked it, but I'm afraid that he may get into gambling.

V. 3. A man figure with a big nose, the figure of a person.

V. 3. He looks like half man, and half animal. (What does that call to mind?) Maybe my boyfriend. (?) He's watching over me, which makes me feel comfortable—it's really in my best interest. On the other hand, I sometimes get mad, I feel like he's telling me what to do.

In this series of responses on several blots, the patient sketches for us her conflicted relationship with her father and, now, her boyfriend: enjoying the dependency, but resenting the domination.

A different sort of shift is seen in the content of this same patient's responses and associations to Card VIII.

VIII. 10" 1. These look like bears.	VIII. 1. They could represent like a struggle—in my life—what's happening to me—hoping that I can live a normal life, and feel well.
VIII. 2. It also looks like a sea—as though looking from the moon down.	VIII. 2. I like water—it's cool and soothing. It's a place of tranquillity, to get away to. The moon has an effect on the tides, and maybe on your moods.

In these two brief responses we see the alternation between her sense of internal conflict and her desire for tranquility and peace.

The following is the Rorschach technique record of a 36-year-old bisexual cabdriver who sought outpatient psychotherapy because of anxiety attacks. Emphasis on interpretation is placed on content sequence analysis.

Card I-17" 1. The central thing—could possibly be a human form, a person with his arms above his head.	1. There are hands coming here. The bottom half looks like a female, seen from the behind.
2. There's an interesting possibility of eyes, and the ears of some kind of animal but the face isn't complete.	2. Maybe it implies something sinister—that makes me think of some of my relationships with other people. I sometimes have a lack of sensitivity to what they want or need—I interpret things as how I want them to be.
3. An interesting symmetry—as though the two sides are pulling away from each other rather than working together.	3. There's a conspicuous central dividing line. There's a sense of two figures, two forces pulling away. (What does that remind you of?) A struggle between what I want to do—what other people expect me to do. What I do to enjoy myself, versus to get approval from other people. (What does that make you think of?) The way that I'm always working so hard—I end up defeating myself in the process. A lot of me is phony, a bluff. I try to make a good impression on other people.

4. With a stretch of the imagination, it could be a woman's lower genital area. It's almost symmetrical, but not quite.

4. It makes me think of that part of a woman. (What do you think of then?) I think I have a preoccupation with sex—I use it in a compulsive way to get approval—it's the easiest and safest way to get approval without establishing ties, to make an involvement with a person in a sexual way. (What do you think of then?) I want to avoid establishing ties—because I'm afraid of rejection. I want to look for support, but I might be rejected. I don't want to rely on anybody for approval or affection. (What does that remind you of?) I think of my father—I was independent in high school, but I was always trying to get someone interested in me. (What does your father make you think of?) He was not a very expressive person—he was very stoic—a man of few words. In terms of my social life, when I was especially sensitive to the reactions of my peers, my parents' ideas about things put a great damper on my social life. I couldn't ever have discussed with my father anything that bothered me.

In the subject's responses to Card I a number of themes present themselves. In the first response the "rear view" may suggest homosexual or bisexual inclinations. The second response with the "eyes" and the sinister association might point to a trend toward ideas of reference. The third response is strongly suggestive of a split in the sexual self, with forces pulling the subject in opposite directions—possibly a repetition of the theme of sexual confusion already noted. The fourth response is highly revealing of aspects of the self, including as it does sexual aspects, feelings toward the father, and ambivalence about relationships with people. Clearly, this individual has a very high capacity for insight.

Card II—18"
1. The red area looks something like a butterfly.

2. It has a strange appearance similar to a face, a conorted face—red, closing in on the eyes, and maybe a mouth that's open.

2. On the sheet here, it looks more like a mask. (What does a contorted face make you think of?) My personality again, a sort of mask, artificial behavior, trying to be what other people want. The mask is more in terms of for me than for anyone else. I have lsss awareness of who I am and what I want.

3. The two black areas could be two figures squatting on their haunches, with their hands up against each other.

3. They look like two old men in robes—surrealistic characters. They could be two people who are in conflict. (What does that make you think of?) Sometimes, I have interesting periods of rage—strange overreactions—it happened recently with someone in my cab. The man assumed that I was cheating him and got angry at me, and started a tirade. I responded the same way—there was an ego confrontation between us. Afterwards, it was hard to write it off, it stayed on my mind. (What do old men in robes make you think of?) Like monks or somebody like that. The religious representation could be conflicts in terms of my parents. Their religious values and mine—their self-denial aspects of Christianity make me impatient and angry, and contribute to my not knowing more about myself.

In responses to Card II we again see the sense of the self as in some way "phony," not genuine, as initially revealed on Card I. The third response again suggests a strong split in the self, with superego aspects prominent.

Card III—9"
1. It looks immediately like two people pulling away at something, in two separate directions.

1. It could represent for me a sense of inner conflict between whatever I really want to be and what I've told myself that I want to be.

2. The red things vaguely resemble something falling, maybe a person.

2. I often feel like I'm floundering around—I don't know what I'm doing. These two people look very feminine. (What does that make you think of?) I can see it in terms of being strongly attracted to women, wanting to relate to women, wanting to relate to a woman on an intimate basis, but the problems that I have in my way of picking up with people who want a certain kind of dependency.

3. The lower half resembles a face, but the top half doesn't bear that out.

3. There seems to be sort of a contradiction—something that gives a certain impression, but the rest of it doesn't bear it out.

Card III responses again suggest contradictions in the sense of self, feminine aspects of sexual identification, and a view of the self as "floundering around."

Card IV—10"
1. It looks like a huge man or an animal falling backwards.

1. What comes to mind is as though it were someone floating on his back in the water. That's something that I can't do. I can't relax like that—I don't feel that I have control—relaxing is necessary in order to float.

2. It could also be an animal running forward, crawling forward. This thing here might be the head.

2. It could have an ominous quality to it. (What does that make you think of?) Being pursued. (What does that remind you of?) The tyranny of the should.

3. All of these little spots, it's not symmetrical.

Card IV responses repeat the theme of being in a helpless position "falling backward," and again a somewhat paranoid "ominous quality." The self is also viewed as quite tense, having difficulty relaxing. Superego aspects again intrude—"the tyranny of the should."

Card V—10"
1. This makes me think of a butterfly, a bat. A thing that flies, it's mostly wings.

2. A sense of opposition to the two parts of this one.

2. A sort of an arch—mutual opposition supports conflict. The pressure coming down here holds it up. (What does that remind you of?) Sometimes I'm able to utilize conflict, it takes off the pressure somehow—remaining ambivalent, I avoid responsibility or commitment, and I avoid being judged, and I avoid failure.

3. There's like a face hidden behind this in the center.

On Card V the theme of inner conflict persists, as well as the superego issue, "I avoid being judged."

Card VI—21"
1. All of these blots seem to be drawn in terms of opposition in one thing. These might be two heads arguing or something like that.

1. This reminds me of cartoon characters—two worms that talk—all they have is big eyes and a mouth. (What does two worms arguing make you think of?) There's something ludicrous about it. There's a lot of absurdity, that I see in my situation and in others. The whole idea of making a worm—giving worms intelligence to behave like humans. Why wish that absurdity on them?

2. This could be somebody standing on top of something, with their arms out, except for the obvious division.

2. He has a very cross-like appearance. The cross on the top makes me think of a church. (What does that make you think of?) What comes into mind is a traffic cop at an intersection. I have religious figures and authority figures associated with that. (What do you think of then?) Standing at the top of something, as if providing some kind of support. Maybe I'm looking for authorities to support that—make decisions for me, give instructions, yet at the same time I'm resisting it.

Card VI again takes up the repetitive theme of inner conflict, a split in the sense of self. Also added at this point is a theme of poor self-concept ("worms"). The religion and authority figure associations in Response 2 suggest a critical superego basis for the poor self-concept.

Card VII—10"
They're all very much the same, they all have symmetry—but little things in them make them less than perfectly symmetrical. They also all resemble a sexual orifice or something.

1. The two heads that are torn apart from each other. The two sections are split away.

1. There's a struggle—between two things—what they want to be, and what they feel they should be.

2. There's a sexual orifice here and in the other blots too. There were those things which might be seen that way.

2. It's seen either from the back or from the front—it could be a rectum, or it could be a vaginal opening.

Card VII repeats the theme of sexual preoccupation seen earlier, with the theme of bisexual ambivalence expressed very poignantly.

Card VIII—15"
1. These are like two animals— maybe bears or something from the side.

2. This area has a tendency to move up. It seems to be more—coming down. It's holding up the other part.

2. The gray is holding down this area. (What does that make you think of?) There are a lot of things that I do to ensure but I don't pursue my interests as far as I might. I create a lot of problems and obstacles, to keep from succeeding or finding out if I succeed.

The Card VIII response again addresses the issue of a split in the sense of self, feeling that in some way he may inhibit or sabotage himself.

Card IX—18"
1. This one looks like eyes that are looking out from something that's obscuring things, like a mask.

1. It makes me think of self-deception that's used as a mask, and obscures a lot.

2. This looks like I feel sometimes, the upper part of the torso looks red, as though it's inflamed or tense. And here is the head, going off in all different kinds of chaos, but the most striking thing on this is the eyes—the eyes looking out from behind.

2. Sometimes I just have a sense that I don't know anything, I'm so busy trying to sort things out that my mind is just complete chaos.

The Card IX responses again point to possible ideas of reference, and also a theme of the self as chaotic and disorganized.

Card X—8″
1. This gives me the impression of a slender, scowling face.

1. That makes me think of discipline, disapproval, someone in the position of judging me.

2. An enthroned person is here, with these people paying homage of some kind.

2. These are subservient guards. And this might be a carpet, leading up to the throne. (What does that remind you of?) Authority—it's useful, but there's something destructive about it, because it causes resistance in me.

3. This could be a destructive aspect of this creature here—it has destructive aspects.

4. This feature strikes me as strange.

4. It's standing by itself—it doesn't seem to be related to the rest. Everything sort of surrounds it. (What does that make you think of?) That could be me being judged—me being isolated too.

On Card X this subject concludes with themes introduced earlier—the prominent superego theme, perhaps relating to the father, and the self seen as judged by the powerful authority figure.

Records included in Chapter 16 further demonstrate principles of content sequence analysis.

▲13

The Consensus Rorschach

A particularly novel and creative use of the Rorschach technique has been its use with two or more individuals, dubbed the "Consensus Rorschach" procedure. In this procedure a protocol is obtained from two or more people who, through some form of negotiation, arrive at a single set of agreed-upon percepts. While traditional scoring can be applied to such protocols, emphasis has primarily been placed on content variables and aspects of interpersonal interaction.

CONSENSUS PROCEDURES IN THE LITERATURE

The Consensus Rorschach procedure was initiated by Blanchard (1959), who showed Rorschach inkblots to social worker colleagues and serendipitously observed that the blots stimulated much discussion and dynamic interaction. Blanchard became convinced of the usefulness of the procedure in a group setting and subsequently administered the Rorschach to groups of juvenile offenders. In 1968, Blanchard published a description of a Consensus Rorschach administration to a group of youths who had been involved in a gang rape. Blanchard characterized the resulting protocol as "a reenactment of the gang rape experience" with respect to the patterns of interactions among the gang members.

Other investigators have continued the exploration of Rorschach technique administration in a group setting. Levy and Epstein (1964) have used the Consensus Rorschach to discuss how a family endeavors to attain equilibrium. They thus focus on the process by which each family member modifies his or her Rorschach percepts so as to become more congruous with the developing family consensus.

Loveland (1967) uses the term "Relation Rorschach" for her consensus procedure, which utilizes just one or two Rorschach cards and tape records the interactions without the examiner in the room for as long as 10 minutes as they strive to reach consensus. Loveland also individually asks each member to indicate in writing all things agreed upon so as to better evaluate the extent of consensus. She focuses particularly on transactional components such as clarity of individual communication, comprehension of the communication of others, and the affective posture assumed toward each other and toward the tasks.

Willi (1969) similarly emphasizes transactional components of the Consensus Rorschach, particularly efforts at domination. In Willi's "joint Rorschach procedure" the Rorschach is administered to each person individually in the traditional way, and then immediately thereafter the subjects are asked to look at the blots again and arrive at a single joint solution. Willi relies on both traditional determinant analysis and the analysis of content and behavioral interactions.

Bauman and Roman (1968) label their consensus procedure "interaction testing." They attempt to derive "group process scores" from the procedure, emphasizing such aspects as dominance, group efficiency, and the emergence of new ideas through group interaction. They present data from a Consensus Wechsler-Bellevue scale but note that the same analytic principles would apply to a Consensus Rorschach.

Cutter (1968) and Cutter and Farberow (1970) present a method for analyzing Consensus Rorschach protocols that they call "the method of content polarities." They focus on the extent to which divergent reactions to the same inkblot reflect polar opposites of various behavioral or role expectations. Thus, for example, they present a family responding to Card VII with the content polarity of "wild gyrations, kissing," which they interpret as revealing conflict over the expression of heterosexual feelings and impulses.

Cutter and Farberow (1968) have also studied the impact of disparate groups on the Consensus Rorschach by serially administering the technique to an alcoholic, three of his friends, three of his roommates, his wife (on two occasions separated by 6 months), and a high-low status pair. Striking differences were observed consistent with the diverse social contexts in which the tests were administered.

W. Klopfer (1969) has presented the Consensus Rorschach as a procedure that can be used in the school setting to help clarify interpersonal and intrapsychic problems. Klopfer proposed that this technique may be particularly useful at the start of each school year.

Dorr (1981) has written about his rather interesting procedure for conjoint testing in marriage therapy. The procedure is extensive, typically involving 1

½ days, and includes several measures in addition to the Rorschach. Subjects are also asked which inkblot they liked the best and the least, and which they expected their spouse to like the best and the least. "The consensus procedure usually reveals the way in which the couple resolves differences—their patterns of confrontation, compromise, defenses, and problem-solving strategies" (p. 551). Dorr was one of the few clinicians to actively consider the issue of time- and cost-effectiveness of his procedure. He noted that payback for the cost was usually easily obtained by the therapeutic process being significantly shortened by his in-depth evaluation technique.

As can be seen from the preceding brief survey of Consensus Rorschach literature, a major shortcoming of the technique is that each investigator goes his or her own route, with methods of administration, interpretation, and even the criteria for determining when consensus has been achieved varying considerably from study to study. However, the Consensus Rorschach nonetheless represents an interesting application of a psychodynamically penetrating method (the Rorschach technique) to the study of social relationships.

The present authors have found the Consensus Rorschach particularly useful in marriage counseling settings. The Rorschach is administered *only once* to both people, using the following instructions:

> I am going to show you both 10 inkblots. They are not made to look like anything in particular, so there are no right or wrong answers. I would like each of you to find three or four things that each blot might look like, and then to agree on one thing that the blot looks like the most. Let me know when you reach this agreement. Here is the first inkblot.

In our experience, this way of administering the Consensus Rorschach does lose some information, but not very much. It drastically reduces the time requirement for the procedure to roughly three-quarters of an hour, that is, one therapy session. In the 45 minutes we are also able to include a Consensus TAT as well (usually consisting of cards 1, 2, 3BM, 6BM, and 13MF).

It seems likely that the reason the Consensus Rorschach is not widely used has to do with its previous prohibitive time requirement. While we agree with Dorr (1981) that the more lengthy Consensus Rorschach can justify itself in the long run in many cases, if the procedure is to be widely used it must become more economical of time.

CASE STUDIES

The following brief case histories of the consensus protocols represent examples of the analysis that is possible using this technique.

As can be seen with Case #2, the Consensus Rorschach can be useful as a therapeutic tool in marriage counseling as well as a technique of assessment. Case #2 was administered in three sittings, as described previously. (See Chapter 14 for further examples of the Rorschach as a tool in psychotherapy.)

Case History #1

Mr. J. is a 32-year-old lawyer. Mrs. J. is 29 and works as a stockbroker. She had previously worked in a secretarial position. The couple has been married for six years. They have no children. They describe an early history of the relationship in which Mrs. J. felt very unsure of herself and emotionally labile, relying on Mr. J. for emotional support, viewing him as very stable. As she has gotten older and in particular as she has been successful in a pressured and demanding job, she has gradually come to rely less on Mr. J. and to perceive him as emotionally cold and dominating. A major complaint of the wife is that Mr. J. withdraws from her when they have a conflict, refusing to verbally work out their difficulties. Mr. J. in particular objects to Mrs. J. spending evenings with her single friends in bars and other places in which he is afraid that she will meet another man. Mrs. J. also indicated privately to the examiner that she had been experiencing some sexual attraction to her female friends. They also report that sex between them has become infrequent and perfunctory.

Consensus Rorschach Protocol #1

Card I

E: Mr. J., on this card you saw a porous rock, and also a bug in the middle. Mrs. J., you saw a fox's face.

Mr. J: I can see the rock—but not a bug too! Maybe it's a bug on a rock (laughter)! If it's a fox, what's this part?

Mrs. J: I don't have to define every part, do I? That's what I see.

Mr. J: I'll go with the fox—that's what it looks like actually.

In Mr. J's response to this blot we see both a poor self-concept image (the bug) and also a projection of the self as rock-like, unemotional and possibly damaged (porous). Mrs. J.'s response is more common and less idiosyncratic. In the interplay between them we see both her increasing willingness to defend herself against his criticism and his quick knuckling under to her increased assertiveness.

Card III

E: Mr. J., here you saw two people leaning on something—a table—trying to talk to each other. Mrs. J.—you saw two—

Mrs. J: They're definitely women—talking to each other.

Mr. J: I can see that—two women talking to each other.

In the interplay between Mr. and Mrs. J. on this blot we again see Mr. J.'s current eagerness to please as he contemplates the possible dissolution of the marriage. Mrs. J.'s image of the two women talking may be a projection of her currently seeking intimacy in relationships with women. Mr. J.'s percept is probably reflective of his wish for more effective communication with his wife, who is becoming increasingly distant.

Card VII

E: Mr. J., on this card you saw two people talking to each other but separating, walking away from each other. Mrs. J., you saw—

Mrs. J: Two little girls facing each other. They have ponytails and they're crying.

Mr. J: Can you see the two people walking away from each other?

Mrs. J: Kind of—but the little girls are clearer to me.

Mr. J: O.K.—I'll go with the two little girls.

Mr. J.'s percept on this blot is consistent with a view of his relationship with his wife as becoming increasingly distant. Her percept, common for this blot, is infused with a depressive image (crying). Again, Mr. J. goes along with the image suggested by his wife in apparent eagerness to please.

Card VIII

E: Mr. J., here you saw two animals—like panthers or something—maybe climbing a tree. Mrs. J., you saw the upper body of a strong woman in a lowcut dress.

Mr. J: (laughter)

Mrs. J: No, wait—here are the arms coming out, here are her shoulders, here's her hair.

Mr. J: Nice hairdo (laughter).

Mrs. J: The dress is cut down, she has a big waist. But I see the animals too.

Mr. J: I don't see the girl.

Mrs. J: Here's her shoulder here. She's got a cap on top.

Mr. J: I see the panthers on the side.

Mrs. J: I can see the panthers too.

Mr. J: Maybe the panthers are on the woman's body (laughter).

Mrs. J: Okay, two panthers.

In Mrs. J.'s response we see the growing self-image of a strong female, an image that Mr. J. ridicules. Mr. J. also reveals some of the hostility that he feels in the relationship ("maybe the panthers are on the woman's body"). Mrs. J. ultimately relinquishes her percept despite early attempts to defend it, suggesting that her general level of confidence remains fragile.

Card IX

E: Mr. J., here you saw two figures trying to look at each other over a wall and you also saw someone spying on them down here at the bottom. Mrs. J., you saw two women facing each other, dancing, with long gowns on.

Mr. J: I really don't see what you see.

Mrs. J: All right—I can see the two figures and the wall.

In his percept, Mr. J. emphasizes the emotional separation that he feels between him and his wife. Mrs. J. presents a response that reflects a dynamic fluid interaction between two females. However, she again surrenders her response in deference to the husband, which increasingly occurred as the administration proceeded.

In the responses presented above, Mr. and Mrs. J. demonstrate a relationship in which a struggle for control is paramount. Mrs. J., being the more dependent and less confident of the two, at times still abjectly surrenders to the husband. At other times, however, she asserts the increased control that she has in the relationship as a consequence of her growing independence and rejection of him.

While Mr. J. remains blocked from genuine emotional expression, he is afraid of losing her and yearns for communication with her. This in itself is a good prognostic indication for the relationship. She, on the other hand, is increasingly looking for intimacy in relationships with other females. This may be indicative of a somewhat confused sexual identification.

It is clear that the early "marriage contract" (Sager, 1976) between the parties has broken down, a contract in which Mr. J. was to provide the stability, while Mrs. J. would provide the emotional spontaneity and expressiveness. If this marriage is to survive, a new contract needs to be negotiated, one directed less by emotional limitations and infantile needs.

Case History #2

Mr. R. is a 38-year-old engineer, while Mrs. R. is a 36-year-old computer programmer. They have been married for five years and have a 3-year-old daughter. The early years of the relationship are described in very positive terms, with an active and imaginative sex life as well. However, Mrs. R. later acknowledged that she had been faking orgasms, never having had one. Mrs. R. describes herself as overworked in her joint role as full-time worker, mother, and housewife, receiving minimal help with housework and parenting from Mr. R. She essentially describes him as selfish, misrepresenting himself as egalitarian during the courtship. Mr. R. deeply resents the deterioration in their sex life, seeing his wife as having misrepresented herself as being sexually free and motivated during the courtship. Mrs. R. also describes her husband as perfunctory and doing the minimum when he does help with household chores.

The Consensus Rorschach was administered to these clients at a time when the counseling process had reached a state of "logjam." Mr. R. had made some significant changes in helping behavior, and some improved communication was seen. However, the therapy process seemed stalled at that point. It was hoped that the Consensus Rorschach might provide clarification as to the nature of the relationship problems that had not yet become apparent.

Consensus Rorschach #2

Card I

Mrs. R: Why are you taping?

E: Because there's often a lot of interchange, a lot of talk—I won't be able to copy it down fast enough. I'll transcribe it at my convenience. On the first blot, Mrs. R., you saw two things on this. First, you said two angels kissing.

Mrs. R: The shoulders and the waists are here.

E: You also said this could be part of a skull but it wouldn't have ears.

Mrs. R: The eyeholes, and the sinus cavities.

E: Mr. R., you saw first of all two people dancing around a center post.

Mr. R: Those are the people dancing about.

E: And you also saw a family of three with the adults on the outside, with a child in the middle.

Mrs. R: What does that make this?

Mr. R: That's a little more abstract.

E: OK—you just have to reach a consensus as to what this blot looks like.

Mrs. R: I think it looks the most like the angels (both laugh).

Mr. R: Two people dancing around two angels (laughs).

Mrs. R: This looks like the figure of someone wearing a long dress—this looks like the body—not wearing a slip.

Mr. R: Right.

Mrs. R: But I don't know what happened to the head. A decapitated person in a dress wearing no slip.

Mr. R: How about just the dress—here's the neck, here's the shoulders.

Mrs. R: It doesn't just look like a dress.

Mr. R: That part does, with two seamstresses fluttering around the dress.

Mrs. R: Those don't look like people to me.

Mr. R: Well, the head and the hair and the arms. It's a dance number that's why I said dancing. Very stylized.

Mrs. R: I see a ghost too.

Mr. R: What would you like these to be?

Mrs. R: I don't think they look like anything (pause). I think I saw a ghost here. Is this the one that I thought looked like a bat? No, that was later. This is a person or a figure—or they look like two other angels with the wings.

Mr. R: OK, I can buy that. Two angels standing around this dress figure.

Mrs. R: OK.

E: So it's two angels—

Mrs. R: This is a figure with a dress.

Mr. R: Standing around this dress figure—

Mrs. R: These look like feet—it lost its head—these look like hands.

Mr. R: Yeah, a real nasty accident.

Mrs. R: This is an exercise in negotiation or interaction, isn't it?

Card II

E: OK, now on the second card—Mrs. R., you saw in the middle a rocket jet taking off—then you said this could be a face with bozo hair.

Mr. R: It looks like it has whiskers on him. And a butterfly—and this little sexual thing. Female reproductive organs.

E: And Mr. R, you said two redheaded women kneeling, facing each other.

Mr. R: Knees, hands, red hair, this is where their faces would be.

Mrs. R: Oh, I thought that would be their hair and this would be—I don't think that would be their face.

Mr. R: I just kind of see the whole thing as redheaded women kneeling.

Mrs. R: But then her hair sticks up in the air.

Mr. R: Yeah.

Mrs. R: I could see two redheaded women if this is their face—and this is just a collar or something. But I did see that as the face.

Mr. R: Here's the eye, the head is pointed down.

Mrs. R: I don't see it.

Mr. R: OK (pause). How about an animal's face with red horns. Eyes, nasal cavity. The mouth is opening.

Mrs. R: Does this mean something, that you see things in the white space, while I see things in the dark space?

Mr. R: That's his job. Although I like the rocket ship blasting off—that's slick. I didn't notice that.

Mrs. R: A lot of times I saw individual things—I couldn't make something out of the whole thing. Or I could make this—it looks like a person with a cat face and bozo hair and this could be shoulders even with shoulder straps or something—these could be the hands holding something with a hole in the middle of it.

Mr. R: I get to an animal hide later.

Mrs. R: This could be the claws of something, but this definitely looks like a butterfly. It's pretty distinct.

Mr. R: Yeah. A person's arm and hair—

Mrs. R: I see a figure, but it looks like an animal to me—these look like claws.

Mr. R: I kind of glossed over the fine points and looked at the general shape of the figure. Well, how about two women holding down a rocket ship.

Mrs. R: These definitely look like hands, I'll give you that.

Mr. R: Yeah.

Mrs. R: This could even be some kind of satanic robe or one of those black robed things.

Mr. R: OK—a flimsy burnoose (laughs), covers you head to foot, like a sack, it has a hood on it.

Mrs. R: I'll give you the two figures if you make this their head. If that's their head, they're cervically dislocated.

Mr. R: OK—here's the face, eyes, the nose.

Mrs. R: No, the faces fit into each other. I mean this to me looks like an ugly face, but a face. But if you want the two figures, the face has to be here. The faces meet there, and this would be their shoulder hanging out or something. But I do like my rocket ship.

Mr. R: OK. So it's two people facing each other with a rocket ship in the middle.

(He sounds eager to please—she sounds grudging)

Mrs. R: All right (grudgingly). This is irritating. Do we have to do this with all the cards?

E: Is it irritating?

Mrs. R: Yes.

E: Why?

Mrs. R: How much difference does it make what we decide it looks like? It looks like what it looks like.

E: You'll see—I'll give you feedback.

Card III

Mrs. R: I saw this as two alien waiters—putting their heads in a pot, pulling something apart—maybe a crab.

E: Then you saw a butterfly.

Mrs. R: And these look like a stomach and trachea.

E: You also said a crab or a skades.

Mrs. R: A mite, yes.

E: And the corner thing you said could be a deformed butterfly. And you also said the red things could look vaguely like an esophagus and a stomach. Mr. R., your response to this blot was two women walking around a basket or a bowl and they could be hermaphrodites.

Mrs. R: You went into that, huh?

Mr. R: Yeah—face, breasts, penis.

Mrs. R: How about two figures picking up something?

Mr. R: Yeah, that was the general consensus right off the bat, without getting into the details of it.

Mrs. R: I didn't try to assign a gender to those.

Mr. R: Hey, guys are into that stuff (laughs).

Mrs. R: So far, every one you've seen was a female.

Card IV

E: Now here, Mrs. R., you said it looks like part of the skull with the spinal cord. These two things could be faces.

Mrs. R: This looks like an animal head of some sort, these look like weird claws, these could be feet.

E: A creature with a tail or feet, maybe a badger.

Mr. R: Yeah, I can see that now.

E: You also said it looks like two people sleeping or reclining.

Mrs. R: Yeah, up here. Maybe a nose, maybe a hand. Somebody laying down on this thing. Here are other faces. This one has a cigarette sticking out of its mouth.

E: Mr. R., you said here an old pair of boots leaning up against a wall.

Mrs. R: I saw this as a whole figure—except that these are a little questionable for hands.

E: Mr. R., you also said you saw part of a dog's face.

Mr. R: Yeah, ears at the top, here's the muzzle, here's the face.

Mrs. R: Yeah, I can see that (pause). I see the boots the most—I don't know if you want to attach it to the rest of the figure, but—

Mr. R: I could go with a pair of boots, leaning up against the wall.

Mrs. R: So what do you do with the top of it?

Mr. R: I don't worry about it.

Mrs. R: You didn't give me that with the angels. All right, make it the boots (sounds discouraged).

Mr. R: Boots! (laughs).

Card V

Mr. R: Here I see a bat!

Mrs. R: Bat or a butterfly.

Mr. R: Yeah, a bat or a butterfly. A switch hitter (laughs).

E: Mrs. R., you said it looks like a bat or a butterfly, more like a bat. You also said two crocodiles or alligators, here at the side.

Mrs. R: Well, we agree on the bat and the alligator—I mean the bat and the butterfly, so—

E: So what's the consensus?

Mr. R: A bat and/or a butterfly.

Mrs. R: A winged creature of some sort.

Card VI

E: Now here—

Mrs. R: This is the Indian totem pole. This looks like the pelt something—and it looks vaguely sexual.

E: You also said this looks like doors into something—doors with walls. Then you said a stylized female reproductive tract. And the pelt of an animal that's been skinned. And Mr. R., you had seen the hide of a skinned animal and also some unusual string instrument like an oddly shaped base.

Mr. R: Here's the neck, here's the tuning keys, and this is the body of it. But I see most clearly an animal skin, a pelt.

Mrs. R: Yes.

Card VII

Mrs. R: Two faces, two kids playing. Two little girls dancing or something.

E: You also had said two cartoon puppies looking at each other and in the middle part, you saw another animal—the head, eye, and body—looking mad or angry.

Mrs. R: Yeah, that was the nose, the eye, the mouth—

Mr. R: Yeah, I can see it.

Mrs. R: I don't know what that is, an ear or a horn or something. The eye would be there. Its nose, its mouth. That's some kind of square body or something.

E: Mr. R., you said two women looking over their shoulders at each other with tiaras or feathers in their hair. "Being so similarly dressed, it's no wonder that they're staring at each other. Women hate that."

Mr. R: You see the faces.

Mrs. R: Yeah, I already said that. Puppies or little girls.

Mr. R: Yeah, OK, and I just said they have a feather in their hair, looking back over their shoulders, holding their hands like this. And the rest is just the dresses.

Mrs. R: Well—I said either puppies or little girls and that was just details or ears on them.

Mr. R: How about little girls.

Mrs. R: All right (sounds resigned).

Card VIII

E: Mrs. R., you saw two animals, badgers or wolverines. You also saw a hip bone, and said that this part looks like a crab, and you saw two faces, ghosts or Ku Klux Klan men.

Mrs. R: Oh, these things. Two eyeholes.

Mr. R: Oh, yeah.

Mrs. R: This is the crab.

E: Mr. R., you said a couple of furry mammals climbing up on top of some structure.

Mrs. R: Two animals. Do we have to make something out of all of it, or can we just go with animals?

Mr. R: Climbing up on top of something.

Mrs. R: Well, they're obviously climbing something (sounds annoyed).

Mr. R: A mountain or something. A peak of some structure.

Mrs. R: This looks like something that's giving them a hand.

Mr. R: Yeah.

Mrs. R: We'll go with two animals.

Mr. R: Yeah.

Card IX

E: Mrs. R, you said this part at the bottom looks like a naked woman. This part looked to you like a dandelion that you blow on. And you also said a pig with a snout, with that round nose.

Mrs. R: Here's the leg of the woman, the feet come out this way.

E: Mrs. R., you also said the eyes look like a ghost. And you also said a solar flare on the surface of the sun. Now, Mr. R., you saw two seahorses facing each other, and in front of them is some underwater vegetation.

Mrs. R: I guess that's the eyebrow.

Mr. R: Here's the snout or muscle on the seahorse. This is the top of the head structure, the body—

Mrs. R: I think you're reaching (laughs).

Mr. R: An inkblot! (laughs) (pause).
How about this—this is the snout, the face of some creature—the nose—with the animal staring down at your naked woman.

Mrs. R: I see that as the face of a horse or something, but I don't know what happens to the top of his head.

Mr. R: He doesn't have a top of his head. He's looking over your naked lady.

Mrs. R: You see the naked lady?

Mr. R: Oh yeah (laughs). Now I do.

Mrs. R: I thought you wouldn't miss that one.

Mr. R: Some kind of face of a creature looking through bushes at a naked lady.

Mrs. R: I see these as more like eyes and a nose.

Mr. R: This whole thing is like a head or a face.

Mrs. R: I see it.

Mr. R: Incomplete.

Mrs. R: I still see my pigs.

Mr. R: Oh—the snout, eyes, ears, kind of.

Mrs. R: Yes. Here's one eye and one ear.

Mr. R: Yeah, I can see that.

Mrs. R: I also like my solar flare (laughs).

Mr. R: Two pigs and a naked lady in front of a solar flare.

Mrs. R: I tend to see it as individual things. I very rarely saw one big thing. This thing looks a little bit like Ducky, in the Land Before Time. The eyes and the nose. A fly (laugh).

Mr. R: (Laughs.) Does orientation count?

E: Hold it any way you want.

Mrs. R: Now this is a face with big Mickey Mouse ears, and this is a coat. This is chaps like a cowboy would have. This is an elephant with a green jacket on and cowboy chaps.

Mr. R: That's pushing it (laughs). But I can see where you're coming from (pause). There's two pigs over the naked lady and the solar flare.

Mrs. R: Yeah, OK.

Card X

Mrs. R: Oh, I hate this card. These are crabs.

E: Mrs. R., you saw crabs in the blue area, then you saw two cartoon bugs arguing, making nasty faces at each other. You saw other crabs here, and over here you saw eyes, nose, and a handlebar moustache, and you said that the part in the center looks like a bunny.

Mr. R: Like looking at the back of a bunny or something?

Mrs. R: Mm—hm.

E: Mr. R, you saw a gentleman with a green moustache and an outrageous pink hairdo, and you said around him are blue crabs and a pair of mice leaning up against his hair.

Mrs. R: Mice?

Mr. R: Well, mice, I mean—some kind of animal. They could just as well be crabs as mice. I saw this as the moustache.

Mrs. R: I see the moustache.

Mr. R: The eyes, the pink hairdo—I see the blue crabs. It's kind of a psyche-delic album cover.

Mrs. R: Can we agree with a man, a handlebar moustache and pink hair without deciding that the eyes are the same?

Mr. R: There's his eyes and his blue shades which he has to wear.

Mrs. R: This looks like a bone of some sort.

Mr. R: And he's going—"What a trip."

Mrs. R: OK.

(After card consensus completed.)

E: All right—how did you feel about it? Did you notice anything?

Mr. R: Yeah, we didn't always see things the same way. Surprise, surprise.

E: Any other feelings, or things that you noticed?

Mrs. R: We had to negotiate to decide what it looked like.

E: And how did the negotiations feel?

Mr. R: In a couple cases they were real easy, in a couple of cases they weren't.

E: Did either of you feel that you gave in more to the other person in the negotiations, or—how did that work?

Mrs. R: On Card II, I felt I gave in.

E: Are you content with that?

Mrs. R: I still think it looks like what I said, but—I didn't care enough to make a big issue out of it.

E: Mr. R., how did you feel?

Mr. R: I thought it was give and take, I didn't count or keep score.

Mrs. R: I was more willing to adapt to what you saw. I didn't think there were too many where you saw what I saw.

E: Mr. R., do you think that's accurate, or not?

Mr. R: Actually, I thought there were times when I came around to what she saw. In not exactly the same way—but there were also times when I wasn't seeing things exactly the way she was.

This consensus protocol reveals a great deal both about the individual psychodynamics of the individuals and also about their relationship. We note that in his responses to Card II the husband remarks that he tends to gloss over the fine points, making a similar remark on Card IV; this is in contradiction to the rather obsessive—complusive style of the wife and is one of the main things about him of which she complains. Further, his suggested consensus response of "two women holding down a rocket ship" on this blot suggests a dynamic of viewing females as suppressive of male assertiveness and sexuality. The negative attitude toward females is further highlighted in his view of women as expressed in his whimsical comment on Card VII and his "women kneeling" on Card II. Also suggested is some underlying difficulty on his part with sexual identity (hermaphrodites on Card III, as well as a reference to "switch hitters" on Card V), which may be related to his somewhat driven sexuality.

Mrs. R., on the other hand, displays a number of contrasting personality characteristics. Strong superego issues are suggested (angels on Card I, satanic image on Card II, disapproving reference to having been confident that he would see the "naked women" on Card IX). Also indicated are a good deal of anger seen in both side comments and the content of her responses, anger that appears to be largely handled in a passive-aggressive manner. Responses pointing to sexual preoccupations and some depression (skulls, etc.) also are present in Mrs. R.'s. record. A somewhat child-like identification on her part is also seen (puppies or little girls, Card VII), with her anger and depression engendered in part by his unwillingness to satisfy her needs.

As regards reaching consensus, their consensus products are frequently poor combinations of their separate responses, indicating the difficulty they have in merging their separate identities and contrasting defensive styles in common endeavor. We see her last comment on Card I as indicating their joint self-consciousness in participating in the procedure, as they initially try to "kiss and make up" and reach superficial agreement. Nonetheless, the acrimony and dynamics surface clearly on the later blots. Mrs. R. feels very much put upon in the marriage, as she does in the consensus administration. She is angry and is unwilling and unable to deliver the love and sexuality desperately desired by the husband.

One aspect of the record that is difficult to convey in the protocol is the tone of voice of the participants. She sounds angry and depressed, while he often sounds eager to please and to win her approval. Nonetheless, he several times simply tramples over her percepts in reaching consensus (Cards IV, VII). She gives in but is resentful.

Interestingly, feedback to the patients about these findings did seem to break the logjam that had developed in the marital psychotherapy. Mrs. R. in particular became more open to seeing her contribution to the marital problems, the differing defensive styles of herself and her husband, and her need to take responsibility for giving herself satisfactions in her life. Mr. R. was able to see more clearly the ways in which he does not satisfy his wife's emotional needs. The Consensus Rorschach procedure thus provided a direct therapeutic effect as well as providing the therapist with a working "road map" of individual psychodynamics as well as how these mesh into the marital dynamics and marital interaction.

Case History #3

Mr. and Mrs. M. are a couple in their 40s. The husband is an accountant; the wife is a housewife who stays home to take care of the children. They sought marriage counseling because of the husband's explosive anger, the wife's depression, and difficulty in agreeing even on very small issues.

At the point that this Consensus Rorschach was administered, they had been in counseling for approximately four months. Mrs. M. reported significant decrease in her depression and Mr. M. was better able to control his anger outbursts. He had also used some individual sessions to work on feelings about his father having been in prison during his childhood. A significant decrease in conflict between the two was noted, and they were now better able to reach agreement on things. However, as we shall see from the consensus record, a number of issues remain incompletely resolved.

Consensus Rorschach Protocol #3

Card I

E: Here's the first one.

Mr. M: First impression is of a wolf's head or a fox.

E: Maybe you could each find several things that it could look like.

Mrs. M: I saw a hideous creature.

Mr. M: A pelvic region.

Mrs. M: Yes. Also a wing or something.

Mr. M: Also in the center a woman with her hands up.

Mrs. M: Um yeah, I see that. But I don't see any more than that.

Mr. M: Looks like dogs' heads, you could play around with that forever.

Mrs. M: Uh-huh. Two profiles with a long nose (laughter). Do you see that?

Mr. M: Um.

Mrs. M: That's about it.

E: Okay, can you reach agreement, a consensus as to what it looks like?

Mrs. M: I think the strongest is the wolf's head.

Mr. M: Yeah, there's no question now that I recognize what I think is that woman's figure—

Mrs. M: Yeah, that's drawing you, me too.

Mr. M: I can agree with the wolf's head because that was the first thing I saw, and on deeper reflection it looks like there's this woman in there.

Mrs. M: Yeah, holding up her hands in supplication (laughs).

Mr. M: (Laughs). I don't know.

Mrs. M: That probably is the more meaningful figure.

Mr. M: I don't know if it's meaningful but it seems to push out.

Mrs. M: Uh-huh. Is that enough?

E: Good.

Card II

E: Now the second one. See what you can do with that.

Mrs. M: Menstrual cycle (laughs).

Mr. M: I have to think about that one (laughs). Looks like a guy with a very bad set of sinuses. (Both laugh.)

Mrs. M: Um, wonder who that is?

Mr. M: Definitely looks vaginal. That seems to be the overwhelming impression.

Mrs. M: Could be—I tend to see faces a lot in things. I can see the eyes and the nose and mouth region and a goatee and big jowls.

Mr. M: And then blood coming from his mouth (laughs). Let's turn this around.

Mrs. M: A bug, a beautiful butterfly.

Mr. M: Could be. Could be. Nope, it looks like a penis down here.

Mrs. M: Hm, I do see it. I prefer to see the butterfly.

Mr. M: OK, I don't have any strong attachment—strong impressions of that one. I see the butterfly. I don't have any strong feelings about this particular one.

Mrs. M: Two mirror images of the State of New Jersey. It's not exactly a flattering representation of New Jersey. That's all I have.

E: Have you reached agreement?

Mrs. M: What's your favorite representation?

Mr. M: My favorite?

Mrs. M: Do you have a strong feeling?

Mr. M: I don't have any strong impressions about this one, honestly. It has a vaginal feel to it. But I can see the butterfly very vividly. I can go with that.

E: OK, good.

Card III

E: How about on this one?

Mrs. M: It's a cow.

Mr. M: A cow?

Mrs. M: It's a cow's face.

Mr. M: You know what I see—

Mrs. M: Two people with breasts over a cauldron.

Mr. M: Yeah, that was the very first thing I saw with a butterfly between them.

Mrs. M: Oh no, that's a force.

Mr. M: A force? OK. Two people with penises and breasts (laughter). That's what I saw anyway. (Both laugh.)

Mrs. M: There are two eyes, this ear, it's almost like a floppy—almost skull-like—

Mr. M: Like Yogi Bear maybe—(laughs). The big blotch is the nose.

Mrs. M: Oh—

Mr. M: I definitely see two people.

Mrs. M: Yeah. We agree—the two people.

E: Okay, great.

Card IV

E: How about here?

Mrs. M: This relates to the first one I saw. Uh, I see the bottom half of sort of an elf—here are his feet and his little pointy shoes. I don't know what this center thing is.

Mr. M: The first thing I saw was some kind of grotesque human figure, sort of shriveled up arms and a head almost like an ape's head. I don't know what the center is. This way it looks like a bat.

Mrs. M: Uh-huh. A flying creature.

Mr. M: A flying creature.

Mrs. M: Or look, it could be a frog the other way.

Mr. M: I don't see a frog. You mean this way?

Mrs. M: Uh-huh.

Mr. M: I guess it could but the head doesn't look right.

Mrs. M: Yeah. I saw the head later, but the strongest would be—

Mr. M: Somebody with shriveled up arms and feet—like a body but shriveled up—I don't see it as an elf. A person with shriveled up arms—no arms.

Mrs. M: I agree if you take it as a whole person not an elf.

Mr. M: OK, I agree it's not an elf. (Both laugh.)

E: So, you agree on what?

Mrs. M: We agree that—I don't want to always be the one to give in.

Mr. M: It's not an issue of giving in, if you see something else tell me—I don't see that much.

Mrs. M: (Unintelligible) on my part what I choose to see. Yeah, I see his figure now most probably I guess. But I prefer not to see that.

E: So what did you see?

Mrs. M: We both see this full figure shriveled up head and arms and large legs.

E: OK.

Card V

E: And on this one?

Mrs. M: A flying—

Mr. M: A bat or rabbit. (Laughs.)

Mrs. M: It's more beautiful than a bat.

Mr. M: A rodent.

Mrs. M: I think it's an insect.

Mr. M: OK, I can deal with that. An insect. A flying insect. A fly. A moth.

Mrs. M: OK. Does it make any difference to you this way?

Mr. M: Not to me. Does it to you?

Mrs. M: I could get philosophical about it. (Laughs.) I see it with almost like a split personality, like divided in half—one being divided in half—arms raised up.

Mr. M: I could see it in a very impressionistic sense.

Mrs. M: That's kind of how I'm looking at it.

Mr. M: I can see that.

Mrs. M: A dichotomy.

Mr. M: I can see that.

Mrs. M: It's an interesting way to look at it.

E: OK, so that's the consensus?

Mrs. M: Yes.

Card VI

E: How about here?

Mrs. M: You first.

Mr. M: A bearskin rug. The first thing I saw was an Indian maiden's head stuck into a bearskin coat.

Mrs. M: Right. I did too. I was very intrigued by this part here. Very nice design. And then I saw a penis and labia. (Laughs.)

Mr. M: I can see that too.

Mrs. M: Or a hot dog. (Laughs.)

Mr. M: I don't see the hot dog too much to tell you the truth. The Indian impression is the strongest for me but what about for you?

Mrs. M: That was my first impression.

E: So what's the consensus?

Mrs. M: An Indian figure.

Card VII

E: OK, how about here?

Mrs. M: These are two nymphs looking at each other.

Mr. M: Two nymphs looking at each other, two faces looking opposite at each other. It looks like a design of faces. Two female faces looking at each other. These two heads looking in opposite directions. See that? It looks like a head tottering on top of a pelvic region. (Laughs.)

Mrs. M: Teetering on top. Male/female. Very interesting. Are we agreed on that?

Mr. M: I guess.

Mrs. M: Well—the male and the female—why does it always have to relate to sex? (Laughter.)

E: So what's the consensus?

Mr. M: Faces looking at each other. The female on top then there's the two male faces looking out—pelvic region.

E: Good.

Card VIII

E: How about on this card?

Mrs. M: Oh, this is pretty. Real weird looking dude. Glasses but also someone who refuses to see and who refuses to hear.

Mr. M: I see two creatures like a wolf or a rodent. I can't even get a good look at it. There's one four-legged creature, there's the other. Right off the top. Then there's this mystical wizard right here. Do you know what he reminds me of? When we were in Colorado and were looking at the woman who does those paintings where you see things—Bev Doolittle—reminds me of a Bev Doolittle painting. Where she introduces all these kinds of Native American—

Mrs. M: This to me would be an evil mind. The rest of this being a rather evil-looking skull like—

Mr. M: I can see that. Also looks a little bit like Donald Duck (laughter). Definitely Donald Duck. The bill, see? The eyes. Donald Duck with a little tuft of hair on top there.

Mrs. M: I did see the animal at first but then it fit into the larger picture where the ears are supposed to be. Cover the ears, the eyes are covered the mouth is covered. I see this one as an evil mind.

Mr. M: OK.

Mrs. M: We'll agree on evil.

E: OK.

Card IX

E: OK, the ninth card.

Mrs. M: (Laughs) Yosemite Sam.

Mr. M: Where? The cowboy image.

Mrs. M: Yeah. Yeah. His ears, eyes.

Mr. M: I see that. Like a cowboy riding the buffalo.

Mrs. M: Oh. The blue.

Mr. M: Where were you looking at it to see Yosemite Sam?

Mrs. M: Here are his eyes, these little slits here.

Mr. M: Oh yeah! And that looks like a big mustache. Yeah.

Mrs. M: It's a fun image, a pleasant image.

Mr. M: I could deal with Yosemite Sam. I looked at it and saw like two dancers in a way, and these two guys riding buffalos, two images of buffalo riders kicking up dust.

Mrs. M: These do have an angelic look though.

Mr. M: Yeah. All dancing around (unintelligible) (laughter).

Mrs. M: It's hard for me to get away from Yosemite Sam.

Mr. M: I'll go with that.

E: OK.

Card X

E: Lastly, on this card.

Mrs. M: Colorful. An Eiffel Tower with fireworks—a celebration.

Mr. M: I could go with that. I also see sea creatures.

Mrs. M: Yeah. Crabs.

Mr. M: Crabs and these are like starfish—

Mrs. M: Seahorses.

Mr. M: Seahorses rather.

Mrs. M: A wishbone.

Mr. M: A wishbone, little, little shrimp, little sea creatures. So it could be that too. These are clearly crabs. I could go with the Eiffel Tower. I also thought of the Taj Mahal in a way with the big lake.

Mrs. M: I don't know the Taj Mahal very well. I was thinking of France and maybe the Champs Élysées.

Mr. M: It could be. I can see the Eiffel Tower. I can go with that.

Mrs. M: Is it a celebration?

Mr. M: Well, they're all eating lobsters. (Laughter.)

Mrs. M: The Eiffel Tower. Crabs or lobsters. And a path. It's a happy picture.

Mr. M: Yeah. No question.

Consensus TAT

E: One more part. I'm going to show you some pictures. I'd like you to tell me what's happening, what led up to it, what the characters are thinking and feeling. Also how it works out. Give it an ending.

Card 1

Mr. M: He's definitely bored, he doesn't want to take his violin lessons. Sick of them.

Mrs. M: He's sorry he ever started.

Mr. M: Doesn't want to practice.

Mrs. M: Mom and Dad are on his case to practice. He hates it.

Mr. M: No question about it. He doesn't want to take the violin lesson.

Mrs. M: So what happens? Mom and Dad yell? Make things worse? Or with our new therapy do Mom and Dad (unintelligible)?

Mr. M: Ultimately he quits the violin and doesn't play it any more. He's lousy. He doesn't want to practice.

Mrs. M: His parents accept the fact.

Mr. M: Accept the fact. Like most kids who take violin and leave it as they get older and lose interest in it.

Card 2

E: Here's the next one.

Mr. M: All right, while her parents toil at the farm, they send the daughter off to school to lead a different life. This is reminiscent of the generation—not only is it a—strikes me immediately as the daughter—by virtue of her clothes she is a schoolchild and that she's not really integrated in the farm—the agrarian aspect—this is a story about sending her to school so that she'll not be a farmer or a farmer's wife.

Mrs. M: Right. I saw myself at first. Going to school and studying a different world. These two do seem disjointed. They don't seem part of the same—it's almost like she's standing in front of a painting.

Mr. M: Right. There's a clear sense they are from different times or just not part of the same picture. I agree exactly with that. An alienation between the three different figures. The two figures who are farming and there's this girl. I don't think there's any connection between them.

Mrs. M: I don't see her as despairing though.

Mr. M: No, I don't think she was despairing.

Mrs. M: But seriously trying to understand.

Mr. M: Either that or looking the other way. Not looking at those people. Looking someplace else.

Mrs. M: Her back's turned.

Mr. M: In one sense, everyone's back is turned to everyone else.

Mrs. M: Um-hum. Is it significant that this figure and this figure are not looking at each other, but looking past each other?

Mr. M: I don't think they're facing each other. I think the girl is closer up.

Mrs. M: So how does this end?

Mr. M: She goes to school.

Mrs. M: OK.

Card 3BM

E: Now this one.

Mrs. M: I have felt this way. Just giving up and you want to just disappear. Feel so totally—just when you're all limp and weak. Paralyzed.

Mr. M: Despair. I can go with that.

Mrs. M: What led up to it? Not being able to pursue her direction, needs, and wants. And how does it end? It looks like scissors on the side. Like they're there. Like that's an option for her to hurt herself but she doesn't. She can't even do that. So she goes on.

Card 6BM

E: OK, the next one.

Mrs. M: This one, definitely Mom's turned her back on her son and he'd like forgiveness but he can't get it.

Mr. M: I see the trouble and the anxiety in the picture. My scenario almost looks like another generational thing. She's turned her back because she's sad. She doesn't look angry. Neither one has an angry face. I think it looks like he's at an age where he's leaving the house or doing something you do later in life and she's kind of sad about it. Maybe he's leaving the house. Or maybe he's telling her he's going to jail for three years. (Laughter.)

Mrs. M: But she's serene.

Mr. M: I see the sadness in her eyes. That's trouble.

Mrs. M: And what happens? He goes his way.

Mr. M: Either he had to give her bad news or goes on his way.

Mrs. M: He has to accept the reality.

Mr. M: No, I think she's the one who has to accept the reality. They both have to accept whatever the reality there is and he walks out.

Mrs. M: I agree.

Card 13MF

E: And lastly.

Mr. M: This guy just murdered this woman and now he's saying "What have I done?" In a psychotic rage he stabbed her. Now he says—he might be a Barton Fink.

Mrs. M: I can see that but I guess she's dead. It's almost like he's turning his back on her sexuality. (Laughter.)

Mr. M: Maybe he's had an illicit affair and now he's feeling guilty. She's lying there in a prostrate condition. Either one. Either he feels guilty because he's killed her or because he feels he had an illicit affair. Something illicit was going on in there.

Mrs. M: Maybe he's covering his eyes and doesn't want to see. Refuses to see. Denial. (Laughs.) And what happens, he goes home to his wife.

Mr. M: I don't know if he's married.

Mrs. M: It doesn't look like a home, it looks like a—

Mr. M: It looks kind of barren. It doesn't look like your typical bedroom. If he's married he may just have sexual guilt anyway. Either that or maybe he's feeling despondent and guilt-ridden because he can't have sex with her— maybe he's impotent or he couldn't get it up or something and now he's feeling lousy. Either way, there's a lot of guilt in this picture. Either a murderer or a philanderer.

(After consensus procedure completed.)

E: OK, folks. Did you notice anything about—what were your reactions?

Mrs. M: Well, I saw my role as keeping it going. Move onto the next thing . . . "OK then, now what do you think happens?"

E: So your role was what?

Mrs. M: To keep things moving.

E: Did you notice anything about your interactions?

Mr. M: I see that in her. I think there's an expectation on her part that that's what she should be. I don't expect it but part of that is her answers and responses tend to be more suggestive while mine tend to be more black and white. This is what it is. Which plays into our roles or how we deal with each other. Not necessarily that I'm aggressive just that "oh yeah this is what it is." I may bend but it starts with "This is what it is." Whereas Mrs. M. is more suggestive and not as aggressive with her responses.

Mrs. M: Because it isn't that. It is a splotch of ink or a drawing or a picture of something, that's all there is.

E: What about the negotiating process?

Mrs. M: I think it went well. Neither one of us had anything to lose then.

E: Did anybody feel they gave in more than the other person?

Mr. M: She probably gave in. Or at least I got the sense she was more accommodating. Even if she didn't see something, she might have said yes she saw something.

Mrs. M: Well I'd see them but I might be more willing to—if I see something first or if I prefer to look at something else I'd go ahead and agree with him even though I didn't prefer to look at that. The crabs—I wanted to see fireworks instead of lobsters.

E: You felt like you gave in?

Mrs. M: I probably did but you know what? He saw my Eiffel Tower.

E: He met you halfway.

Mr. M: Yeah, but the difficulty with this is people see what they see and sometimes it's not a matter of negotiation. I mean I can't say she's wrong if she saw the Eiffel Tower and I didn't. So in some sense the accommodation may be a denial of your own reality in order to be accommodating. How can I say I want you to compromise and say you didn't see it and say you saw a crab if you didn't see a crab?

Mrs. M: I compromised in ways—I mean I always saw what he was talking about. I wouldn't give in if I didn't see that possibility.

E: OK, so did you both feel good about this?

Mr. M: I guess.

The analysis of this record begins with Card I, on which Mr. M. reveals sexual preoccupations and Mrs. M. indicates a strong superego presence and a feeling of being emotionally needy. In addition, she subtly controls the direction in which they are going.

On Card II, Mr. M. continues with his sexual preoccupations and also gives a rather unhealthy response in which he indicates that he unconsciously feels emotionally wounded. Her New Jersey response is interesting, given negative feelings she has about living in New Jersey or in the Northeast at all. In terms of consensus, Mr. M. again gives in.

On Card III, it should be noted that Mr. M. does not resolve the sexual identity issue very well but that in terms of consensus it is quite good, and is the best mutual consensus that we've seen so far.

On Card IV, Mr. M.'s emphasis on the shriveled up arms suggests a feeling of not being very effective in his environment. Mrs. M., in contrast, indicates a feeling that she gives in reaching consensus, which is a complete reversal of what we have seen so far. This, by the way, is something we have often found in marital relationships—often there is a misperception of who holds the power in the relationship.

On Card V, Mrs. M. indicates a feeling of being very split in her emotions in some way, a powerful ambivalence being present. However, there is no indication as to the specific nature of it. She again gets the consensus that she wants in the end.

On Card VI the situation is a little different—however, Mrs. M. is the one who states the consensus.

On Card VII, Mr. M.'s response of a head tottering on a pelvic region is unusual and is probably a powerful image indicative of how he really sees himself—with his primitive impulses often intruding on the intellectual aspects of his life. Some fear of feminine dominance is seen, which, by the way, is something with which he grew up.

On Card VIII the wife indicates depression and the comment about "evil" suggests strong superego issues again. Mr. M.'s response of the child-like cartoon character is suggestive of unresolved oral needs. It should be noted that Mrs. M. *again* gets her response to be the consensus response.

On Card IX, superego issues are suggested for Mrs. M. by her "angelic" comment. The "Yosemite Sam" comment is also interesting, in that it may reflect her inability to get away from emotional issues having to do with her father, who lives in the Southwest. Needless to say, she again gets her percept to be the consensus percept. On Card X, they do manage a good integration of his percepts with her percepts, ending the Consensus Rorschach procedure on a healthy note.

On the TAT, on Card 2, Mrs. M. seems to see herself as somewhat disconnected from her rural upbringing. There's also an emphasis on the lack of emotional contact between people, which is something about which she complains.

On Card 6BM, we also see Mr. M.'s anxious laughter regarding his father's jail sentence, a topic with which he is nowhere near being at peace.

Mrs. M.'s response of the male turning his back on female sexuality is an important response despite her laughter. This later turned into a major topic in the psychotherapy. There are also indications of Mr. M. seeing sex as illicit, interfering with his sexual performance.

In short, we have a picture of two individuals troubled by emotional issues in their growing-up years and caught in the later stages of a struggle for power in the relationship. The Consensus Rorschach served as a very helpful road map of directions in which it would be useful to proceed.

▲ 14

The Rorschach Technique as a Tool in Psychotherapy

Accepting the concept that the Rorschach is more of a clinical technique than a test per se opens the door to much more of an integration of the Rorschach with the psychotherapeutic endeavor. Rather than just useful as a "test" to answer particular referral questions, the technique lends itself to becoming an integral part of the therapy process. It is our belief that in the future the Rorschach technique will serve more as a psychotherapeutic tool than as an evaluation instrument. This use of the Rorschach may include such things as sharing the results of the evaluation with the patient as part of the therapy and encouraging the patient to react to and interpret his or her own responses. As noted by Finn and Tonsager (1992), "Considering psychological assessment to be a therapeutic intervention is a major paradigm shift in how assessment is typically viewed" (p. 286).

Sharing with the subject clinical observations in general and the meaning of Rorschach percepts and associations in particular is certainly not entirely new, but it is an approach that in our experience is not widely practiced. Craddick (1975) has noted that "outmoded but not extinct" procedures still often characterize the clinical and evaluation experience, with secrecy and deception prevailing, and the subject denied access to his or her own records.

Viewing evaluation as having the potential to merge with and contribute to the psychotherapeutic process dates back at least to Jung (1961), who wrote that in the early 1900s he treated a schizophrenic woman who when given feedback about the results of her association test quickly got better and was able to be discharged from the hospital. Jung felt that the process of assessment may provide a key to the client's untold "secret story," and that by enabling the client to tell his or her story, the psychotherapeutic process is begun. Jung noted that, therefore, it is difficult to draw the line as to where assessment ends and psychotherapy begins.

In a 1960 article, Harrower suggested discussing some of the patient's projective test responses with him or her, a procedure she calls "projective counseling." This stands in marked contrast to what has come to be regarded as the more traditional approach as exemplified by Klopfer and Kelley (1946), in which they warned of the potential damage that can be done by sharing Rorschach interpretations with clients.

Following Harrower, a number of other authors have written of sharing clinical information and projective data with patients. For example, Stein, Furedy, Simonton, and Neuffer (1979) described giving psychiatric patients access to their psychiatric records. They noted positive results from this procedure. Roth, Wolford, and Meisel (1980) allowed *selected* psychiatric patients limited access to their own psychiatric records in the presence of a staff member. Positive results were again described. In a similar context, Brodsky (1972) described a positive outcome.

Pertaining specifically to the sharing of psychological evaluation information, Fischer (1970, 1972) has written of giving feedback to patients as an integral part of the therapy relationship.

> If the evaluation is to facilitate positive change, the client must experience his limited possibilities for experience and behavior, as identified by the psychologist, as constrictions in *his* own way of living . . . if he is to grasp these suggested means of expanding his mode of life as feasible, he must experience them through positive relationships. The first of these should be his relationship with the evaluator. (Fischer, 1970, p. 71)

Craddick (1972, 1975) similarly viewed the Rorschach in particular, if properly used, as having the ability to integrate with and enrich the psychotherapy experience. Similar to our own position in this regard, Craddick (1972) viewed assessment procedures, especially projective techniques, as "[permitting] the person to tell certain things about himself that he might otherwise be unable to describe" (p. 107). Craddick also viewed the relationship and type of administration as pivotal in obtaining a revealing Rorschach: "A basic premise of my approach is that one can only share oneself in a situation that permits mutual trust" (Craddick, 1975, p. 279). Craddick worked toward the examiner and the subject jointly interpreting the record.

Two of the present authors, Aronow and Reznikoff (1971), have also described a case study in which a particularly striking figure drawing was used to facilitate therapeutic change. The post-psychotherapy drawing suggested that the sharing of projective technique–based information was instrumental in bringing about both insight and change.

Dorr (1981) has written a fascinating exposition on the use of sharing assessment-based information with patients in a consensus marital evaluation situation. The procedure involved (gently) interpreting results to the marital partners, which led to greater understanding of both individual and marital dynamics. However, Dorr cautioned that this procedure must be used judiciously and with clinical acumen, since "the test results have the potential to hurt" (p. 554). Follow-up was recommended in this connection.

Richman (1967) has similarly reported on the sharing of evaluation-based data with patients, noting that it is not uncommon for psychologists to share such information for psychotherapeutic purposes. Richman stated that "the method's efficacy is largely a function of the skill and experience of the counselor, the motivation of the client, the presence of a positive working relationship, and a respect for the person being tested" (p. 62). Worth noting is that Richman's interest in this procedure began serendipitously, when a mother insisted on feedback on her son's testing. Richman found that the sharing of information resulted in a therapeutic breakthrough in the mother's understanding of her contribution to the problems and the need for outside intervention.

Mosak and Gushurst (1972) have also written on the sharing of test-based information with patients. They stressed that such sharing should be simple, direct, easily comprehensible, personally relevant, and rendered nonjudgmentally. They stressed the need to remain on guard for negative reactions and to deal with these immediately. They also noted the potential of this sharing to "open up" the patient for psychotherapy and emphasized certain special uses of the technique, such as to identify hidden "blocks" in psychotherapy, to bring into the open aspects of functioning that might otherwise be difficult to talk about (notably sexual problems), and to provide closure by testing or retesting at the conclusion of psychotherapy.

Schlesinger (1973) emphasized that the truism "all clinical work takes place in an interpersonal context" has often been neglected. Schlesinger also noted the continuity between the diagnostic process and the treatment process. The patient should be encouraged to participate as much as possible in the evaluation endeavor:

> I believe that some of the most valuable information to be gained from testing comes from the patient's reactions to his own responses, reactions that are more likely to be given spontaneously and fully if the atmosphere in the testing situation encourages the patient's free participation. When the patient is invited to share in his own diagnos-

tic study, it is possible additionally to see to what extent he can think about his own behavior in psychological terms. (p. 512)

J. Allen (1981) also wrote about the strong links between assessment and psychotherapy. Furthermore, he suggested allowing the patient to speculate about the meaning of his or her projective responses in particular. "[This] view of psychological testing suggests that therapeutic interventions are likely to be part of the diagnostic process" (p. 256).

Appelbaum (1990), in writing of sharing data with assessment subjects, has observed tremendous initial trepidation, a reluctance to do harm or to be wrong. However, he stated that his fears inevitably proved to be groundless.

Pope (1992) has suggested that feedback about the results of psychological assessment may be the most neglected aspect. He pointed out that feedback is a "dynamic, interactive process." He discusses 10 aspects of the feedback process, ranging from such issues as informed consent to assessing and understanding the patient's reactions.

Gass and Brown (1992) have discussed the issue of test feedback in the context of the neuropsychological evaluation of patients with brain dysfunction. They have remarked that the provision of such feedback is an important therapeutic intervention in its own right, yet few patients report receiving such feedback. They suggested a six-step framework for feedback that takes into account the special circumstances of the neuropsychological evaluation.

Finn and Tonsager (1992) have introduced something novel to the discussion on feedback: namely, a strictly empirical study of its effects. In their investigation, subjects selected from a college counseling center's waiting list were randomly assigned to an MMPI test feedback group or to a group that received only examiner attention (32 subjects receiving feedback, 29 in the control group). The test feedback was based on a "collaborative model" previously developed by the authors. As contrasted with the control group, the subjects given feedback reported a significant decrease in distress and increase in self-esteem. Interestingly, the positive results of the feedback were stronger two weeks later than at the initial time of feedback. These authors' strictly empirical findings suggest to them the therapeutic importance of insight. "As the inscription over the oracle at Delphi instructed, it is important to 'know thyself.' This [approach] . . . suggests just how valuable and beneficial such knowledge can be" (p. 286).

Bellak (1993) has discussed the specific use of the TAT in psychotherapy and suggested that as a therapeutic tool it may be particularly useful in short-term psychotherapy. Bellak also allowed the patient to interpret his or her own stories. "This way the patient may actually learn to look for common denominators in his behavior, and the process of *working through* may be started" (p. 161). Bellak presented a number of case examples in which TAT stories and other projective materials were used to further the psychotherapy.

This author also made the point that "all the principles of careful psychotherapy must be observed. . . . No one inexperienced with psychotherapy generally should use the TAT in therapy either!" (p. 167).

In our experience (and in the experience of other authors summarized above), the Rorschach technique has four principal uses in association with psychotherapy:

1. A road map of dynamics, conflicts, ego strengths and weaknesses, and so forth prior to the onset of therapy. This is the more traditional use to which the Rorschach has been put in connection with psychotherapy.
2. An assessment of progress, either during the course of therapy or at the very end. The latter is particularly helpful if there is a "before" measure to provide contrast.
3. A tool to clarify blockages that may occur in the course of psychotherapy and that might otherwise be impenetrable.
4. An actual tool for insight and change in psychotherapy when one shares the interpretation of the responses with the subject(s). This last use of the Rorschach is, of course, the most demanding in terms of clinical acumen and timing.

The first use of the Rorschach listed is nothing particularly new; all previous chapters on psychodynamic interpretation are relevant, and Shafer's text (1954) is highly useful for this purpose.

The second use, assessment of progress, is illustrated by the Rorschach record presented as Case #1 in this chapter. Use of the Rorschach in a before-and-after psychotherapy situation is presented by two of the present authors in a previous article (Aronow & Reznikoff, 1971).

The third use listed, the identification of blockages that are impeding progress and subsequent breaking of the logjam, is presented in Cases #2, #3, and #4 in this chapter. In our experience, this use of the Rorschach optimally merges with the fourth use listed, sharing the interpretation of the responses, since this is frequently what does in fact serve to break the logjam.

Case History #1

Ann is a 32-year-old homemaker who has recently returned to college to get a degree in education. She grew up in a large family in which boys were favored, the mother was harsh and cold, and the father was warm in early childhood but later ignored her. She entered psychotherapy with several concrete objectives: to become better able to express warmth; to strengthen her feminine identity and regularly experience orgasms; and to (possibly) divorce her husband of many years, whom she describes as cold, distant, rejecting, and unemotional.

At the time of the Rorschach evaluation the patient had been in therapy for approximately seven months. The therapist administered the Rorschach. The purpose of the testing at this point was to assess progress to date and to identify areas that still needed work.

Rorschach Protocol #1

Card I. 5″ 1. Well—a combination of things. Looks like a devil and a butterfly—so like me. (Laughs.)

1. (What does that make you think of?) Actually, now it looks more like a pumpkin—there are also hands. It looks like a headless woman—it looks like breasts on the side. (What does that make you think of?) Mom. It looks like she is coming for you—to spank you. That's the look. (What do the devil and the butterfly make you think of in your own life?) The devil is frightening—the butterfly means freedom. They can do whatever they want. I never feel that freedom. I always feel I have to be somewhere for somebody. I usually feel restricted.

2. Could be some kind of a crab.

2. (What does a crab remind you of?) The beach. We spent a lot of time when I was young at the shore. But there was always the shadow there, there was never freedom—the shadow was always there of the family that I lived in—we didn't have any fun. You'll be reprimanded if caught smiling.

3. Two little birds on the top. Spaces seem something like a devil—first and foremost.

3. (What do birds make you think of?) Being very happy, very free. There are evil spaces here, though. (What does that call to mind?) They are from an evil face. (What does that make you think of in your own life?) Someone who would be mean to you.

Card II. 8″ 1. Looks like a female singing.

1. (What does a female singing make you think of?) She seems to have her mouth wide open. (What does that make you think of in your own life?) Nothing.

2. Two men kneeling, clapping hands—doing that Russian dance.

2. (What does that bring to mind?) A happy time—I love to dance.

3. Clown-like eyes.

3. I don't like clowns too much. They have scary faces. They're not natural looking.

4. Two men with turbans clapping hands.

4. Having a good time together. (What do two men having a good time make you think of?) Guys have fewer restrictions. Girls didn't have that kind of fun in my house. (Laughs.)

Card III. 6″

1. Looks like two men dancing—little black men in formal attire—holding a top hat at the bottom—dancing in a circle.

1. (What does that make you think of?) Nothing.

2. Bottom part looks like a bug-like face with claws. It could be an ant or a spider.

2. (What does that call to mind?) I had a little spider I was taking care of—he was like a friend. It was stupid. He was always there—we thought he was like a buddy.

3. Middle looks like a butterfly.

3. (What does a butterfly remind you of?) It's free and pretty and let's throw in feminine. (What does that make you think of in your own life?) Nothing. (Laughs.) Actually, I looked it, pretty, but I didn't think that I was. (What do you think now?) Halfway—I'm sort of in between now. I notice that I'm more feminine with females—with men I feel I have to hang onto the tougher side—I feel they wouldn't like me for me. Females are kind of like silly—they don't do well in repartee. Only men have a shrewd way of thinking, they stay on top of a conversation, they have an edge.

Card IV. 10″

1. Looks like a giant sasquatch lying on his back, with two big feet up front.

1. (What does a giant sasquatch make you think of?) Jack—the big oaf, my husband. It could be Dad too, lying down. Inactive. A big lump. A waste. Lazy.

2. The back of a bear, lying on his stomach, legs extended on either side.

2. It's sensual—it's something I'd like to lie on top of—it would feel nice and soft and furry—a bearskin rug.

Card V. 4″

1. That's a bat—or—

1. (What does the bat make you think of?) A bat in a bat cave. Really ugly. It bites.

2. A bunny rabbit on his tippy toes with a giant cape.

2. (What does the bunny rabbit make you think of?) I don't know. I think of toe dancers. (What does that make you think of in your own life?) I could be soft underneath—but there's a tremendous shield around me for protection—dainty feet underneath. Pretty, but don't touch. (What does the cape make you think of?) Look at what I have—but I can close it up any time.

Card VI.   13"   1. The top looks like a totem pole.

1. (What does a totem pole make you think of?) It also looks like a giant penis. (What does that make you think of?) Not getting any (laughs), my situation, the reason I came here— not having an orgasm, wanting one real bad. But I'm less frightened now. It's more exciting than disgusting, which is great. A few months ago I would have said something entirely different. I also see a set of legs open and a penis—I used to wish for one—I don't any more. I think that's great. I'm not so afraid of being vulnerable. I felt horny last week—I was able to look at porno movies. In the past, I would be the male in my fantasies about it. Monumental progress.

2. Bottom—some kind of a coat—like a skin to an animal.

2. (No associations)

3. Bug look at the bottom again. It's pretty.

3. (What does it make you think of?) I like bugs, nature. I like the outdoors. They have their own little freedom, they can do anything they like. I feel like I can't. (Why?) It comes from the past— everything that you did, you'd be told was wrong. There was no place to go. My house was confining from day one.

Card VII.   8"   1. This looks like two ladies facing one another—a do on their head.

1. (What do the ladies remind you of?) They're pretty, and feminine. I like their faces, they're like ballerinas. I was disappointed as a kid that I couldn't continue with my ballet lessons. It was the only feminine thing in my life. For some reason, for a while my family let me be feminine like that.

2. Underneath, it looks like two males with something on their heads looking outward.

2. (What do they bring to mind?) They have big stomachs. They're kind of looking down at you, like you did something wrong. I don't see them smiling.

3. Or it could be the two ladies with their hands like this.

3. (What do they call to mind?) Just like an Egyptian stance—they're having fun. That makes me think of me and my sister.

Card VIII.   12″   1. Two animals crawling up the side— beavers?

1. (What do they make you think of?) They look like they're being sneaky and cautious, trying to get around something. (What does that make you think of in your own life?) It was just a way of being careful not to be the one under the gun. Try not to be noticed like with my family.

2. A corset effect— older corsets.

2. (What does that bring to mind?) An old-fashioned feminine lady with a tiny waist—I like that old bustle look. You knew she was a female. I don't like the new females that much.

3. Gray—could look like outstretched— dog or mammal, four legs and a tail.

3. (What does it call to mind?) I don't know—nothing.

Card IX.   18″   1. Orange part looks like bugs—partially turned over.

1. When I was young I caught a bunch of lightning bugs—I put them in a jug. During the night, it bothered me that they were trapped and I released them. That's sort of like myself. (What do you mean?) They were caught in where they were at. I don't like restrictions.

2. Center part could be something with his back toward me— blue like a spinal section.

2. (What does that make you think of?) Someone with his head low, contemplating something. (What does that remind you of?) Someone brooding and sad, in a dilemma or something. (What does that make you think of in your own life?) I imagine—some sad times. One time in particular I was standing in my bedroom, singing out my window a Disney song.—someone will come and get me out of here. Maybe I was 10 or 11. I remember most of all a great loneliness that brings a sadness to my mind. (Patient cries.) Anything would be better than there.

Card X.   9"   1. That looks like two little lobsters.

1. (What do they bring to mind?) They're fighting, angry, going at one another. That makes me think of my entire youth and my family.

2. Center looks like mean eyes with a long mustache.

2. My uncle John (laughs). He scared me—he was very loud. He was my father's brother. He used to give me a quarter but I didn't like him. (Why?) He was mean and loud. I didn't know if he would yell at you or not.

3. Gray on top could be dancing mice—hands up in celebration. Or boll weevils. I'm heavy into bugs.

3. (What does that make you think of?) Fun—having a good time. Most things in nature have a good time because they are free—I've never been free mentally. I was always under someone's thumb. Like my husband complains about my cooking—he has a lot of gall. But my freedom is more from myself. It's easy to blame others for your not being free—that's like a chicken's way out.

This Rorschach record reveals capacity for insight, seen in Ann's ability to interpret her own responses, to relate them to her own self-identification, history, and psychodynamics.

Ann sees herself as presenting a hard, masculine exterior to the world, with a soft, more feminine self hidden inside. Males are seen as admirable and strong and having the best of this world, but hostility toward males is also present. Females are seen as weak, but there is a growing ability to accept this side of herself and to experience it as positive as a result of psychotherapy.

Many responses refer to the family of origin as distant, cold, and threatening. The loneliness of her childhood at one point prompts her to break down in tears.

A strong need for emotional freedom is frequently expressed, both from external restrictions and by implication from internal inhibitions. Anger and a sense of the self as sometimes "walled off" and protected from others are seen.

How she starts the Rorschach technique and how she chooses to end it are quite instructive. She begins with a contrasting image—the devil and the butterfly—reflecting her ambivalent identification as the "wise guy, masculine, hostile person" but also the feminine and sensitive Ann underneath. She ends her associations with an acknowledgment that she is indeed in charge of her fate, and that it is a cop-out to simply blame others and her past for her problems.

The assessment of progress indicates that she is engaged with the necessary dynamic issues of her life and has a good deal of insight as well as an ability to express her emotions and accept responsibility. However, the repetitiveness of themes of emotional pain from her childhood suggests that this aspect has been somewhat neglected in therapy and must be dealt with more fully.

Case History #2

Mr. and Mrs. L., a couple in their mid-50s, have been married for 22 years. There were no children in the marriage. Mr. L. is a vocational counselor, Mrs. L. a homemaker. The presenting problem involved Mrs. L.'s recent discovery that her husband had been having an affair, which led to his revealing that he had had numerous affairs throughout their marriage.

Both marital partners described very difficult childhoods characterized by considerable emotional deprivation. Their sex life was quite sporadic, with Mr. L. needing to be extremely dominant. A counselor with whom they had previously worked attributed the husband's sexual acting out to a need to compensate for a physical disability, an interpretation with which the present therapist was largely in accord until the Rorschach was administered.

The purpose of the evaluation was to clarify both individual and marital dynamics, to assess ability to change, and in particular to break a logjam that had developed in the therapy, with the husband quite ambivalent about whether he wanted to change his long-standing sexual pattern. At this point the patients had been seen (largely in individual sessions) for approximately three months.

Rorschach Protocol (Consensus) #2

Card I

Mr. L: I saw a fox or a wolf. This is a pointy nose, to me. These are the ears. These are the eyes.

E: You said you saw the face of a fox or wolf.

Mr. L: This is a grinning look and this is the nose and the face.

E: You also said a bat in flight.

Mr. L: It's a possibility, the other way around. I think I saw a bat—yeah, here's a bat, the wings here, this is the little head, the little tentacles coming out of the mouth.

E: Now Mrs. L, you said you saw a bat. Then you said you also saw a vagina.

Mrs. L: I did?

E: Then you said it looks like little hands on top.

Mrs. L: I don't see a wolf. I see maybe a cartoon cat or something. Possibly a bat. I don't see a wolf.

Mr. L: A fox more, see this snout. This is the face coming up on each side. It reminds me of that wolf on the "Road Runner" who chases that coyote in the cartoon.

Mrs. L: If you go from like here down, like these are the ears.

Mr. L: No, the ears are here. These are the ears—flappy, like Wiley Coyote.

Mrs. L: Does he have four eyes?

Mr. L: No, this is part of the snout. These are the eyes on the side. The pupils are here. This is the face. You know the "Road Runner" show? Or I can transform that into a bat also if we have to agree on something.

E: Have you reached agreement?

Mrs. L: No, not really. I'll go with a bat, but you know, as far as a fox, I don't see any fox at all.

Mr. L: How about a coyote?

Mrs. L: Nope—just down here I see ears, and a nose—that would be a fox.

Mr. L: What do you see?

Mrs. L: I see a bat. I see little hands.

Mr. L: Yeah, I see that too.

Mrs. L: There's a face over here, and there's a face over here, maybe a dog or something.

Mr. L: Looks more to me like an ape of some kind. The snout and the lower jaw jutting out here.

Mrs. L: It could be.

Mr. L: But to me it's so pronounced, the coyote effect, it's my main one.

Mrs. L: I don't see it at all.

Mr. L: All right, well, we're at a stalemate there. I can buy the bat, but the fox or coyote would really be my first.

E: You have to tell me when you've reached agreement.

Mr. L: Oh? We're supposed to?

Mrs. L: The bat, that's it. As far as anything else, I don't see the fox.

Mr. L: (Laughs.) I can see a bat in there too but the coyote is the main one.

Mrs. L: He's got four eyes, how can you see a fox?

Mr. L: No, these aren't eyes here, just part of the grinning apparatus, like he's grinning. The cheek bones don't signify anything. The eyes are up here. These are the ears drooped—this is the round puffiness of the face, this is the snout. If you can't see it, you can't see it.

Mrs. L: I don't—I see a pumpkin-like face, that's what I see.

Mr. L: Well, it does have some sort of appearance like that, but it still looks more like a coyote to me. I can see a bat here too. These are the little appendages, the little head, the wings jutting out, the tail down here. I can buy a bat.

Mrs. L: I'll buy a bat.

Mr. L: All right, we've reached agreement.

Card II

E: OK, now on this second one, Mrs. L., you said the little red things on top are two thumbs.

Mrs. L: See the thumb? This is a nail.

Mr. L: They don't mean anything to me.

E: Then you said little rabbits. Or two elephants with their trunks together.

Mrs. L: Here's the rabbit with ears and its little paws—could also be two elephants.

Mr. L: That's what I saw—two elephants.

E: Mr. L., you also said a red splotch where you squashed a bug and there's blood.

Mr. and Mrs. L: Yeah, yeah.

Mr. L: I saw two bears with their snouts together like in the circus holding something up.

E: Two kodiak bears nose to nose, juggling.

Mr. L: Juggling something like they were holding something between them. These are the ears coming back. The noses like a little kodiak bear or something.

Mrs. L: You see the thumbs, I'll see the bears.

Mr. L: I can buy your thumbs, but they didn't have any meaning for me. This was the main thing that had the meaning to me, I think. Thumbs are not really significant. But I can see something like a thumb there. But it doesn't have any meaning at all.

Mrs. L: Look, it's supposed to have meaning.

Mr. L: The bear is the main focus that I focused on. I didn't focus on the rest of the picture too much.

Mrs. L: Well, there is a little paw here and a little paw there. If you have a bear, then you just have a piece of a bear.

Mr. L: Yeah, it's a bust.

Mrs. L: If you hold it this way, then you have a complete rabbit.

Mr. L: I don't see any rabbit.

Mrs. L: Don't you see two ears here?

Mr. L: No.

Mrs. L: And two little paws here?

Mr. L: No, I can't see a rabbit.

E: Have you reached agreement?

Mrs. L: I'll go with bears, it's immaterial.

Mr. L: Well I think it is, we're doing this for a reason. I saw bats in the other one, so I was willing to compromise on that.

Card III

E: Here, Mr. L., you said it looks like two African women. For some reason they have penises coming out, looks like they are holding water jugs, and Mrs. L., you said it looked like two skinny dancers in formal clothes, for one thing. Then you said the little red parts could be a horse with a long tail or a cat crying. You also said these two things could be dancers with high-heeled shoes on. You said the red things in the middle could be lungs.

Mrs. L: You know, like two male dancers with those tuxedos.

Mr. L: I can see that too.

E: Mrs. L., you said these two things could be kidneys.

Mrs. L: These could be lungs, and these could be kidneys.

Mr. L: At first I saw the Africans with their jaws jutting out, like the women on the Discovery Channel with the short-cropped hair. Chins jutting out, these look like two busts here, I thought these appendages were arms. I thought they were just holding a water jug. I couldn't figure it out, this looked like a penis on each side coming out.

Mrs. L: I just disregarded them because they didn't fit. These look like horses galloping, he's got his head turned. He's got a long tail there.

Mr. L: Yeah, I can see that. I didn't look at it that way.

Mrs. L: Well, you are allowed to turn it around.

Mr. L: I don't know, I just didn't. The first thing I saw is what I said.

Mrs. L: I've never seen a woman with a pointed jaw like that.

Mr. L: Come to my office someday.

Mrs. L: Maybe with a nose like that I could see.

Mr. L: We have some women come in that look like that, flat heads, the jaw comes forward. A lot of black women look like that. Maybe I see more black women than you do. They could be two waiters too, in formal attire.

Mrs. L: Waiters, okay, I could go with waiters. My first impression was they were waiters too.

Mr. L: I thought they looked female because these look like busts to me. But I don't know what the bottom represents. I couldn't understand that. I thought it was something bisexual.

Mrs. L: That's rather deep. I went for the simple one.

Mr. L: Are we going to agree on something there?

Mrs. L: Well, they're two males. We agree on that. We agree on the little horses.

Mr. L: What are these breasts here?

Mrs. L: They could be lapels or ruffled shirts.

Mr. L: I could see it that way too. So are we going to go with that they look like two waiters then?

Mrs. L: I'll go with waiters.

Mr. L: Well, what are they doing here then? What is this?

Mrs. L: Something else. I thought two lungs, no—those are kidneys, the lungs are up here.

Mr. L: It's not as easy as it was the first time. I guess I could go with waiters, although what they are doing I really don't know. The first one came better to me as a bisexual person. I could see waiters there in formal tuxes. I could see when you turn it sideways, a horse with a long tail. I didn't look at it that way. I looked at it frontways.

Mrs. L: Well, you're allowed to turn it around.

Mr. L: Yeah, I know, but I just looked at this part here and I disregarded the red.

E: So your agreement is . . .

Mrs. L: Two formal waiters and two horses.

Card IV

Mrs. L: I saw Bigfoot.

Mr. L: That's what I saw too.

E: Mrs. L., you saw Bigfoot but no head, things on the side could be buzzard skeletons. A straight thing in the middle; a trunk of a tree; a little tiny head on top; you said it could also be an animal, fuzzy and hairy. Mr. L., you saw "a science fiction-type thing. Could be Bigfoot; a tail or a large penis, looks like a grotesque penis. Then, looking the other way around, it could be a mystical symbol; wings, head with a crown—like in Egypt—a ritual symbolistic creature."

Mr. L: Like the Phoenix or a fire bird.

Mrs. L: I could go with that.

RMr. L: We're in agreement.

Mrs. L: Except that it's not a weird penis.

Mr. L: I said possibility, not that it was; like a tail or an oversized penis. When you turn it upside down doesn't it look like that to you, too?

Mrs. L: Yes, I never thought of turning it upside down, but—

Mr. L: Do you see the wings jutting out on each side? The little crown on top there?

Mrs. L: Uh-huh.

Mr. L: Well, it looks like we're pretty much in agreement.

E: Okay, what is the agreement?

Mr. L: Bigfoot. I think we both think it is Bigfoot.

Card V

E: Mr. L., you said this looks like a bat in flight, and upside down, still a bat.

Mr. L: Either way it looked like a bat to me.

E: Mrs. L., you said that's a slug from my garden, the things on the end are alligators, and the rest of this is a butterfly.

Mr. L: I only see just one thing—this would be part of the wing structure to me. I can see alligator heads at the end, but they don't have any significance in the whole picture. I'm trying to make sense out of it, maybe I shouldn't. I see it as a moth.

Mr. L: Those butterflies that have things hanging on their tails, not a Monarch, but—ones that fly in the early spring. But to make sense, I can't see a moth with alligators hanging on each side of it.

Mrs. L: No, well, we're not making one thing out of it. I couldn't pin down just one object. The first thing that hit me was the slug, the butterfly, and the alligators.

Mr. L: I saw it as a bat in flight.

E: So, do you have a consensus?

Mr. L: I could go with a moth or butterfly.

Mrs. L: I could go with that.

Card VI

E: Mrs. L., you said this has something to do with Indians; like feathers, and the spear they have it on, and like a skin that they put on the tepees; a foot with a big toe on it.

Mrs. L: I saw a foot with a big toe. Is that the same thing you saw? (Laughs.)

E: Mr. L., you said the top part looks like a totem pole, the skin of an animal, a bear of some sort, maybe Eskimo, with an Aleutian totem pole over it; a kodiak bear, a hunting type. Someone shot a kodiak bear, the totem over it symbolizing power.

Mrs. L: I don't see a bearskin, I see—

Mr. L: These are the front paws, the back paws, this is the back of the skin, the color design on the kodiak bear, and the head is missing, and the totem is here.

Mrs. L: I thought more of something of a flat-haired animal, like a reindeer or something.

Mr. L: That would be too big for a reindeer.

Mrs. L: A bearskin would be more solid in color.

Mr. L: No, the golden bear has a black streak down its back, they're two-toned.

Mrs. L: OK, if that's what you want.

Mr. L: No, it's not what I want, it's what I see.

E: So you're going with that?

Mrs. L: OK, a totem pole.

Mr. L: Yeah, it's a totem pole with a design of feathers.

Mrs. L: It's a ceremonial pole with feathers and a skin, solid in color.

Card VII

E: Now, Mr. L., on this one you saw "sexual connotations; the heads of two women, hands outstretched, pelvic area here, and a vagina. As if Siamese twins are sharing the same pelvic area." Mrs. L., you said storm clouds, with dark edges, not angry, just stormy, and pig faces; two little girls with ponytails sticking straight up in the air; little pigs, could be monsters, with horns like the devil.

Mr. L: I don't see all those other things. All I see is two girls with braided ponytails facing each other. This is a common denomination, they are both attached to this area, the pelvis area and the vagina, with little busts. Young girls. I'm being honest, that's what I see.

Mrs. L: Don't you see a face? Or an eye like a snout with two ears?

Mr. L: Yeah, eyes here and a snout.

Mrs. L: More like a pig.

Mr. L: Yes, I can see that but I don't know the relationship to the rest of the picture. I take it all in one and you break it up.

Mrs. L: I don't see anything sexual at all. It looks like clouds to me with black edges.

Mr. L: I don't see any clouds.

Mrs. L: Well, I agree on the little girls, but not on anything sexual because I don't see it.

Mr. L: You don't have to. I don't think we're here so that we have to do everything together. I can see a face here below the girls, but it has no relationship to the pictures. But you pointed it out, I didn't see it before. This doesn't look like clouds. It looks like a pelvic area. The black area is the sex part.

Mrs. L: We don't agree.

Mr. L: We don't agree.

E: This one you're not going to agree on?

Mr. L. We agree on part of it—the two faces, girls facing and pigs. But I don't see how the pigs fit in with the picture. But I still see what I said before. Do you ever get anybody who agrees 10 out of 10?

E: (Laughs.) Sometimes.

Card VIII

E: Mrs. L., you said this looked like two nice animals, not bears, a strong animal, a cheetah or a hyena. You also said the top part looks like a mountain or a castle in a fairy tale; the green is an insect, not a praying mantis. The head is like a mosquito. These things aren't wings. Fourthly, you said the red on the bottom is the insides of a person when a doctor cuts you open—the spine, lungs, et cetera. Mr. L., you said, if anything, science fiction; first of all two lizards, like the creature in "Aliens" that comes out of a fellow's chest.

Mr. L: It reminds me of those little things that came out and ran around the floor.

Mrs. L: Now I see an animal—strong—just look at the back on him.

Mr. L: Yeah, well, that thing that was inside the guy was strong when it got out—sharp little fangs and all.

E: A creature holding onto a paw you saw?

Mr. L: This is the mother creature—it looked all like science fiction to me. This was like the creature coming out of the birth sac. She's pulling them out of their birth sac. These are tentacles from science fiction. Their tails are still in there. They're being warmed coming out of the birth sac.

Mrs. L: Well, I'll go along with animals coming out of the birth sac, although I don't see it, but I'll go along with it. To me, this looks like a Disneyland Castle on top of a mountain.

Mr. L: I don't see that—anything Disney at all. I see it as a science fiction movie—it reminds me of "Aliens." We don't have to agree on all of these. We can agree on part of them or something.

Mrs. L: I just don't see science fiction. I see normal things.

Mr. L: All right.

E: So?

Mr. L: No agreement.

Card IX

Mr. L: This was a weird one to me.

E: Mr. L., first you said it doesn't look like much of anything, the shadowy area looked like a penis. Then you said a vagina of a woman, the uterus is here, as if a penis is entering the vaginal area—there's an ejaculation area here, you said.

Mr. L: This loop looks like somebody took an x-ray of a penis going into the pelvis area, this would be the vagina, this would be the excretion area.

Mrs. L: Excretion?

Mr. L: Having an ejaculation.

E: Mrs. L., you said first impression, two lobsters—

Mrs. L: Spider crabs.

E: You said inside of somebody—dark spots are the tonsils.

Mrs. L: This is the tonsils, the throat.

E: Mrs. L., you said it could be fingers on the bottom. "This stuff on the top is screaming, although I don't see a face or anything. And two little mice here."

Mrs. L: I see the little body of a mouse with his tail, throat, tonsils, and lungs. This is like a spider crab.

Mr. L: What's this blue area here?

Mrs. L: Nothing—I didn't see anything there. I looked right here—at this smeared part. I could hear screaming.

Mr. L: If I look at it over again, this looks like "Brunhilde" from that cartoon—the green thing—this is her eye, this is the big snout she has. See her on both sides. Now I'm beginning to see something different. You know that "Brunhilde," the cartoon? Can you see that now?

Mrs. L: Yes, I can see that.

Mr. L: I guess these could be spidery. I can see the relationship to a spiny lobster. I can rechange my thinking on that. Then the other area doesn't have much meaning then. Now, yes, I can see "Brunhilde" very defined. The spiny lobsters. I don't know about the rest of it. Do we agree on part of the picture?

Mrs. L: Uh-huh, yes.

Mr. L: We get 50 percent agreement.

E: What's the agreement?

Mr. L: We both see the character from the cartoon "Brunhilde" on each side. And this looks like a spiny lobster. And I don't have any significance for the rest of it, but she has the significance that she sees—the crying out or something here, which I don't see. We both agree to the orange and green. The rest then I have to disregard the original. I don't see much else in there—that would be the most pronounced thing that I could see.

Card X

E: Mrs. L., you said you saw crabs, two more crabs, and then holding it upside down a little astronaut, two daffodils, two monsters on the top—gremlins, the head of a penis, and you said it could also be a vagina.

Mr. L: I saw an oriental figure, Confucious, with slanty eyes, a fu-manchu moustache coming off the nose. This is like the animal skin fur that they wear—like a cloak—holding a crab in each hand. A Kubla Khan oriental headdress like they wore in those days, the helmets. The red is the robe.

E: Then you said this is the penis and the sexual organs are here.

Mr. L: Yeah, it would be the Year of the Crab. A Chinese type of symbol. The oriental king or monarch.

E. You said it looks very oriental, hands outstretched holding a crab.

Mr. L: You can see those little slanty eyes coming down? The mustache on each side?

E: You also said his penis is exposed and this is a brassiere—maybe he's interchangeable between male and female. The penis here, but also breasts.

Mr. L: To me that looks like something from one of those oriental—Kubla Khan-type era. This is the helmet that they used to wear in those days.

Mrs. L: I can't put that all together. I see pieces of the same—but I don't see it as one figure.

Mr. L: Soon as I saw this, it was so pronounced, like that fox and coyote. Those two things were the most pronounced to me. These are appendages holding a crab in each hand. Why he's doing it, I don't know. Except that it could be an oriental symbol for the Year of the Crab.

Mrs. L: I agree with you on the crabs. As far as this penis and vagina here, I'd go with that.

Mr. L: Does this look like a brassiere to you of some sort?

Mrs. L: Yeah—that could be a brassiere.

Mr. L: This doesn't look like any headdress at all to you?

Mrs. L: No. This is a little monster and that's a little monster and they're talking to each other. This is a daffodil—I'd go with sea horses on that.

Mr. L: Well, we see a couple of things here. We agree on part of the picture.

E: So, what's the agreement?

Mr. L: We have a partial agreement. Upside down we see an astronaut being held up by two sea horses. The other way she sees crabs on each side and crabs on the bottom. I can see four crabs here. She sees two sort of science fiction animals arguing with each other.

Mrs. L: Like the ones from "Gremlins" or something like that.

Mr. L: But I still see the ornamental headdress of an Asian and I see these slanty eyes and a mustache, so we can't agree on that part of it. What do you think this red is? I can buy flowers—daffodils.

Mrs. L: I don't remember seeing anything in that red at all. These could be like little islands—but—overall, I don't see anything at all in the red.

Mr. L: This looks like his robe—like a fur robe. That's what it looks like to me. We agreed that could be a bra and a penis—upside down and that way. And a vagina, below could be like a bisexual individual. I think we both agree on that or am I putting words in your mouth?

Mrs. L: Not bisexual. Male and female.

Mr. L: Wouldn't that be bisexual or am I using the wrong terminology?

Mrs. L: You're using one person. I'm using two people. Woman—Man.

Mr. L: I see them attached as one. That's the problem I have with this—it's one person—this whole thing. You're breaking it up into segments.

Mrs. L: You've got a dirty mind.

Mr. L: I don't know if I do or not—that's for him to decide.

(Both laugh.)

Mr. L: I'm being honest. You know, in the Orient, females weren't allowed to act. The males took the part of the females and the male. This is what I see—part man, part woman. I can't change my mind on it—I see it. I can see the astronauts and the sea horses upside down, but the rest of the picture doesn't make much sense. I can see two crabs on the top and these look like crabs on the side. But it still looks like an oriental figure in the Year of the Crab and it looks like something that's part woman and part man. Maybe it has some Freudian meaning—you don't have to agree. Just tell him what you think and I tell him what I think.

Mrs. L: Yeah that's it.

E: Do we have agreement?

Mrs. L: We have an agreement to disagree.

Mr. L: I seem to get one solid picture and she got little things out of pieces—maybe she looked more closely than I did.

(After consensus procedure concluded.)

E: How did you people feel about doing this? Did you notice anything?

Mr. L: I thought it was very interesting. I don't know where it will lead to—but I found it interesting.

E: How did you feel about reaching agreement on things? Did either of you feel that one of you gave in more than the other? Or what feelings did you have about reaching agreement on things?

Mrs. L: I think I gave in on a lot of points.

Mr. L: I'm sorry you feel that way.

Mrs. L: Well, I'm not in the best of moods right now, so—

E: Mr. L., you didn't feel that way?

Mr. L: No, because I see that coyote there, but can also settle for a bat. She saw a bat so I was willing to compromise on the bat. But I still see the dominant part in my mind, the coyote, but I can accept a bat. There's a couple of things I can accept. I don't think I forced my dominance.

E: You felt you were willing to compromise?

Mr. L: Yes, I guess I always feel like that but in the end she doesn't feel I am because I try to persuade her. She sees a lot more in these pictures than I do.

E: Did either of you notice anything else about the whole thing? Anything that strikes you—about what you saw, or the other person saw, or about your interactions?

Mrs. L: I think I don't like his explanation of all these penises.

Mr. L: I only saw them in a couple of pictures, not all of them.

Mrs. L: In a bisexual manner, so—

Mr. L: Well then, maybe I'm a latent homosexual. I don't know. Maybe I'm a latent homo—maybe I'll find out when I'm 70.

Mrs. L: Weird, to me.

Mr. L: Maybe "E" can explain it to me. You know, if I'm supposed to be honest about this.

Mrs. L: Yeah, we're supposed to be honest about it.

Mr. L: Here, I'm trying to be truthful and you're upset because I'm being truthful.

Mrs. L: No, I'm not upset about that.

Mr. L: When we got to the diner and all, you felt pretty good. Why all of a sudden you got all tensed up when we got here. I don't understand.

Mrs. L: Because you keep going on with this "If we get back together, if we get back together."

Mr. L: When did I say that?

E: I don't think that pertains to the procedure.

This consensus protocol reveals a great deal, both about individual psychodynamics and also about the relationship. First and foremost, Mr. L.'s sexual identification is markedly confused; he goes so far as to specifically make this interpretation himself. This is very likely the predominant factor responsible for his compulsive womanizing. The horrible "alien" percept bursting from the chest on Card VIII may well be a manifestation of his fear of hidden homosexual wishes bursting forth. Further orality is indicated on his part, and feelings of emotional coldness are evident, as well as some paranoid tendencies. Problems in ego functioning are suggested at several points.

For Mrs. L., it is evident that she is still very angry and hurt. She fights hard for her percepts and rarely gives in. Evidence of depressive affect is seen, as well as a poor self-concept. However, in contrast to her husband's sexual ambivalence, she endeavors to establish her own clear sexual identity. A child-like, dependent orientation is also clearly present; she is in emotional pain, and self-preoccupation is seen.

As regards to the relationship, it is clear that they are not satisfying each other's emotional needs. The consensus procedure is characterized by a raw power struggle, with each sometimes giving in grudgingly. Several times they fail to reach any consensus at all. A few times the examiner has to remind them that they are supposed to reach a consensus. They are clearly miles apart emotionally at this point in time, and without significant change the marital prognosis can only be considered guarded.

When the technique results were discussed with the husband, the issue of sexual identification was gingerly approached. The patient became tearful, indicating that he had known this about himself at least on some level for a long time. He went on to describe homosexual experiences that he had previously concealed, despite a detailed history having been taken. For the first time he became actively motivated in trying to use his sessions for self-exploration, now viewing his sexual acting-out not as something laudable but as expressive of deep emotional difficulties. With his permission, this was shared with the wife, who was able to accept it and to at least understand his behavior. Nonetheless, extensive marital difficulties remain, and the prognosis is still guarded.

It should be noted that the intervention described was not undertaken lightly. It was judged that Mr. L. was capable of handling the information and that the relationship with the therapist was sufficiently strong for such an intervention to be successful.

Case History #3

In this case the subject is a 40-year-old divorced woman who sought psychotherapy because of depression and many problems of adjustment following her separation and divorce. The psychotherapy became bogged down, with no clear direction to pursue. The Rorschach technique was therefore administered, over two therapy sessions.

While many of her other responses and associations were revealing, a crucial point was reached on Card V. One of her responses on this blot was "Smokey the Bear (laughs). His profile and the ranger cap." Her associations were as follows: "It makes me think of being a Girl scout, camping out. It was lots of fun—with lots of memories. But the memories are strange—I seem to remember pictures, not feelings—that seem to tell me something. I can see the lake, the graveyard, like flipping through someone else's photo album. (What does that make you think of?) It makes me upset that I don't have feelings about it—why don't I remember how I felt?"

In subsequent psychotherapy sessions the patient used this insight from the Rorschach administration to open up the general area of her reluctance to deal with emotions. She was able to connect this with her lifelong fear of being like her alcoholic, depressed, overly emotional mother. It should be noted that these themes had been touched on before, but the centrality of the conflict and the extent to which it was interfering with the therapy were only now apparent.

Case History #4

In this case the people involved in the Consensus Rorschach were a couple in their 30s who had a very young child. The technique used was that presented in Chapter 13, with the Consensus Rorschach administered to both parties at the same time, together with the Consensus TAT.

Mr. K. had had a highly traumatic childhood, being separated from his parents at a young age for over a year and being raised by a strict and domineering grandmother. Mrs. K.'s childhood could generally be described as normal, although at the moment of seeking therapy she was in quite a panic at the prospect of losing her husband and being left with a small child.

Rorschach Protocol (Consensus) #4

Card I

E: Let's start with the first inkblot.

Mrs. K: Looks like an insect.

Mr. K: A bat.

Mrs. K: A bat?

Mr. K: Yeah.

Mrs. K: It looks more like a beetle cause it's round here.

Mr. K: It looks like it has two little hands on it. I don't know, it looks like a bat—an insect. A Halloween mask—the eyes looking at us.

Mrs. K: Oh yeah. The eyes like a jack-o-lantern.

E: Can you reach agreement as to what it looks like?

Mrs. K: I agree it looks like an insect.

Mr. K: Looks like some sort of satanic animal. (She laughs.) Evil.

Mrs. K: It looks evil to you? I don't think so.

Mr. K: I don't know.

Mrs. K: The eyes and the mouth are all I see right now. Here are the eyes, here is the mouth.

Mr. K: It looks like a cat that's been run over. (Laughs.)

Mrs. K: This does look like a cat's face—the ears on top. Kind of distorted though.

Mr. K: A mask.

Mrs. K: Yeah, an evil mask.

Mr. K: It looks like an evil-looking cat.

Mrs. K: OK, I'll agree with that.

Card II

E: How about this second inkblot?

Mr. K: A spaceship?

Mrs. K: These don't look like eyes to you? This looks like two people talking to each other. Don't they? You don't see that? (Laughs nervously.)

Mr. K: They look like worms.

Mrs. K: No, two people. See, this is an eye and a nose and a mouth, and a little eyebrow on top. It looks like they're talking to each other.

Mr. K: Oh yeah.

Mrs. K: I don't know what the rest of it is, but that's what the top looks like.

Mr. K: It looks like an airplane.

Mrs. K: Oh yeah—I see that—a jet.

Mr. K: I don't know what the black thing is. Two faces. A neck of a chicken, I don't know.

Mrs. K: No.

Mr. K: The two faces have stopped talking.

Mrs. K: Yeah.

Mr. K: Two faces on top—and a spaceship or—

E: So what's the thing you agree on that it looks like the most?

Mr. K: Two faces on top—

Mrs. K: And a spaceship—or an airplane.

Mr. K: Down here—a blast.

Mrs. K: Yeah.

E: Okay, you've reached agreement?

Card III

E: Now this one.

Mr. K: Two people.

Mrs. K: Two people, working on something together. Here's a heart. There's affection between them.

Mr. K: Yeah. They're doing something together.

Mrs. K: Yeah. Two women standing over something that looks like a kettle— over a fire. Two women preparing dinner. Preparing a meal.

Mr. K: They look like men.

Mrs. K: They look like men? Then what are these?

Mr. K: (Laughs.) They look odd.

Mrs. K: Big-breasted men?

Mr. K: I can't make out what those red things are.

Mrs. K: No, it's definitely something between them.

Mr. K: It looks like something that's holding down someone's head?

Mrs. K: No. It looks more like a muskrat that's hanging upside down.

Mr. K: Yeah, that could be. It looks like a bird.

Mrs. K: No, I don't think so.

Mr. K: It looks like a dead bird upside down.

Mrs. K: Where are the legs?

Mr. K: Over here.

Mrs. K: Oh.

Mr. K: I still don't know what the middle is.

Mrs. K: So, are we agreed? You don't think they look like two women?

Mr. K: They look humanoid—they look like two monkeys to me. (She laughs nervously.) The things on top look like birds—like a dead bird hanging upside down.

Mrs. K: Could be.

Mr. K: With a trail of blood or something. And the thing in the middle, I have no idea.

Mrs. K: I don't know what that is either.

Mr. K: It looks like a hedge—a wall hedge—two tall bushes on either side— like looking from far away.

Mrs. K: Yeah, that could be. But—

Mr. K: It looks like a door in the back.

Mrs. K: Oh yeah, I see what you mean, because it's dark in the center there. Yeah, that's OK. OK—I'll go with that.

Mr. K: So what is it? A muskrat, a dead bird?

Mrs. K: I see a muskrat.

Mr. K: I don't see that. Well, it could be.

Mrs. K: Well, some kind of an animal.

Mr. K: It's not alive.

Mrs. K: It's not alive.

Mr. K: The hedge and a door at the end.

Mrs. K: And two people.

Mr. K: Humanoid, I'd say.

Mrs. K: They're working over something.

Mr. K: Yeah, doing something. That's about it.

E: Okay, so is there something you agree on?

Mrs. K: Yeah, I think we agree on one thing—there are two people working on something.

Mr. K: I don't know about people. Two—

Mrs. K: They're not people?

Mr. K: Two humanoid kind of figures.

Mrs. K: Two people.

Mr. K: They are doing something together. The middle is like the hedge. On either side the far end is like a door. Looks like a swinging door.

Mrs. K: No, it's not swinging. No, it's not a swinging door.

Mr. K: It's got the Western top.

Mrs. K: Oh, I guess you're right—I see that.

Mr. K: And—that's it.

Mrs. K: OK?

E: OK.
Card IV

E: Let's try the next one.

Mrs. K: Looks like a dog. Like an Eskimo.

Mr. K: It doesn't.

Mrs. K: No really, these are his arms, this is his legs, this is his head—he's like all bundled up 'cause he's out in the snow—and these are like his snowshoes.

Mr. K: Actually it looks like some sort of rug.

Mrs. K: Like a rug? Oh, yeah I guess so.

Mr. K: Except I don't know what that tail—

Mrs. K: Yeah, I don't know what that thing is in the middle. Maybe it's some animal—some type of animal with a tail?

Mr. K: Maybe some type of animal.

Mrs. K: (Sighs.)

E: So how are we doing? Do you have an agreement?

Mrs. K: I don't know (Laughs nervously.)

Mr. K: Some sort of rug or something—but—

Mrs. K: Like a fur rug. Yeah, some kind of animal but I don't know what kind of animal it would be. Yeah, I'll agree with you on that.

Mr. K: Yeah, but it doesn't look like anything—that's the closest thing I can see.

E: OK, great.

Card V

E: Let's give this one a try.

Mr. K: Looks like a bird.

Mrs. K: That's what it looks like to you? A bird?

Mr. K: Looks like a butterfly.

Mrs. K: It does look like a butterfly.

Mr. K: Insect legs here—except the head looks like a rabbit.

Mrs. K: A rabbit with long ears? (Laughs.)

Mr. K: Doesn't it?

Mrs. K: Yeah, it does look like a butterfly and that's what I thought it was.

Mr. K: Looks like a rabbit with butterfly wings or a butterfly with a rabbit body.

Mrs. K: (Laughs.) A butterfly with a rabbit body! Yeah.

Mr. K: I think it's more like a rabbit with wings.

Mrs. K: I don't think it's a rabbit.

Mr. K: The head over there?

Mrs. K: It looks like a bird.

Mr. K: Not a bird. No.

Mrs. K: No? Are those ears or antennas?

Mr. K: This looks like a rabbit's legs at least.

Mrs. K: It looks like a rabbit with wings?

Mr. K: A rabbit with wings, that's what I see.

Mrs. K: I don't know if the body is really a rabbit body. Rabbit ears don't stick up like that. Only in cartoons.

Mr. K: Only in cartoons. It still looks like a rabbit.

Mrs. K: Okay, I'll go with a rabbit.

Mr. K: A rabbit with wings.

Mrs. K: A rabbit with wings.

Mr. K: Fluffy wings.

Mrs. K: Very fluffy wings.

E: OK, good.

Card VI

E: Try this one.

Mr. K: An Indian symbol. It is definitely a rug. (Laughter.) Look at it.

Mrs. K: I don't see anything.

Mr. K: It looks Southwestern on top. This looks like a rug, this is like the head.

Mrs. K: It doesn't look like a body, doesn't it look like a—

Mr. K: A bear—

Mrs. K: No—I don't see anything in there.

Mr. K: Yeah, definitely like some sort of fur. This is like an Indian—

Mrs. K: You don't see this—like a person's body? This is their head and this is their body? Like a bellybutton.

Mr. K: No.

Mrs. K: They're touching.

Mr. K: No.

Mrs. K: No? A little butt. You don't see that? (Laughs.) In a way, yeah.

Mr. K: Definitely not.

Mrs. K: Definitely not. OK, so we won't agree with that.

Mr. K: Some sort of Indian thing. Look at that!

Mrs. K: Yeah, this looks like what you would see like in a totem pole.

Mr. K: Yeah, hanging.

Mrs. K: But I don't know what the rest of this is.

Mr. K: Looks like a fur rug to me.

Mrs. K: Yeah. It's got the arms and the legs.

Mr. K: No, if you look straight down it looks like a fish.

Mrs. K: A fish? OK, so we agree it looks like a totem pole and like a rug. Yeah, sure. Isn't that what you meant?

Mr. K: No not a totem pole. Have you ever seen those things hanging like on the side of teepees and stuff? Like called a shield. Like in the movies.

Mrs. K: No.

Mr. K: You don't watch movies.

Mrs. K: Sorry. But definitely Indian.

Mr. K: But definitely Indian in nature. The thing on the bottom—

Mrs. K: OK. I agree with the body like a hide.

Mr. K: A hide.

E: So that's what you agree on.

Card VII

E: Here's the next one.

Mr. K: Like two heads trying to kiss.

Mrs. K: Yes. Definitely. I don't know what the rest of it is.

Mr. K: Yeah, I don't know what the rest of it is.

Mrs. K: Yeah. But yeah, two heads.

Mr. K: Like two heads trying to kiss but their bodies are moving back towards the back, not towards each other.

Mrs. K: Yeah, they're pulling apart. Yeah.

Mr. K: I don't know what the thing is on their heads.

Mrs. K: It's like a feather.

Mr. K: (Unintelligible)

Mrs. K: Something like that or a hat.

Mr. K: No, hairdo? Big hair.

Mrs. K: Like pigtails.

Mr. K: Yeah but it's going up.

Mrs. K: Yeah, flying up in the breeze.

Mr. K: Up? I don't think so. But it's like two heads trying to kiss.

Mrs. K: Uh-huh.

Mr. K: Their bodies are like repelling away from each other.

Mrs. K: Right.

Mr. K: And the thing on their heads—I haven't the slightest.

Mrs. K: OK. Well I think they're either feathers or pigtails.

Mr. K: Happy?

Mrs. K: Yeah. OK?

Mr. K: Uh-huh.

E: Well, OK.

Card VIII

E: OK, let's try this one.

Mrs. K: Don't they look like bears?

Mr. K: Maybe possums.

Mrs. K: Yeah, yeah, I'd say they're possums.

Mr. K: Possums on the side.

Mrs. K: Yeah. I don't know what they're climbing up.

Mr. K: No, they're just there.

Mrs. K: Yeah.

Mr. K: I don't know, maybe some sort of skeleton?

Mrs. K: Yeah, that's what it looks like. I was thinking this looks more like a pelvis bone?

Mr. K: Yeah, I can see that.

Mrs. K: But I don't know how the rest of this—this could be like the rib cage.

Mr. K: No, I don't think (unintelligible). Definitely a skeleton here—

Mrs. K: Yeah.

Mr. K: I think it's like a fish skeleton—like a prehistoric skeleton.

Mrs. K: Definitely doesn't look anything like—

Mr. K: Like a prehistoric skeleton.

Mrs. K: What are these muskrats or possums doing?

Mr. K: I like muskrats. They're just there on the side.

Mrs. K: Yeah. (Laughs.)

Mr. K: They're not doing anything. They're like all like hanging out. The bottom you say is a pelvis?

Mrs. K: Yeah, it looks sort of like a pelvis the bottom there. I don't know. If they say it had to be something.

Mr. K: Yeah, well . . .

Mrs. K: That's it.

E: So what's the agreement?

Mrs. K: There are two muskrats or possums on the side and there is some type of skeleton from a prehistoric animal.

E: All right.

Card IX

E: And how about here?

Mrs. K: (Laughs.) I don't see anything here. What do you see? These maybe look like some kind of feet but they're not really attached to anything. Like claws.

Mr. K: This is almost just like a seaside like a shore, a strip of land.

Mrs. K: Oh like you're looking at a map?

Mr. K: Yeah. Like a map of England.

Mrs. K: Uh-huh.

Mr. K: Up to a point. All this is like little islands—

Mrs. K: Islands.

Mr. K: Yeah, see around here and then this (unintelligible).

Mrs. K: I don't know what that is—

Mr. K: This looks like big fluffy pillows or something. Clouds. Definitely fluffy, they're not hard.

Mrs. K: Those? I don't know what they are.

Mr. K: I don't think they're like rocks or anything, maybe just the floor. Or like cotton balls.

Mrs. K: Could these be shoulders and this a neck or the chest? I don't know where the head would be.

Mr. K: No, I don't think these are shoulders at all.

Mrs. K: I don't know.

Mr. K: Stylized shoulders.

Mrs. K: Yeah, definitely.

Mr. K: Two little breasts.

Mrs. K: Yeah, those little marks there. But then this would be the head, but I don't see anything that looks like a head there. It looks just really weird.

Mr. K: It's like a lobster or something, like a crayfish.

Mrs. K: Oh, the red? Yeah, could be.

Mr. K: So what is it?

Mrs. K: (Laughs.) I don't know.

Mr. K: OK, it's a stylized torso. Man or woman?

Mrs. K: I don't know.

Mr. K: Looks like a woman to me—not a very good-looking woman—

Mrs. K: (Laughs.) Just the torso of a woman—and then what would the rest of it be?

Mr. K: I think the chest is of a woman. The shoulders of a man.

Mrs. K: Right.

Mr. K: The orange top is some sort of a crayfish or the shoreline of some sort, like on a map. And the middle—

Mrs. K: The middle doesn't look like anything, to me anyway.

Mr. K: It's almost like a hollow shape, like this is open.

Mrs. K: I don't see it. I don't see it having three dimensions.

Mr. K: That's it.

E: So what's your decision?

Mrs. K: On the bottom, the pink is a torso of a woman and on top there's some type of crayfish.

Mr. K: Yeah. I could go with that, yeah. It looks more insect-like. If you would look at the whole thing then what is it? What is the word? Sea line?

Mrs. K: Seashore line.

Mr. K: Seashore line, yeah. (Unintelligible)

Mrs. K: Yeah, I don't know what it is.

E: OK.

Card X

E: And finally this last inkblot.

Mr. K: (Laughs.)

Mrs. K: This looks like an animal—

Mr. K: A pig?

Mrs. K: Yeah, a lot of legs. I see a lot of animals in here. These look like little bulls—

Mr. K: What?

Mrs. K: Bulls. Like a bull, like a cow. Yeah like a bullfight, those types of bulls. They're standing on their legs, and there are their little arms, the head, and this is—they've gotten the thing already—on their heads, their tail. You can't see that? (Laughs.)

Mr. K: I can see how you could see it, but yeah the bodies don't look that but the bodies don't look—

Mrs. K: None of this stuff looks like a bull should be. Don't these look like some kind of animals?

Mr. K: No, I don't think so. Doesn't look like there are too many animals in this thing.

Mrs. K: What do you think this is? A goat's head.

Mr. K: I think the outline looks like the hair of a woman. Just like something on her head—no face. The face is (unintelligible) on the neck.

Mrs. K: Oh, her face is there?

Mr. K: Yeah, no face.

Mrs. K: So it's like a wig?

Mr. K: No, I think it could be just a wig with an ornament on it. I think it's like a female form, not like a wig or a mask.

Mrs. K: No. No, definitely—if it would be a wig it would be a woman.

Mr. K: Yeah, of some sort—

Mrs. K: Ornament on top.

Mr. K: Yeah, or like a weird map of Italy. Like somebody was drunk and drew it. (Laughs.)

Mrs. K: Could this be two eyes and a nose? (Unintelligible)

Mr. K: (Unintelligible) . . . the whole face.

Mrs. K: Yeah.

Mr. K: That doesn't look like a mouth.

Mrs. K: No, it doesn't.

E: So can you reach an agreement?

Mr. K: A ceremonial mask—the whole thing here—here are the eyes—there's no one in it but this is where the head would fit?

Mrs. K: Yeah, yeah, I could see that. And the bulls on top?

Mr. K: OK. (Unintelligible)

E: I'm sorry, what?

Mrs. K: He said you explain to him what it is. (Laughter.) Ceremonial mask, with the bulls on top and some kind of big tick animal on the side.

E: Very good. One more thing I would like you to do is briefly look at a few pictures and make up a story to go with the picture. Include such things as what's happening, what led up to it, what the characters are thinking and feeling, and also how it works out. Give it an ending. Make up a story.

Card 1

Mrs. K: Well he doesn't look happy. Maybe doing his homework—is that what it is?

Mr. K: Yeah it looks like homework stuff.

Mrs. K: So he probably came home from school and he wanted to go out and play but—

Mr. K: Had to do homework.

Mrs. K: His mom said no, you have to do homework first.

Mr. K: Yeah.

Mrs. K: And now he's sitting there very upset—

Mr. K: Half asleep.

Mrs. K: And he's just doing his homework.

Mr. K: (Unintelligible.)

Mrs. K: In the dining room.

Mr. K: Yeah, could be. He's not understanding whatever he's looking at.

Mrs. K: No, he's not doing it, just sort of looking at it. He's resigned to the fact that he's not going to go out and play.

Mr. K: Well, I think now he's like trying to do this stuff and he's like not getting it.

Mrs. K: Um. I guess he does have that blank look.

Mr. K: Yeah, it's like what the hell?

Mrs. K: Do you want more of a story than that?

E: No, that's OK. Do you want to give it an ending?

Mrs. K: An ending? His mom makes dinner and then he doesn't have to do his homework anymore because he has to eat dinner.

Mr. K: Yeah, he's gonna spend some time there just looking at this—

Mrs. K: To him it's going to be hours.

Mr. K: Yeah he's looking at this stuff trying to—

Mrs. K: And then his dad will come home and his dad will explain it all to him.

Mr. K: Well, I don't think so.

Mrs. K: Yeah, yeah. Or his older brother.

Mr. K: No.

Mrs. K: Makes sense of it all.

Mr. K: No, tomorrow he's gotta go to school and remember this whole thing.

Mrs. K: After dinner somebody will sit down with him and go over it and explain it to him. But they'll notice during dinner how upset he is. You don't believe that?

Mr. K: No. This is like before—he's gonna do his homework and he's going to close the books—

Mrs. K: And forget about it?

Mr. K: No, tomorrow he's gonna have to try to remember, explain it, and know this stuff—it won't be easy.

Mrs. K: I think somebody's going to help him with it later—before he has to go back to school and that everything will be all right and that he will be happy.

Mr. K: No.

Mrs. K: Yeah, it will have a happy ending.

Mr. K: Well, OK.

Mrs. K: Is it too sad to have a happy ending?

Mr. K: Well, look at his face.

Mrs. K: Well, yeah, but he'll get over it.

E: OK.

Card 2

E: Let's try this one, a story for this.

Mr. K: A farming village. The girl is the only one going to school—everyone else has to work.

Mrs. K: It looks like she's leaving to go to school. These are her parents—her mother and her older brother working on the farm, but they want her to go to school.

Mr. K: But she feels that she should be there working.

Mrs. K: Right.

Mr. K: She looks kind of guilty maybe?

Mrs. K: Uh-huh, but she's been given this opportunity.

Mr. K: Everyone else—

Mrs. K: Everyone else is toiling away.

Mr. K: Definitely a farm, the seashore in the background. The—

Mrs. K: Uh-huh.

Mr. K: Hills (unintelligible) the mother don't look too happy—

Mrs. K: No, because she has to stay there and—

Mr. K: She's resigned to whatever—

Mrs. K: She's resigned to her life but she wants something more for her daughter.

Mr. K: Yeah. But I don't know about the brother.

Mrs. K: Well he looks kind of young to be her father.

E: How's it going to work out?

Mrs. K: In the end? She is gonna go to school, get great grades, she's gonna go to college, she's gonna come back, she's gonna support them, she's gonna be the medical doctor in town, she's gonna make millions of dollars.

Mr. K: And her mom will probably die before she does any of that.

Mrs. K: Yeah, her mom looks pretty old. But her mother will be happy because she knows that she did the best for her daughter.

Mr. K: Just before she dies, she knows her daughter has made it.

Mrs. K: That's right.

E: Good.

Card 3BM

E: How about this one?

Mrs. K: Oh, it's very sad.

Mr. K: Not a happy scene. This is a suicide.

Mrs. K: Why?

Mr. K: It's a woman who just killed herself. This is a gun—

Mrs. K: That's a gun? Just looks like a woman who's just sad and she's sitting in her living room. Maybe . . . that looks like a knife or something?

Mr. K: Unless she's either dead or she's crying.

Mrs. K: Yeah, it's very sad.

Mr. K: She's dead—she doesn't have very good posture—she can just tip over. (Laughter.)

Mrs. K: I don't think she's dead—

Mr. K: She's crying.

Mrs. K: Yeah.

Mr. K: This looks like a gun or some sort of—

Mrs. K: She looks like a young girl, don't you think?

Mr. K: Well, late 20s maybe, late 20s, yeah, she's not a teenager—

Mrs. K: No, I thought she's a teenager—

Mr. K: No.

Mrs. K: What's the story? I think she's lonely, she's upset and she's just crying. You think it's a suicide?

Mr. K: No, it's—she's definitely crying I think. Although I don't know, I think she might be dead. From her position the bottom half of her body is not—

Mrs. K: No, she's supporting herself.

Mr. K: Yeah, yeah. Definitely crying though. She's not very pretty.

Mrs. K: She's not very pretty? How can you tell? She's big—

Mr. K: Big bottom—look at the shoulders—

Mrs. K: Big woman.

Mr. K: I don't think she's proportioned. She doesn't have a happy life.

Mrs. K: No.

Mr. K: Just like Cinderella, they left for the ball—

Mrs. K: Oh yeah, they left her behind—

Mr. K: They left her behind.

Mrs. K: And so she's upset—

Mr. K: She's just lonely—

Mrs. K: Lonely and upset?

Mr. K: Hates everything.

Mrs. K: And so, how does it end? Like Cinderella, the fairy godmother comes? (Laughs.)

Mr. K: No, she takes this gun over here and—

Mrs. K: I think things get better.

Mr. K: Maybe. . . . But there is no Cinderella story.

Mrs. K: Yeah. It looks very sad.

Mr. K: She grows up, she gets over it but—

Mrs. K: She's always sad.

Mr. K: I don't think she's sad. She'll learn to deal with it and gets away from this house, this place.

Mrs. K: Uh-huh. And these people.

E: OK, good.

Card 6BM

E: Give this one a try.

Mrs. K: They look really worried, like they're looking outside?

Mr. K: Like "Mom, I'm gay!" (Laughter.)

Mrs. K: Doesn't it look like she's looking out the window waiting for someone to come home?

Mr. K: Yeah, initially I thought he had just told her that he has to leave home and—

Mrs. K: And she's just staring—

Mr. K: Yeah, and she's sad—but look at his face—it looks more serious then. Like he just embezzled her money and the cops are about to come.

Mrs. K: Yeah, she's looking out the window and the cops are coming. (Laughs.) She looks like she's sort of in shock.

Mr. K: Yeah. Disappointed.

Mrs. K: She's disappointed? No, that's not disappointment. It's more like— because her eyes are so wide open. In shock maybe?

Mr. K: Yeah, she doesn't know what to say or do.

Mrs. K: She's obviously not looking at him. She's looking away, she has no idea what to say.

Mr. K: He just confessed something. It wasn't good. He doesn't look happy.

Mrs. K: And she's worried and (unintelligible).

Mr. K: Yeah, he is sorry. Look at his hands.

Mrs. K: Yeah, he's very sorry, sorry he has to tell her this.

Mr. K: Yeah, he's not happy either.

Mrs. K: Maybe he came home to tell her that her husband died.

Mr. K: No, looks like her son.

Mrs. K: No, to tell her that her husband, his father, died.

Mr. K: No, it's not that kind of news. It's like a disappointment. Like what the mother expects would never happen.

Mrs. K: Yeah.

Mr. K: He feels bad and sorry.

Mrs. K: Uh-huh.

Mr. K: How does it end? I guess they discuss it. But there's really nothing they can do about it.

Mrs. K: Right, it looks like there is nothing that can be said really.

Mr. K: Nothing you can do. He just told her something. She's disappointed, he feels sorry, and there is really nothing they can do about it to make things right again.

Mrs. K: Yes. That's it.

Card 13MF

E: Now the last one.

Mr. K: Is she dead?

Mrs. K: She doesn't look alive but why isn't she dressed? At least he's fully dressed. He's very upset, probably going to cry. I think she is dead the way her arm is down like that.

Mr. K: No.

Mrs. K: Maybe he just came in and found her like that. I'm not sure it's her room. It looks like his room—a hard table and books. It looks like she had been sick and staying at his house and he came in and now she is dead—

Mr. K: No.

Mrs. K: Think maybe he killed her?

Mr. K: I don't think it's that at all. I don't think she's alive. If she was alive her arm would be next to her in the bed.

Mrs. K: She'd be a lot more comfortable looking.

Mr. K: Yeah. She looks dead.

Mrs. K: I think he killed her, and now kind of regrets it. Can't believe he did it.

Mr. K: Yeah, but where's the weapon?

Mrs. K: He strangled her.

Mr. K: He scared her to death.

Mrs. K: I think it ends that he gives himself up and admits his guilt.

Mr. K: No. This is not his room. This is like a hotel or motel room because the bed is so low. She doesn't look comfortable, she looks dead. He won't turn himself in. Maybe it's her place. He's definitely sorry, I don't know whether he killed her. I don't think he killed her. She's dead.

E: Can you folks agree?

Mrs. K: He doesn't agree with my ending.

Mr. K: She's just going to stay there.

Mrs. K: What happens to him?

Mr. K: Maybe he didn't kill her. Maybe she likes to sleep with her arm over the side. But he's definitely sorry. It's not a happy picture. There's stress, there's tension, and just sadness.

(After consensus procedure completed.)

E: OK, good. That's the procedure. What are your reactions to it? How did you feel about it? Did you notice anything about you, or the other person, your interactions? Did anyone feel they gave in more than the other person?

Mr. K: The first part was kind of fun, trying to figure out what was in there. But the stuff in the pictures—

Mrs. K: I thought that was easier.

E: Did you notice anything about your interactions?

Mr. K: I think we agreed more on the inkblots.

Mrs. K: Yeah.

E: Did anyone feel they gave in more than the other?

Mrs. K: I thought we did equally.

Mr. K: You were sympathetic with that girl who was crying, the one we thought was dead first.

Mrs. K: Oh yeah. It was sad.

Mr. K: Women tend to be sympathetic to other women in that type of situation.

E: Did you feel also that it was about 50/50 in terms of giving in?

Mr. K: I gave in more.

Mrs. K: You could see things more than I can.

This Consensus Rorschach and TAT first of all reveal that the parties differ in the emotional mental health that they bring to the situation. He reveals some paranoid and strongly depressive aspects of functioning, while her responses are generally within the normal range. She frequently tries to reach a consensus with him, but he often resists it. She evidences some disturbance at his inability to see the popular people response on Card III. On Card IV, her Eskimo response shows she feels a coldness in the marriage. The Card V response of the husband is quite revealing—the rabbit with wings is clearly a projection of his self-concept—that is, a superhuman being who is covering up an underlying poor self-concept.

Mr. K. consistently gets Mrs. K to give in, although she evidences some assertiveness at points and disturbance at many of his percepts—for instance, his comment on Card IX, "not a very good-looking woman." On the TAT, he struggles against giving a happy ending to the story, while she is rather desperately seeking a happy ending.

Both patients had come seeking traditional marriage counseling, with the husband coming with a good deal of resistance (for example, even showing resistance to getting out of the car). The Consensus Rorschach was administered to these clients after the taking of comprehensive histories to help decide how therapy should proceed. It was suggested to the clients that the best procedure would be for the husband to come for a time by himself to work through emotional difficulties of his childhood before dealing with specifically marital issues. It is interesting to note that this came as news to the wife, who was not aware of the very difficult childhood that Mr. K. had had. The couple agreed to this suggestion, and the appropriate therapy was therefore able to proceed.

Case History #5

In this case the patient is a 28-year-old married male who sought psychotherapy because of alcohol difficulties, anxiety, and low self-esteem. He described coming from a large family. The father was noted to be alcoholic but affectionate; the mother cold and critical. After the patient had been seen four months in once-per-week psychotherapy, he had stopped drinking altogether, but significant progress had not been made with his other symptoms. The therapy became bogged down, and the reason was not clear. He had also stopped bringing in dreams, which might have shed light on what was happening. The Rorschach technique was therefore administered to the patient.

The Rorschach record proved quite revealing, but it was the responses and associations on Card I that proved to be pivotal. His first response on Card I was "It looks like—a mirror image of someone reaching up to the sky, a woman." The associations to this percept were as follows: "(What does that make you think of?) My mom—asking for help during troubled times. She had trouble making the adjustment going from an upper middle class family to a struggling family. The struggle was to accept this life. She's still there—I really respect her for that."

The patient's second response to the first inkblot was "It also looks like a butterfly." The associations to this percept were: "(What does a butterfly bring to mind?) The warmth that my mother gave us. It was beautiful—there's nothing like it. (Pause.) It wasn't easy for her to show it, though."

In the session following the Rorschach technique administration the patient reported considerable agitation, including sleeplessness, as well as a resumption of remembering his dreams. He indicated a conscious welling up at anger at his mother, anger that had largely been repressed and intellectualized. This not only brought the patient in touch with his deeper feelings toward his mother, but also brought home to him the extent to which he was out of touch with his emotions. This constituted a breakthrough for the patient, who was then able to proceed in therapy in a variety of directions.

▲ 15

Report Writing

GENERAL CONSIDERATIONS

Until its principles are mastered, report writing is perhaps the most difficult aspect of psychodiagnostic activity for even the more experienced psychologist. Rorschach technique interpretations are highly complex and inferential; organizing and integrating them so they can be communicated in a meaningful way is sometimes a task of near monumental proportions. This chapter will endeavor to highlight some critical aspects of report writing. For a more comprehensive treatment of the subject, the reader is referred to books by Huber (1961), Walter Klopfer (1960), and Tallent (1993). While specific features of the Rorschach report as such will be addressed, it is to be recognized that ordinarily the Rorschach is included in a battery of psychological tests yielding more extensive data. The principles of synthesizing and communicating the findings are essentially the same whether one or more psychological procedures are administered.

The most frequent and serious difficulty in Rorschach reports results from the writer losing sight of the fact that he or she is evaluating a particular person and, instead, becoming immersed in a welter of technical Rorschach details. Dwelling on the various percentages and ratios found in a Rorschach summary table is worse than useless. If an individual who is comparatively unfamiliar with the Rorschach reads this type of report, he or she would not only find it patently incomprehensible, but would very likely regard it as an exercise in obfuscating self-puffery calculated to display the erudition of the writer.

Almost equally disruptive to a reader is a Rorschach report that directs minimal attention to the referring questions and instead launches into a host of issues tangential or unrelated to why the patient was referred for assessment. For example, if the principal referral question asked was whether organicity is present, then writing a report that focuses essentially on the patient's psychosexual adjustment is obviously not very helpful. Of course, very often referral questions are vague or nonexistent and the psychologist, by default, must decide what to include in the report. If the psychologist typically receives such referrals, it is strongly recommended that he or she educate the referring agent with respect to framing specific referral questions in the context of information that the Rorschach and other psychological procedures can realistically provide.

Some referents have the misapprehension that all background information about a client should be withheld from the examiner and that the Rorschach report should be a "blind diagnosis." The rationale behind this is that having other data of various types about the client establishes preconceptions that then serve to color and possibly distort subsequent Rorschach interpretations. While there is doubtlessly some element of truth in this, not having full information about the client creates a much greater potential for misinterpretation. Such variables as education and occupation are critical in providing a meaningful context for interpreting a Rorschach protocol. Other facts in the patient's history might be of equal importance—a recent loss of a loved one, for example. Thus, all relevant information about the client who is being assessed should be available to the psychologist when the psychological evaluation is undertaken. Of course, this does not mean that such data should be indiscriminantly regurgitated in a psychological report, especially when it can be obtained in other readily accessible records.

Behavioral observations during the evaluation sessions are as important as the Rorschach responses themselves in drawing a meaningful personality picture of the client. Such observations should be included in a separate introductory section of the report and, wherever pertinent, integrated in the body of the report. A problem sometimes arises when one tries to reconcile general subject behavior and the actual Rorschach percepts. An example of this may be an individual who comes to the evaluation situation and acts in a very diffident passive-compliant manner, but produces Rorschach associations that are rife with aggressive and rebellious elements. Such an incongruity is likely to be spurious rather than real and explainable on the basis of the different levels on which the person functions. In this illustration the individual's passive submissiveness may result from defensive efforts to deal with unacceptable guilt-producing, angry, destructive thoughts and feelings.

A neophyte Rorschach worker may be greatly discomforted by Rorschach percepts that ostensibly do not seem to fit with behavioral impressions. With further Rorschach experience, however, the psychologist will grow considerably more adept in understanding the interplay between behavior and inner living.

It must be recognized that the psychologist preparing a Rorschach report is working with complex hypotheses and suppositions about personality structure that, in turn, are derived from a set of inferences about the inkblot percepts per se. This conjectural framework may result in much hedging and qualifying on the part of the report writer, with the assessment abounding in words like "might be," "seems to," "suggests," and the like, and sometimes reliance upon what has been characterized as the "Barnum effect." The Barnum effect derives from P. T. Barnum's assertion that "a sucker is born every minute." In terms of report writing, it means the inclusion of very general interpretations that virtually anyone would regard as essentially descriptive of them. An example of this type of interpretation might be, "the client evidences conflicts."

Avoiding more definitive and specific interpretations at any cost is hardly likely to give the reader confidence in the findings. The report writer should try to give key statements in the workup a kind of "level of confidence rating." Thus, when there is a great deal of data to support a given assertion, this might be indicated by a statement such as, "There is strong evidence of. . . ." On the other hand, if the protocol contains somewhat minimal or contradictory indications to corroborate an interpretation, then the statement could be prefaced with, "There is some suggestion of. . . ." Occasional interpretations based on slender evidence that help to clarify certain psychodiagnostic aspects are not inappropriate in a report, as long as the referent is made aware of their problematic nature.

The comparatively inexperienced psychologist attempting to interpret the Rorschach often feels a bit bewildered by the plethora of personality data and, therefore, may cling to a "cookbook approach" to interpretation, mechanically looking up given ratios and percentages in a Rorschach textbook and paraphrasing the general interpretations assigned to them. This invariably makes for a highly fragmented, stereotyped report in which the person who has been evaluated frequently is lost in the course of the presentation. To be at all meaningful, a report must be person-centered rather than instrument-centered. With additional evaluation experience accompanied by good supervision and feedback, the psychologist naturally grows more confident and is usually willing to abandon a majority of cookbook interpretations, focusing instead on the unique constellation of personality features of the individual as they emerge on the Rorschach and other procedures.

Documentation, that is, citing various ratios or other technical aspects of the record, has no place in the body of a psychological report, except in the learning context. It is presumed that the referring agent is retaining a competent professional with sufficient expertise not to be called upon to "defend" his or her conclusions. Including scoring or tabulation details of a Rorschach in a report serves more as a disruption than an aid in communicating what is being presented. On the other hand, there are times when the content of the client's own words dramatically capture what the interpreter is trying to convey. To illustrate this, a woman whose Rorschach indicated that she was just barely beginning to emerge from a severe depression gave the following response to Card IV: "It looks like a dead old tree stump but here at the top a few little green shoots seem to be coming out." To the outer blue details of Card IX, a man whose Rorschach indicated that he experienced life as very unstable and directionless said: "A amoeba constantly changing its shape." In such situations it might be helpful to quote the material verbatim in the report.

A question that sometimes arises with respect to the Rorschach is whether the psychologist working with it must be totally conversant with a personality theory in order to write good reports. This is perhaps best answered by stating that there certainly must be a capacity for viewing behavior within some conceptual frame of reference, though this need not be in terms of one highly developed and specific personality theory. Flexibility may well be the best posture with regard to theory. Some understanding of theoretical underpinnings of personality is doubtless necessary to integrate various components of a Rorschach protocol in report form. At the same time, being rigidly committed to a particular personality theory may result in procrustean report writing, with all patients arbitrarily squeezed into a fixed theoretical model.

It is worth mentioning that many reports suffer from an overemphasis on symptoms and pathology and dwell only to a minimal extent, if at all, on assets and strengths. It clearly is far easier to delineate the flawed aspects of personality than to identify those that signify at least some modicum of health, especially when a client is in the throes of significant emotional difficulties or on the brink of psychiatric hospitalization. Even the most emotionally disturbed, chronically ill individual has some areas of strength, although these may be very circumscribed and not at all obvious. A careful identification and description of such assets should form an essential portion of the report, especially from the standpoint of assisting in treatment planning.

Whenever possible, the Rorschach should not be administered alone but rather in conjunction with other psychological procedures. A battery usually makes the job of report writing far simpler. Results obtained from one personality procedure can amplify and complement the data on another. If the procedures run the gamut from structuredness to relative unstructuredness and also tap various levels of conscious control, some very interesting contrasts can be established. Having the Sentence Completion Test and the Rorschach technique in the same battery, for example, with the former being far more subject to the client's censorship, permits the examiner to gain considerable insight into the client's defensive operations. When an intelligence scale is included in a battery with the Rorschach, the psychologist is able to compare how the client utilizes his or her intellectual resources in familiar versus less familiar and well-defined situations.

WRITING THE REPORT

What will be offered in this section of the chapter will be an approach to the actual writing of the report. Various other authors have presented outlines on this subject that are doubtlessly of equal merit. Furthermore, sometimes an institutional or agency setting requires a particular type of report with the inclusion of specific interpretive material. As a consequence, the psychologist working in such a setting may have to comply with the report writing demands of his or her position.

This outline emphasizes the Rorschach rather than psychological reports based on a more extensive battery. As alluded to earlier, however, the principles are essentially the same.

Any approach to report writing should be prefaced with the strong recommendation that considerably more time be devoted to thinking through what is to be put in the report than to the actual writing. Also, apart from the formal content of the report as such, the writer must attend very carefully to the matters of syntax, vocabulary, and punctuation. A report that is ungrammatical, no matter how insightful, will lose some of its value. Continuity is also an exceedingly important aspect of report writing. A logical sequence of ideas must be reflected in the way the interpretive material is presented. The usefulness of report writing is significantly diluted when it is written in a rambling, desultory fashion, skipping from area to area with insufficient attention to continuity.

In most cases an outline of some type is helpful in formulating a case and organizing the report. If a battery of psychological procedures is administered, then the kind of report that discusses each of them one at a time should be scrupulously avoided. This type of report is typically rife with redundancy and lacking in meaningful cohesiveness.

What follows is an outline for the content and organization of a Rorschach report. In no sense is this outline meant to be used in all instances. There may be clients who produce Rorschachs yielding little information on some of the areas covered in this outline. On the other hand, the outline is not intended to be all-inclusive, and there may be some Rorschach findings that do not readily fall into any one area.

History and Background Information

This section should succinctly summarize the background history of the subject that is relevant for the particular evaluation situation. It should be relatively brief and should not, for example, rephrase information readily available in the social work summary found in the client's folder.

Behavioral Observations

The behavioral observation section describes the major dimensions of the client's behavior during the evaluation session. Just as the name implies, the behavior should be reported at an observational-descriptive level, rather than an interpretive one. Typically included in such a section is a description of the client's appearance and the reason the individual states he or she has been referred for psychodiagnostic evaluation. It is often very helpful to highlight changes that may take place in the client's behavior as the evaluation session progresses.

Interpretation of Findings

This section of the report should provide a coherent survey of what the examiner is able to glean from the responses, with the following principal areas covered.

Intellectual Components of Personality

This would include any evidence of intellectual impairment; covering intellectual efficiency and potential, the way the client seems to meet practical problems, as well as his or her abstract reasoning ability. Also important would be an assessment of conventional thinking and, by contrast, the capacity to form original ideas. Level of aspiration and range of interests should also be included, as well as some assessment of intellectual ties with reality.

The Emotional Aspects of Personality

Subsumed under this area is a general evaluation of the client's inner resources, drives, controls over such drives, affective conflicts, degree and type of reactivity to emotional stimuli, mood state, presence of anxiety, and an estimate of the appropriateness of responses to emotional stimuli.

Concept of Self

This portion of the report evaluates how critically and realistically the self is regarded. Is the individual inclined to be inordinately expansive, for example, or are there unwarranted propensities for self-derogation? The concept the individual has of his or her psychosexual role and the amount of introspectiveness and self-understanding manifested are also to be included.

Interpersonal Relations

This section would tap attitudes toward males and females of different ages and in a variety of roles. It covers group indentification, general comfortableness in dealing with others, and the types of interactions that are likely to take place within a social context.

Diagnostic Aspects

At the outset it should be mentioned that the writer of a report is probably best advised to think in terms of a more general diagnostic formulation rather than a diagnostic label such as found in *DSM III-R*. A label is a kind of shorthand that is readily understood by professionals in the field; it communicates a considerable amount of information about an individual being assessed in parsimonious fashion. Labeling, however, makes for stereotyping and undercuts the interplay between an individual's basic personality structure and the pathology present. In formulating a diagnostic statement, amount and type of anxiety should be addressed. Reality appreciation should be carefully evaluated; there should be a thorough assessment of the kinds of defense mechanisms operating and their effectiveness in dealing with anxiety and the demands of the environment. It is important that as much or more attention be directed toward the individual's assets as to his or her maladaptive patterns of behavior.

Prognostic Evaluation

This involves an overall assessment of the individual's strengths and weaknesses and an estimate of the adequacy of controls, reality testing, and motivation for self-growth.

Summary and Recommendations

This section should succinctly review the salient features of the report and state recommendations where relevant. Not infrequently, statements about personality not found in the report proper are included in the summary. This is inappropriate. No new material should be included in a summary.

The writing of a Rorschach technique report is clearly a formidable task that demands the investment of much energy and effort. It is not enough to be a highly skilled and perceptive Rorschach evaluator—one must be capable of incorporating and communicating findings in a written report that provides a comprehensible and informative personality assessment of the client. Sample reports are included with protocols in Chapter 16.

▲ 16

Sample Protocols

The following three Rorschach protocols include summary, tabulation, and location sheets. The first and last protocols were obtained by the traditional inquiry technique, with scoring of determinants thus possible. The middle protocol was obtained with the Rorschach Content Technique (see Chapter 11). The three protocols also differ in that the first is from an intact individual who served as a volunteer subject, while the second protocol was obtained from a schizophrenic outpatient; the latter protocol was also part of a larger battery. However, interpretations derived from the other assessments, with the exception of the WAIS, have been deleted from the report on the second test protocol. Reports for each follow the Rorschach protocols. The third protocol was obtained from an elderly subject.

Because of the context of the evaluation, there is no history and background information section in the first report. For didactic purposes, the origin of interpretations is indicated in parentheses in all reports, but under normal circumstances in a clinical, school, or other applied setting, such material would not be included in the report.

Much appreciation is expressed to Betti Schleyer, M.A. of Fordham University, who provided the first Rorschach protocol and report in this chapter.

PROTOCOL #1   Rorschach Response Form for Linda; 38 Years Old; 10/19/79

		Response	Inquiry	Loc	Det	Content	
I. 10"	1.	Well, of course, it's obviously a bf.	1. (a) The bf was the whole thing. (b) The middle part is the body and these are the wings. These would be markings on the wings.	W(S)	F	A	+ P
	2.	Two hands reaching out on top	2. (a) Up here were the hands.	d	M	Hd	+
	3.	A Halloween mask almost like a cat—its eyes and mouth are elongated, pulled out.	3. This was the cat—here are the ears, eyes, nose—the whole thing.	W(S)	F	(Ad)	+
	4.	v I must have Halloween on my mind—I see the mask again—the ears of the cat are at the top. I don't see much more.	4. These would be the eyes—it's more menacing upside down.	W(S)	FM	(Ad)	+
			A1. It almost ll a pumpkin. (a) The whole thing.	W(s)	F	(HD)	+
II. 5"	1.	I see a pretty bf at the bottom—delicate looking.	1. Down here is the bf. (What about it made it look delicate?) The parts of it that seem to fall out from the body—it wasn't just chunky.	D	F	A	+ P
	2.	The middle section almost reminds me of a spaceship.	2. The middle section was the spaceship. This line indicated the part that would come off, the capsule—here's the nose of it.	S	F	SPaceship	+
	3.	These two sections ll two dancing bears holding something in the middle like a candle v>^ that's it.	3. Here were the bears—they're holding something in the middle like a torch or a candle. (b) They looked furry to me and blobby—here's the front leg and the back.	W	FM·Fc	A	+ P

		Response	Inquiry	Loc.	Det.	Content	
			A1. Here on the (location) chart without any color I see a tiger mask—here are the eyes with the pupils, here's the mouth, jowls, but I don't see it on the card with color.	W	F	(Ad)	+
III 5"	1.	I see 2 waiters in a restaurant all dressed up in tuxedoes carrying st. The ll sophisticated, elegant people—almost as if they were puttinG a tablecloth on a table together.	1. Seemed to be like somebody you'd see in a restaurant. Their getup looked elegant to me—like they're putting st on a table.	W	M	H	+ P
	2.	v (laughed) I see 2 Africans—l African because they have large skulls—back to back—doing a dance because 1 foot is up in the air. I don't see the red things as part of it but they're there.	2. They're here—this is 1 foot and the other foot is kicking up in the air—they look African because of the elongated head. They seem to have beards and hair.	W	M	H	+
IV 13"	1.	I don't see anything right off. This is a very menacing picture—it almost ll some kind of monster with padded feet and hands.	1. The whole thing was the monster. (What do you mean by "padded"?) This is all furry and this is more like the paws of a bear—his feet are very large so they just kind of plod around (demonstrates with hands).	W	M·Fc	(A)	+
	2.	v upside down it ll a leaf when the leaves are turned over—the underside doesn't connote beauty because it is dark and isn't that graceful.	2. Like a geranium leaf, a very textured leaf—it has variations in the green like the shading here, like when a leaf turns over like when it's going to rain. The bottom is a lighter color than the rest of the leaf—this part is the turned over part.	W	Fc	Plant	+

239

			Loc.	Det.	Content	Score
3.	v stem of a plant >	3. This part here. (b) Just the general shape.	D	F	Plant	+
V. 8" 1.	A bat—isn't very appealing >v I don't have any response to this, ll a bat. I don't see anything else.	1. The whole thing was the bat. (b) The different parts ll a bat. (c) It's just there.	W	F	A	+ P
VI. 12" 1.	Ll a skin of an animal that you put down as a rug on the floor.	1. I don't remember—like a bearskin rug, just take this part off. Here is the head, paws, hind parts. (b) Just the shape.	W	F	A$_{obj}$	+ P
2.	>v I see at the top st like reaching out like the first card—it's all part of the object but yet they're going beyond the limits of the object— going beyond what's there, reaching out.	2. It looks more like hands on Card I—belonging to it but going beyond it.	de	M	(Hd)	+
3.	^ You can see some sort of totem pole at the top—you have a face and arms sticking out. This section doesn't seem to belong to the rest of the card—it's more graceful.	3. The top part ll a totem pole.	D	F	(H)	+
VII. 6" 1.	Ll 2 women facing each other with a feather sticking up out of their heads—almost as if one was mimicking the other. They're connected, they're wearing a muff.	1. This was the face and the feather— ll they are mimicking each other, almost like their faces are straining forward.	W	M	H	+ P
2.	The second section ll a gargoyle with a horn in the front of their head and you can see the eye and nose.	2. This section here is the gargoyle— here's the eye, nose, mouth, horn— ll st you'd find on an old building carved in stone.	D	Fc	(H)	+

	Free Association	Inquiry	Loc.	Det.	Content	
3.	>v ... the gargoyles upside down ll elephants' heads w trunks but as a whole I don't see anything	Upside down these were the elephants.	D	F	A	+
4.	But the white section ll the top of a decanter where you have the head and neck of the bottle and going into the bottle.	This was the decanter—this is the top and here's the bottle. (b) Just the general shape of it.	S	F	Obj	+
VIII. 20"						
1.	Oh, color. I immediately c 2 rodent animals on either side connected to the mess in the middle but I can't make much of the middle.	These 2 here were rodent-type animals.	D→W	F	A	+ P
2.	v I don't know. The only other thing is the middle section ll somebody's backbone w vertebrae coming out of it—I don't get much else out of it.	Here are the vertebrae, the spinal cord and the vertebrae coming off it.	D(S)	F	At	+ P
IX. 24"						
1.	The section at the top sort of rm of that painting of the unicorn in the Met—the way it almost seems suspended in air as if it were a horse and there were feet dancing up in the air.	The top section reminded me of the unicorn. (b) It's a horse-like animal, its feet are up in the air flailing—it's like some force is holding it suspended in the air.	D	FM.Fm	(A)	+
2.	v Upside down the orange sections ll lobsters. The colors are pleasing to me.	Upside down it ll lobsters—these would be feet and maybe coloring 2.	D	FC	A	+
3.	It ll the green with these fingers on the bottom is reaching out to the pink or wanting to include it in some way.	These things down here were the fingers—ll they were trying to include the pink. Other than that the colors are artistic. I don't c anything else.	D	M	Hd	+

241

X. 5"

#	Response	Inquiry				
1.	A very busy picture—I almost automatically think of spring and flowers, birds, gardens, and bugs.	1. This is what reminded me of spring. Everything is placed as though it were delicate and light—floating.	W	Fm	Nature	+
2.	These 2 brown things ll beetles.	2. These things remind me of brown bugs.	D	FC	A	+
3.	The yellow reminds me of birds.	3. All 4 were birds, kind of floating around. (b) The shape and color and position.	D	FC	A	+
4.	The blue reminds me of spiders, friendly spiders. I wouldn't mind having them around because they're friendly.	4. Here were the spiders—a pleasing kind of bug.	D	FM	A	+ P
5.	The only thing which doesn't fit is the gray section at the top because it kind of detracts from the pleasing aspect of it. v Upside down it reminds me of a flower—the 2 sections of it and the, I guess they're called pistils, on the inside—it almost makes me think of a picture of a plant's reproductive system they'd have in a biology book—the gray could be the roots of it all.	5. This green section reminds me of the reproductive system of a flower.	W	FC	Botany	+
6.	Actually, it reminds of a uterus and ovaries as well.	6. The same section reminds me of a uterus. (b) Just the general shape.	D	F	At	+

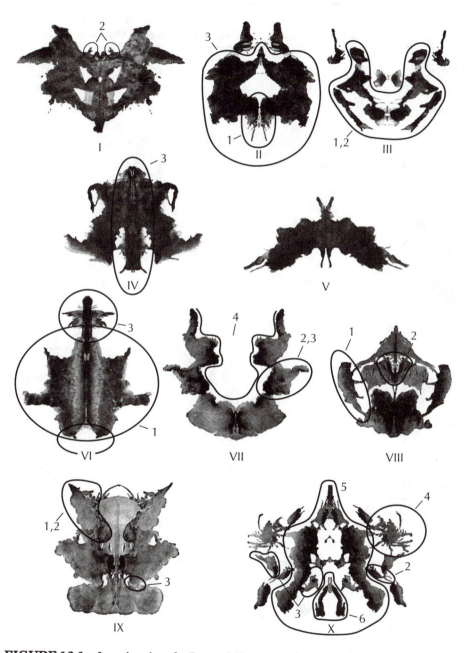

FIGURE 16-1   Location sheet for Protocol #1

PROTOCOL #1 Summary Sheet

		Location	Deter-minants	Content	Form-Level	Populars-Originals	Percept
1.	1.	W(S)	F	A	+	P	Butterfly
10″	2.	d	M	Hd	+		Hands
	3.	W(S)	F	(Ad)	+		Mask
	4.	W(S)	Fm	(Ad)	+		Mask
Add.	5.	W(S)	F	(Hd)	+		Pumpkin
II.	1.	D	F	A	+	P	Butterfly
5″	2.	S	F	Spaceship	+		Spaceship
	3.	W̸	FM·Fc	A	+	P	Bears
Add.	4.	W̸	F	(Ad)	+		Mask
III.	1.	W̸	M	H	+	P	Waiters
5″	2.	W̸	M	H	+		Africans
IV.	1.	W	M·Fc	(A)	+		Monster
13″	2.	W	Fc	Plant	+		Leaves
	3.	D	F	Plant	+		Stem
V.	1.	W	F	A	+	P	Bat
8″					+		
VI.	1.	W̸	F	A_obj	+	P	Skin
12″	2.	de	M	(Hd)	+		Something
					+		reaching
	3.	D	F	(H)	+		Totem poole
VII.	1.	W	M	H	+	P	Women
6″	2.	D	Fc	(H)	+		Gargoyles
	3.	D	F	A	+		
	4.	S	F	Obj	+		Decanter
VIII.	1.	D	F	A	+	P	Rodents
20″	2.	D(S)	F	At	+	P	Vertebrae
IX.	1.	D	FM·Fm	(A)	+		Unicorn
24″	2.	D	FC	A	+		Lobster
	3.	D	M	Hd	+		Fingers
X.	1.	W	Fm	Nature	+		Garden
5″	2.	D	FC	A	+		Beetles
	3.	D	FC	A	+		Birds
	4.	D	FM	A	+	P	Spiders
	5.	W̸	FC	Botany	+		Flowers
	6.	D	F	At	+		Uterus

PROTOCOL #1   Tabulation Sheet

Location		Determinants			Content	
W	5	F	13(+2)		H	3
W(S)	3(+1)	M	6		(H)	2
Wˣ	5(+1)	FM	1		Hd	2(+1)
		Fm	2		(Hd)	1
D	13	Fc	2			
D(S)	1	FC	4		A	10
		Multiple	3		A	2
d	1	Deter-			(Ad)	2(+1)
de	1	minants				
		FM·Fc	M·Fc	FM·Fm	At	2
S	2				Masks	2
					Plant	2

Number of responses	31(+2)	W:M	13:7
Rejections: Cards		Sum C	2
Number of Populars	10	M:sum C	7:2
Number of originals		m:c	6:4
Average R/T chromatic	11.8″	VIII-X%	35
Average R/T achromatic	9.8″	FK+F+Fc%	55
F%	42	(H+A):(Hd+Ad)	17:5
F+%	100		
A%	45		
H%	26		

ApperceptionW 42%D 45%d 3%Dd+S 10%

PSYCHOLOGICAL REPORT

NAME: _____Linda_____ AGE: ___38___ DATE: ___10/19/79___

Technique Administered

Rorschach technique

Behavioral Observations

Linda was neatly dressed, as is appropriate to her job as a guidance counselor in a parochial school. She was friendly and helpful to the examiner, offering coffee both before and after the procedure. She displayed a small amount of tension before the testing began, but this dissipated during the course of the session. She referred several times to the emotional or aesthetic impact the cards had on her, with statements such as, "This isn't very appealing." She had volunteered to take the Rorschach and stated afterwars that it had been an interesting experience; she thanked the examiner sincerely.

Interpretation of Findings

Linda is currently operating at an intellectual level of average to very superior (A% = 45, W = 13). However, her limited range of interests and lack of flexibility in her approach to new situations interfere with an optimum realization of her intellectual potential (A% = 45, F% = 42). She tends to rely upon an overemphasis on conventionality (P = 10), although she is capable of being receptive and responsive to the outside world (R = 31), at least in a mechanical way (sum C = 2). She is able to handle practical problems (D% = 45) and shows good organizational ability (W% = 42), but perhaps over-emphasizes global approaches at the expense of attending to small details (d% = 3). Although she has an active fantasy life (Card VII—gargoyle, Card IX—unicorn), her intellectual ties to reality are unwavering (F + % = 100). She displays a level of aspiration appropriate to her abilities (W:M = 13:7) and is able to draw on her inner resources when necessary (7 M's, M's usually good form). Apparently finding her impulses threatening, Linda is quick to impose intellectual controls on her affective reactions, which results in a lack of spontaneity (14 A's to 8 H's, but only 5 FM's to 7M's—therefore avoids use of FM much more than M, sum C = 2, all FC). This suppression and denial of both the awareness and expression of impulses contributes to conflict and tension, with impulses striving to be acknowledged perceived as destructive outside forces that threaten the organization of her personality (Fm = 3). She appears to be struggling to maintain her personality integrity in the face of these forces. This inner conflict and related feelings of vulnerability prevent her from fully attaining her creative potential and lead her to respond to new situations in a stereotyped way, at least initially (F responses usually given first).

This conflict also prevents Linda from fully attending to the outer world, especially in terms of its emotional impact (F = 13, sum C = 2). Her self-control is achieved at the expense of emotional involvement (M:sum C = 7:2, F% = 42). She often views the world impersonally (F% = 42), although her interpersonal sensitivity (Fc = 4) does allow her, at least superficially, to achieve friendly relationships (F% = 42, FK + F + Fc% = 55, CF = 0). It is difficult for her to respond to emotional stimuli in general (longest RT to Cards VIII and IX), and she experiences particular inability to deal effectively with emerging dysphoric feelings (partial rejection of Card V). She is intellectually self-assertive and may also tend to be somewhat self-critical (W(S) + D(S) + S = 5, (H) = 2, Hd = 2, (Hd) = 1).

Linda's self-preoccupation gives rise to a degree of impairment in object relations (threatening masks on Cards I and II, monster on Card IV). Consistent with the fact that she is in a religious order that demands chastity is evidence of a lack of interest in, and/or fear of emotional involvement with men (perceived Card IV as "menacing," had trouble seeing anything in Card IV at all, cut off the phallic part of Card VI instead of integrating it into a W response). On the other hand, some concern with the general issue of generativity and childbearing is apparent (reproductive system responses to Card X).

There are several significant indications that Linda is experiencing strong needs to make changes in her life. She is aware of her need for the acceptance and approval of others and has accepted this need (Fc = 4, mostly furry). She is also aware that this need has been frustrated in the past (subjective shading disturbance), and that emotional stimulation can be pleasant (positive comment on colors of Card IX). Within the framework of her good social skills (FC = 4, FC:CF + C = 4:0) and empathetic ability (7M, 3H) she is frequently able to lower her defenses in social situations (less constricted in Inquiry phase than Association phase). Most reflective of her strivings for greater interpersonal and affective gratification is her response to Card I: "two hands reaching out on top." In the same vein on Card VI, she saw: "At the top something . . . part of the object but yet going beyond the limits of the object—going beyond what's there, reaching out." Finally, one of her percepts to Card IX was: "It looks like the green with these fingers on the bottom is reaching out to the pink or wanting to include it in some way." She clearly feels a need to "go beyond the limits" of her comparatively constricted personality and, from the rest of her record, it appears likely that she has the emotional strength and inner resources to do so.

Summary and Recommendations

Linda is an intelligent, well-organized woman with good inner resources. However, at this time she is overcontrolled and there is conflict over the expression of her feelings and impulses. While she has more adequate social skills, she feels easily threatened and vulnerable in interpersonal situations and may, therefore, generally limit the degree of her involvement with others. She is currently experiencing a sense of personal dissatisfaction and is engaged in a process of self-assessment with justified confidence that she can identify assets that will enable her to derive more gratification from her interactions with the environment. This client would have a good prognosis in counseling, should she be so inclined.

		Response	Inquiry	Loc.	Cont.	FQ	P
I. 10"	1.	What people eat—I only know the word in German—crab. (Some people see more than one thing. Do you see anything else?).	It makes me think of food (What does food call to mind?). Food is poisoned. (What do you mean?). I'm always afraid that food is poisoned—even I thought that bananas are injected with poison—I never taste food from a stranger or someone I don't know very well.	W	A	+	
	2.	"Adler" in German—an eagle.	High in the air. (What does that call to mind?). An airplane. (What does an airplane make you think of?). Having a crash—I'm always afraid that airplanes will crash.	W	A	+	
II. 22"	1.	I don't see anything—I have no imagination. I'd say it's an animal.	An animal can be a sweet thing— and it can be a beastlike lions in a jugnle—when kept in a house—it's very sweet and loving. (What does that bring to mind?). Depression.	D	A	+	
	2.	A dog.	They're kissing each other (What does that bring to mind?). Sex. (What does that make you think of?). Masturbation. Some people masturbate because they can't get fulfillment with other people. (What does that make you think of in your own life?). A doctor once when I was 19 asked if I masturbated and I said I don't know what it is—I went home and tried it out. It was a stupid question—he made me do it.				P

		Response	Inquiry	Loc	Cont		
				W	H	+	P+
III. 25"	1.	Two persons playing ball.	Childhood. (What does that make you think of?). Loneliness (?). I never had any friends. (Why?). Because I was with foster parents—I had a laot of food I didn't want—I never was hungry, I never wanted to eat (Find one more thing that this blot might look like). They don't have heads like persons—they're like animals in caricature. (What does that make you think of?). They're good-natured.				
				D	Obj	+	P
IV. 45"	1.	This ll 2 pairs of boots.	A pair of boots is sadistic. (What does that make you think of?). Getting hit. (What does that call to mind?). Getting hit. (What does that call to mind?). When I was 7, a mother always was spanking her little girl with a stick—I imagined I was her.				
	2.	That—I DK what it is—It ll a jumpsuit.	It's itchy—every material bothers me. (What does that remind you of?). Wool. I could never wear wool—I was forced screaming into wool sweaters—I couldn't wear them.				
				W	Food		
V. 35"	1.	2 pieces of meat.	Makes me think of throwing it in the toilet. When I was a little girl, I threw it in the toilet. I could never eat meat. (What does your not eating meat call to mind?). I could get stuck in my throat, and people die. (Find one more thing that this blot might resemble. (It looks like a				

Card	No.	Response	Inquiry	Loc	Content	FQ
VI 26"	1.	A bf.	butterfly. (What does a butterfly remind you of?) Pulling out their wings when I was a little girl. (What does that remind you of?) I was a sadistic fiend I guess—generally I'm very kind to animals.	W	A	+
	1.		No—I didn't pull out their wings—I would catch them, put them in a box, and give them food—I never pulled out their wings. (Find one more thing that this blot might look like.) It's shaped like a leaf. (What does that make you think of?) Plants and growing—plants never grow in my apartment—there's always darkness in my apartment.	D	A	+
VII. 55"	1.	I'd say animals—but there's a tail up on their head—they don't look right.	1. I don't know—it doesn't make sense.	D	Na	
	2.	It could be a dance on the snow.	2. Falling down. (What does that make you think of in your own life?) I was falling down when I was ice-skating—I never went on the ice again.	D	(H)	
	3.	This all 11 embryos to me. All the cards 11 this.	3. Children. (What does that make you think of?) I'm glad I don't have any—I'm sick, I can't give them an education—I'm glad I don't have children, but I love them very much.			
VIII. 3"	1.	This is a skeleton of a human body.	1. A dead person. (What does that make you think of?) My father died before I was born—I still love him.	W	A+	

		Response	Inquiry			
IX. 50"	1.	This is a candle.	(What does that call to mind?) A lot of sadness—for my mother too—she then didn't want to have me anymore. (Find one more thing that the blot might resemble. (2 fishes. (What do they make you think of?) Nothing special—a fish has to be in the water. There are some very nice fish around. I don't like to eat fish because they have bones.	d	Obj	—
	2.	A glass vase with water, flowers are around.	1. Romance. In restaurants when I was younger—I used to be very happy. (What does that remind you of?) Being in love—it's a wonderful feeling.	W	Bot	
			2. It's just romantic.			
X. 15"	1.	They all have the same shape. This ll a flower	1. Makes me think of being in love—a person gvets flowers when they're in love—a beautiful garden of flowers in the sun. (What does such a garden make you think of in your own live?) There will always be darkness in my life—except for childhood. But I didn't want to go into the garden—I always wanted to be in the room—It was safer.	D	Bot	
	2.	An insect.	2. An insect—a bee who has bitten me several times in the garden—I had a swollen foot and I couldn't go to school.	D	A	+

252

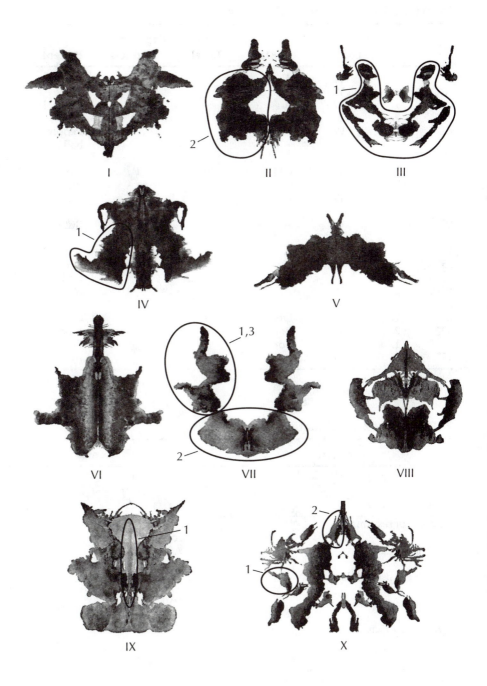

PROTOCOL #2   Summary Sheet

		Location	Content	Form-Level	Populars—Originals	Percept
I.	1.	W	A	+		Crab
10″	2.	W	A	+		Eagle
II.	1.	W	A	−		Animal
22″	2.	D	A	+	P	dog
III.	1.	W	H	+	P	People playing ball
25″						
IV.	1.	D	Obj	+	P	Pair of boots
45″	2.	W	Obj	+		Jumpsuit
V.	1.	W	Food			Pieces of meat
35″						
VI.	1.	W	A	−		Butterfly
26″						
VII.	1.	D	A	+		Animal
55″	2.	D	Nat			Snow
	3.	D	(H)			Embryo
VIII.	1.	W	At	−		Skeleton
3″						
IX.	1.	d	Obj	+		Candle
50″	2.	W	Bot	−		Vase of flowers
X.	1.	D	Bot			Flower
15″	2.	D	A	+		Insect

PROTOCOL #2   Tabulation Sheet

Location		Content	
W	9	H	1
D	7	(H)	1
d	1	A	7

Number of responses	17	Average R/T achromatic	34.2
Rejections: Cards	0	A%	41
Number of popopulars	3	H%	12
Number of originals	0	VIII-X%	29
Average R/T chromatic	21.6		

Apperception	W 53%	D 41%	d 6%

PSYCHOLOGICAL REPORT

NAME: _____Ida_____   **AGE:** ___44___   **DATE:** ___2/3/77___

Techniques and Tests Administered

Rorschach technique, WAIS, TAT, Bender Gestalt test, Rotter Incomplete Sentences Blank, Psychological Data sheet, Figure Drawing.[1]

History and Background Information

This patient first came to a hospital in 1965, at which time she was described as suspicious of people, withdrawn, unable to do office work. The patient has had two hospitalizations in the past.

The patient was born in Germany; her father died before her birth. The mother was reportedly depressed and suffered "bad health" after the patient's birth. A stepsister was reported to have had arguments with the mother about boyfriends. The patient liked this sister, who was attentive to her. In 1940, the patient was evacuated from Germany to a foster home in another country because of the war. The patient states that she later learned that a further reason for this evacuation was the fact that her mother was half Jewish. The patient states that, "I was very unhappy about being sent away and thought at that time that my mother had abandoned me." A "key scene" she recalls from her childhood involved her foster mother telling her that she did not love the patient anymore.

The patient's schooling was interrupted as a result of the war; she states that she terminated school in the eighth grade. She held various typing and secretarial jobs following the war, arriving in the United States in 1959. Since that time, she worked as a secretary. The patient is single and has never married.

The patient states that she has a "sleeping problem" and usually doesn't get up before 1 o'clock. "Sometimes I stay in bed all day because I feel sick." The patient complains of severe headaches, palpitations, and sweating. She also describes herself as withdrawn, with minimal social life.

Behavioral Observations

The patient is a tall, thin woman who arrived appropriately and well dressed for her session. She spoke English with a thick German accent; she spoke in a flat, emotionless voice throughout the session.

---

[1]To demonstrate the applications of the Content Rorschach, only the WAIS and the Rorschach are used to document interpretive statements in this illustrative case report.

The patient immediately began excusing her performance as the session began. She stated that she was "not a good talker," had no imagination, was very sick, had little education, and so on, and that the examiner would have to take these facts into account. She often gave up easily on tasks; she would sometimes continue if the examiner insisted.

The patient had little emotional contact with the examiner; she avoided eye contact and largely just responded to questions and directions. She was, however, observant of what went on in the session. At one point, when the examiner took out a handkerchief, she blurted out, "Do you have a cold?" While the patient generally avoided interacting with the examiner, when testing was concluded, she gave a shy smile and shook the examiner's hand before leaving.

The patient completed all tasks presented to her. She also took several tests home with her and later returned them; she typed in extensive answers to questions about her background history.

Interpretation of Findings

On the WAIS, the patient obtained a verbal IQ of 78, a performance IQ of 70, and a full-scale IQ of 73. This places her present level of intellectual functioning in the borderline mental defective range.

From her scores on subtests, however, it seems likely that her premorbid level of functioning lies in the average range. Her scores were considerably lowered by the high degree of confusion present at this time, by her different cultural background, by her relatively low level of education, and also by her poor frustration tolerance. The patient performed best on tasks involving some social skills. Her ability to abstract and her capacity to distinguish essential from unessential details are also among the best preserved of her abilities.

Ego functioning is problematic at times. Reality testing sometimes fails under stress (extended F + %), resulting in distorted perceptions of the environment. Object relations also show some impairment (low H%, past and present described social isolation—e.g., see comment regarding few childhood friends on Card III). There is also evidence of difficulty maintaining the defense of repression, resulting in the eruption of inappropriate and sometimes primitive material into consciousness (masturbation comments on response II-1, comment on Card VII that "all the cards look like embryos," presence of Rorschach Confabulations).

The patient is an individual who has been deeply scarred by the early events of her life (repeated references to trauma in associations to percepts). While she longs for close relationships with people, she also associates "oral supplies" with danger and hurt ("poison" association to food on Card I, negative association to food on Card III, reference to food getting stuck in the throat on Card V). It seems likely that the patient's perceived rejection by her mother and her stepparents is connected with her reluctance to accept affection (reference to rejection by both parents on Card VIII-1). The patient consequently insulates herself from potential hurt with her guarded, insulated defensive style ("crab" as her first Rorschach percept, almost phobic reaction to wool sweaters on Card IV-2, and patient's general demeanor during testing).

While the patient is frightened of receiving affection and attention from others, she is also unfortunately in the position of wanting it desperately. She appears to still manage to get gratifications from others in two ways. First, the patient seems to find it acceptable to get sympathy and concern from people through her "sickness," that is, through display of symptoms, both mental and physical. Second, the patient seems to be gratified by attention from others that is accomplished by aggression; a sadomasochistic orientation is seen (comments on IV-1, V-1, and VI-1 about sadistic boots and tearing the wings off butterflies). An early association of physical abuse with parental attentiveness is reported (comments on IV-1 about envying a girl who was being spanked).

The patient has difficulty accepting her basic drives, both sexual and aggressive (airplane crashing on Card I-2, and nonacceptance of masturbation on Card II-2). A primary means by which she deals with her unacceptable impulses is through the defense of projection, resulting in the paranoid flavor that suffuses her record (eagle and poisoned food comment on Card I, projection seen in masturbation associations in response II-2).

Significant depression is seen. The patient clearly experiences her present life as rather cold and unsatisfying (comments about plants not growing for her, snowdance, and darkness in her life in responses VI-1, VII-2, and X-1, respectively). However, it should also be noted that some hope and potential for better social and general life functioning are present (more optimistic associations and comments on cards IX and X, patient's tentative "engaging" with the examiner at the conclusion of testing).

While the patient "uses" her sickness to get attention and caring from others and may thus tend to magnify her complaints, those working with her must recognize that she is nonetheless fragile and seriously disturbed. At times the distinction between reality and fantasy is blurred for this patient (contradictory comments about whether she tore the wings off butterflies on Cards V and VI). The general diagnostic impression is one of schizophrenia, paranoid type.

Summary and Recommendations

This patient's verbal IQ of 78, performance IQ of 70, and full-scale IQ of 73 place her present level of intellectual functioning in the borderline mental defective range. Mental confusion, poor frustration tolerance, a low level of schooling, and her cultural background are all contributants to these low scores. Her premorbid level appears to lie in the average range. Ego functioning is poor, with problems seen in reality testing, object relations, and the maintenance of repression. Perceptual disturbances associated with schizophrenia are present.

This patient is deeply distrustful of others. She has withdrawn from relationships to narcissistic self-preoccupation. She rejects oral supplies from others, which is probably traceable to early rejection by her mother. While she is frightened of the oral supplies, she still craves them. She accepts attention from others through sympathy for her symptoms and when the attention she wants is linked with aggression (i.e., through masochism on her part). She has great difficulty accepting her basic sexual and aggressive drives, projecting them onto others, resulting in strong paranoid trends. While her desire for sympathy from others may result in her magnifying her symptoms, it must be kept in mind that she is nonetheless fragile and seriously disturbed. The diagnostic impression is one of schizophrenia, paranoid type.

The patient needs a long-term psychotherapy relationship with a supportive therapist who can gradually bring her out of her shell while at the same time shoring up ego defenses. Her therapist should continually be aware of the fragility of this patient's adjustment. Participation in a supportive socialization group might also be considered at some point, given her loneliness and her desire for closer relationships with other people. Biofeedback might also be considered as an adjunctive procedure for her headaches; however, the use to which she puts her physical symptoms must also be kept in mind.

PROTOCOL #3   Rorschach Response Form for Carol; 76 Years Old; 1/9/92

I. 4"	1.	Bird of some sort. these things are wings. There is a head with horns and a slight tail. It's like a bird of prey.	1. Ll bird because of the wings. Wings seemed to be spread out. Some birds have different layers of wings. These are horns or feelers. They help them balance so they can attach themselves to something.	W	Fc	A	+
II. 16"	1.	This is cute. It ll two heads of dogs. Two cute little dogs standing on hind legs.	1. The eyes and the snout make it ll a dog. Connected with something so they are balancing—performing dogs. Here are ears and feet. If performing, what are they doing? Toenails on feet. Ll an eye because of indentation with white spot for eyes. Ll ears because one would be on near side and other on far side.	D(S)	FM	A	—
	2.	I don't know what the red spots are supposed to be. I can't see anything in the red spots. Ll some little gadget. I can't associate them with little dogs.	2. I still don't know what the red is.	D	C/F	Obj	
III. 35"	1.	(Laughs.) I can't connect these all together. A couple of people trying to balance themselves. At first they looked ll they are being blown with the wind.	1. Ll people because they have head, neck, body parts, arms, and legs. Ll they are alancing because of wind—it's the position they are in—or, they could be bending over. Top part ll a jacket/coat and this is the pants. The shape of the coat and the pocket—differences in color and part white.	D	MF·Fm·FC	H	+ P

	Response	Inquiry	Location	Determinant	Content	
III.	A1.	This is crazy. I told you I was an R.N. This ll a pelvis with vertebrae.	A1. This could be a spinning thing that they are trying to control.	D	mF	Obj	+
	A2.		A2. This could be a fan they are holding.	d	M	Obj	+
	2.	Red spot in the middle is a bow or a tie.	2. Dark down the middle is vertebrae. White spot in the middle is the disk.	(D)S	FC'	Hd	+ P
	3.	These hanging down don't connect with picture at all. Ll chicken with a long, long tail. Chicken don't have long, long, tails. If I look at it right side up, it ll it's falling off of something.	3. Knot is in the middle and these two loops are loop parts. Not have streamers down so it's like a bow tie.	D	F	Obj	+
∧∨	4.		4. Now I'm wondering what made it ll at a chicken, which it did when I first looked at it. It's a chicken with combs or feathers on top. Ll a comb because of little nib nabs—specks on top. When picture right side up, it ll it's falling because it's upside down.	D	Fm	A	+
IV. 39"	1.	They don't get easier as they go along. Whatever it is, I don't know. This ll something that has big feet. There are two feet. Center part could be a spinal column. I don't see a head. Kind of a furry thing. Upside down it doesn't ll anything. Top part ll a part of a arm (out of proportion with the rest). There's a difference in color—in shading. Some of fur is light and some is dark.	1. Feet look out of proportion. Ll spinal column because of straight lines going down like bone. Could be a tail, too. Whole thing is fur—the shading of gray to black makes it ll that. Ll arm because it's the top of the animal and it is bent out and I can't think of what else it could be.	W	Fc	(A)	+
	A1.	This ll a beak on something else. It is shaped like a beak, like a "V" pointing down.	A1. This ll a beak on something else. It is shaped like a beak, like a "V" pointing down.	dd	F	Ad	+

	Response	Inquiry				
V. 2" 1. ∧∨	(Smiles.) How pretty. Bf. I saw them in our garden this summer. There are tentacles on either side and the wings are spread apart. I like it upside down better.	Ll bf because of antennaes/feelers and wings. It is graceful looking. Wings are spread apart.	W	F	A	+ P
> 2.	These two things ll chicken legs separate from the bf. (Laughs.) Roasted/toasted.	Ll cooked chicken because of the shape of the bone and knob. Here's the meat. Ll cooked because of how it looks when I cook them.	d	F	Food	+
VI. 17" 1.	At first glance I would say it ll a fur rug hanging on the wall.	Ll fur rug because ll something I've seen. Ll fur because of colors and shading.	D	Fc	Aobj	+
2.	(Turns card around for a while). Top part not ll rug on wall but I don't know what it is. I can almost see two eyes, and a long beak or nose in between and little things—whiskers—under head.	Ll eyes because of two little light-colored spots. Dark part going down is nose/beak—the line in middle. The two thing ll whiskers just because they are thin and sticking out of head.	d	cF	Ad	+
3.	Ll a scarf or shawl extending. Not arms but feathers or wings of some sort. There is a shading of colors from light to medium to dark. Enough of that guy.	Ll shawl because like thin silky material. Silky because of light coloring on outside—very light, not heavy at all.	D	Fc	Obj	+
A1.		Ll asparagus spears—crispy or fresh because taut. Bottom 2 are wilted ones.	dd	F	Food	+

		Free Association	Inquiry				
VII.	17"						
	1.	They are not connected at all. The top 2 ll fried shrimp. Throws me for a loop, but it's the first thing I thought of. What the rest ll, I don't know.	1. Ll shrimp because of shape. When have batter, they ll they're puffed up. Wouldn't be bad to have for dinner. Looks fried because of irregularity of shape.	D	Fk	Food	+
	2.	The more I look at it, I see 2 things down here. Ll something with ears, eyes, nose, and mouth. Don't know what it is. Long ears like a bunny. I know what it is. Rest of face not like a bunny. I know it's paper folded over so both sides are the same.	2. Ll eyes because I can almost see pupils—slanted and white in background and dot in middle is pupils. Nose is protruded out. Color not mean much on this. At the end of the nose are black nostrils. There's a tooth in mouth that shines; it's white. Ll mouth is open so see tooth.	D	FC·FM	Ad	+
	3.	I don't think anything about the center part. After looking at it for a long time though, the center part ll eyes looking at me, mouth and teeth in the mouth. Bottom one got me—can't figure it out.	3. I can't remember saying that. Can't see anything there.	Denial			
VIII.	28"						
	1.	This is so pretty. 2 pink animals. There are the head, legs, and tail. They are moving, walking, climbing	1. Ll animals because have head, body, tails, and legs. Ll head because of shape of head and has a mouth. I don't see eyes. Could be ear sticking up. See 3 legs and a tail.	D	FM	A	+ P
	2.	Maybe the top is a tree of some sort. Can't see these 2 big animals climbing up a tree. But it's just a guess.	2. Ll a tree because it grows up to a point. I'm trying to associate it with 2 animals. Maybe it is a separate thing.	D	F	Pl	+

	Response	Inquiry	Loc	Det	Content	
A1.		A rope holding onto bottom things. Bottom is suspended by the top.	dd	mF	Obj	+
3.	These 2 bottom things could be rocks, but they never would be that color unless come from unknown place I haven't heard of. (Laughs.) Not relateld at all to whole thing.	The irregularity of them, the edge makes them ll rocks. Saw rocks that ll them in Colorado.	D	F/C	N	+
4.	I think this is torn cloth. It's being torn apart.	The color makes it ll cloth. Ll someone tried to rip it apart and these are threads that aren't ripped.	D	Fm	Obj	+
IX. 25"						
1.	This is the right side up, huh. (Laughs.) I'm supposed to see something? The colors are orange, green, pink, and are pretty. Ll a Painting. Ll modern art.	The whole thing ll modern art—the colors make it look that way.	W	CF	Art	—
2.	This ll some kind of spiral going up in the center. It's a little cloudy (or paint rubbed around a little). I can't make out anything definite. I don't see anything definite in the whole thing. I can't figure anything out except modern art. I worked in elementary school with kids who dis this!	Looks cloudy because looks smudged in comparison to other parts.	D	c	N	—
X. 22"						
1.	I see all kinds of things in this one without studying it—just looking at it quickly. Blue things ll crabs if don't study it. It's caught something in its claws. Just an oval thing. I can't name it. Maybe it's a leaf curled up.	Ll crabs because has lots of claws. Ll leaf because of color and it's curled up and is an irregular shape.	D D	FM FC	A Pl	+ P +

No.	Response	Response (Inquiry)	Loc	Det	Content	FQ
2.	Bottom green thing is an archway to something. Wherever you go, you walk through there.	The shape makes it ll an archway. It's an entrance way tht looks inviting. Go in and see what's inside. Looks fancy like Dallas. Dallas's symbol is horns. Ll horns because two straight things sticking up; it's the shape.	D	FK	Archi	+
3.	If I study it real closely, I almost see a face. Head of a youngster with a bonnet and thing sticking out. Just a head. Not connected with rest of what's down there.	I don't remember where I saw this or saying it.	Deni al			
4.	I see glasses if I look quickly. See nosepiece and ear things. Not ll it if I study it.	Ll glasses because of the shape.	D	F	Obj	+
5.	These two things ll what football players put under their chin. I hate football. Things go under chin so they don't get knocked crazy.	Ll those things because they're brown. Looks convexed, oval shape with thin strips.	D	FK·FC	Obj	−
6.	These two yellow things ll high-heeled shoes. I don't know what the orange things are.	Ll high-heeled shoes because of archway, heel, and instep. People wear them now; ankle-high shoes are in.	D	F	Clothing	+
A1.		Flowers growing out of something. Ll flowers because have petals and stems. Ll petals because of shape.	dd	F	Pl	+

PROTOCOL #3   Tabulation Sheet

Location		Determinants		Content	
W	4	F	6(+2)	H	1
		M	(+1)	Hd	1
D	19(+1)	FM	3		
D(S)	2	Fm	2	A	6
		mF	(+2)	(A)	1
dd	(+4)	Fk	1	Ad	2(+1)
		FK	1		
		Fc	4		6(+3)
		cF	1	Obj	1
		c	1	A Obj	
		FC'	1		2
		FC	1	Nature	2(+1)
		F/C	1	Plants	1
		CF	1	Architecture	1
		C/F	1	Clothing	2(+1)
		Multiple Determinants		Food	
			M·Fm·Fc		
			FC'·FM		
			FK·FC		

Number of Responses	27(+5)	Obj%	26
Rejections: Cards	None	W:M	4:1
Number of populars	5	Sum C	3
Number of originals	0	M:sum C	1:3
Average R/T chromatic	37.2″	m:c	5:7
Average R/T achromatic	15.8″	VIII–X%	44
F%	22	FK+F+Fc%	41
F+%	91	(H+A):(Hd+Ad)	7:3
A%	33		
H%	7		

Apperception(W): 15%D: 78%d: 7%Dd+S: 0%

PSYCHOLOGICAL REPORT

NAME: ___Carol___   **AGE:** __76__   **DATE:** __1/9/92__

Technique Administered

Rorschach technique

Behavioral Observations

Carol was nicely dressed and well spoken. She is a high school graduate who subsequently became a registered nurse and worked in the field for two years and then married and became a full-time homemaker. She has several children and grandchildren.

During testing, Carol evidenced a great deal of anxiety in her words and her actions. She was concerned about responding correctly and glanced frequently at the examiner as well as voicing her uncertainty aloud. She responded well to mild reassurance by becoming more daring with the task, for example, turning the card around to look for other associations and noting additional percepts during the Inquiry phase. The entire administration took 1 1/2 hours, during which Carol was very patient and cooperative.

Interpretation of Findings

Carol is currently functioning at a somewhat above average level (R = 27 (+5); utilizes a variety of determinants with satisfactory form). Her approach to intellectually challenging situations is largely a common-sense, pragmatic one (D = 78%). She tends to be characteristically a bit self-doubting, feeling that interrelationships and "connections" in her environment tend to elude her (a number of responses that did not "connect"; denied several responses in the inquiry). At the same time, concerned with her self-presentation, Carol may typically strive to move beyond mere minimal compliance with the cognitive demands made of her (5 additionals).

There are strong indications that Carol is overly sensitive to the world around her (Fc = 4) and may initially react to it in a highly emotional manner (M:sum C = 1:3). However, her excellent reality appreciation (F + % = 91) quickly moves to the fore and she endeavors to distance herself from her disruptive feelings and to treat them almost as if they were essentially abstract concepts (F/C and C/F responses, Card IX—"modern art"; long R/T chromatic).

At this juncture, Carol very anxiously views her surroundings as potentially quite threatening (many shading percepts; "bird of prey" on Card I) and her own life as now rather overwhelming and unstable ("balancing" percepts on Cards I, II, and III). She experiences acute needs for emotional sustenance at basic levels (numerous food and mouth responses) but feels removed from others (only 1M and 1H) and without their genuine support. Her interpersonal contacts may not infrequently leave her with the sense that she is like the "performing dogs" she saw on Card II, striving to win approval.

While Carol retains a definite capacity to see positive aspects of her environment (Card V—"graceful looking" butterfly; Card X—flowers), she feels as if she has been pulled in opposite directions by powerful, destructive forces and damaged in the process (Card VIII—cloth, being torn or ripped apart). In a defensive effort to maintain some degree of self-integrity, she projects her inner distress onto the world, which takes on a transiently even more negative coloration. Mobilizing massive denial, however, she then manages to largely dispel her dysphoric outlook and replace it with a more hopeful one (Card VII—"eyes looking at me, mouth and teeth," but then rejects percept and sees the next card as "so pretty"). There is some evidence that she may have some troubling somatic concerns that she endeavors to intellectualize on the basis of being an "R.N." (Card III—"pelvis with vertabrae"; Card IV—"spinal column").

Summary

Carol is a woman with good intellectual resources and reality testing, who fundamentally approaches life in a very practical manner. Currently she is distressingly experiencing herself as in a state of some disequilibrium in endeavoring to cope with a world perceived as rather uncaring and at times even hostile. She has a great deal of social sensitivity but now apprehensively views herself as largely without the basic emotional support from others she desperately needs. Although she often feels very anxious, with some indications of specific health concerns, she can contain her apprehensions and manage a more positive outlook at least for a delimited period.

▲ References

Alcock, T. (1963). *The Rorschach in practice.* Philadelphia: Lippincott.

Allen, J. G. (1981). The clinical psychologist as a diagnostic consultant. *Bulletin of the Menninger Clinic, 45,* 247–258.

Allen, R. M. (1966). *Student's Rorschach manual.* New York: International Universities Press.

Allport, G. W. (1937). *Personality: A psychological interpretation.* New York: Henry Holt & Company.

Allport, G. W. (1961). *Pattern and growth in personality.* New York: Holt, Rinehart & Winston.

Allport, G. W. (1962). The general and the unique in psychological science. *Journal of Personality, 30,* 405–422.

American Hospital Association. (1987). *Hospital statistics.* Chicago: Author.

American Psychological Association. (1985). *Standards for educational and psychological testing.* Washington, DC: Author.

Ames, L. B. (1975). Are Rorschach responses influenced by society's change? *Journal of Personality Assessment, 39,* 439–452.

Ames, L. B., Metraux, R. W., Rodell, J. L., & Walker, R. N. (1973). *Rorschach responses in old age* (rev. ed.). New York: Brunner-Mazel.

Ames, L. B., Metraux, R. W., Rodell, J. L., & Walker, R. N. (1974). *Child Rorschach responses* (rev. ed.). New York: Brunner-Mazel.

Ames, L. B., Metraux, R. W., & Walker, R. N. (1971). *Adolescent Rorschach responses* (rev. ed.). New York: Brunner-Mazel.

Anastasi, A. (1976). *Psychological testing* (4th ed.). New York: Macmillan.

Anastasi, A. (1988). *Psychological testing* (6th ed.). New York: Macmillan.

Appelbaum, S. A. (1965). The effect of altered psychological atmosphere on Rorschach responses: A new supplementary procedure. In M. Kornrich (Ed.), *Psychological test modifications.* Springfield, IL: Thomas. (Reprinted from *Bulletin of the Menninger Clinic, 1959, 23,* 179–189.)

Appelbaum, S. A. (1990). The relationship between assessment and psychotherapy. *Journal of Personality Assessment, 54,* 791–801.

Arnow, D., & Cooper, S. H. (1984). The borderline patient's regression on the Rorschach test. *Bulletin of the Menninger Clinic, 35,* 25–36.

Aronow, E., & Reznikoff, M. (1971). Application of projective tests to psycho-therapy: A case study. *Journal of Personality Assessment, 35,* 379–393.

Aronow, E., & Reznikoff, M. (1973). Attitudes toward the Rorschach test expressed in book reviews: A historical perspective. *Journal of Personality Assessment, 37,* 309–315.

Aronow, E., & Reznikoff, M. (1976). *Rorschach content interpretation.* New York: Grune & Stratton.

Aronow, E., & Reznikoff, M. (1983). *A Rorschach introduction: Content and perceptual approaches.* New York: Grune & Stratton.

Aronow, E., Reznikoff, M., & Rauchway, A. (1979). Some old and new directions in Rorschach testing. *Journal of Personality Assessment, 43,* 227–234.

Arthur, B. (1965). The forced confabulation technique: An extension of the Rorschach method for use with children. In M. Kornich (Ed.), *Psychological test modifications.* Springfield, IL: Thomas.

Bartlett, F. C. (1916). An experimental study of some problems of perceiving and imaging. *British Journal of Psychology, 8,* 222–226.

Bauman, G., & Roman, M. (1968). Interaction product analysis in group and family diagnosis. *Journal of Projective Techniques and Personality Assessment, 32,* 331–337.

Beck, S. J. (1930). Personality diagnosis by means of the Rorschach test. *American Journal of Orthopsychiatry, 1,* 81–88.

Beck, S. J., Beck, A. C., Levitt, E. E., & Molish, H. B. (1961). *Rorschach's test I. Basic processes* (3rd ed.). New York: Grune & Stratton.

Bellak, L. (1993). *The TAT, CAT, and SAT in clinical use* (5th ed.). Needham Heights, MA: Allyn & Bacon.

Biederman, L. & Cerbus, G. (1971). Changes in Rorschach teaching. *Journal of Personality Assessment, 35,* 524–526.

Binet, A., & Henri, V. (1896). La psychologie individuelle. *Anné Psychologique, 2,* 411–465.

Blanchard, W. H. (1959). The group process in gang rape. *Journal of Social Psychology, 49,* 259–266.

Blanchard, W. H. (1968). The consensus Rorschach: Background and development. *Journal of Projective Techniques and Personality Assessment, 32,* 327–330.

Blatt, S. J. (1986). Where have we been and where are we going? Reflections on 50 years of personality assessment. *Journal of Personality Assessment, 50,* 343–346.

Blatt, S. J. (1990). The Rorschach: A test of perception or an evaluation of representation. *Journal of Personality Assessment, 55,* 394–416.

Blatt, S. J., & Berman, W. H., Jr. (1984). A methodology for the use of the Rorschach in clinical research. *Journal of Personality Assessment, 48,* 226–239.

Blatt, S. J., & Brenneis, C. B., Schimek, J. G., & Glick, M. (1976). The normal development and psychopathological impairment of the concept of the object on the Rorschach. *Journal of Abnormal Psychology, 85,* 364–373.

Blatt, S. J., & Lerner, H. (1983). Investigations in the psychoanalytic theory of object relations and object representation. In J. Masling (Ed.), *Empirical investigations of psychoanalytic theories* (Vol. 1). Hillsdale, NJ: Analytic Press.

Blatt, S. J., & Ritzler, B. A. (1974). Thought disorder and boundary disturbance in psychosis. *Journal of Consulting and Clinical Psychology, 42,* 370–381.

Blatt, S. J., Tuber, S. B., & Auerbach, J. S. (1990). Representation of interpersonal interactions on the Rorschach and level of psychopathology. *Journal of Personality Assessment, 54,* 711–728.

Bleuler, E. (1950). *Dementia praecox or the group of schizophrenias* (J. Zinkin, Trans.). New York: International Universities Press. (Original work published 1911.)

Brodsky, S. L. (1972). Shared results and open files with the client. *Professional Psychology, 3,* 362–364.

Brown, F. (1953). Reply (to critique of S. Charen). *Journal of Projective Techniques, 17,* 462–464.

Brown, F. (1960). An exploratory study of dynamic factors in the content of the Rorschach protocol. In M. H. Sherman (Ed.), *A Rorschach reader.* New York: International Universities Press. (Reprinted from *Journal of Projective Techniques,* 1953, *17,* 251–379.)

Buros, O. K. (Ed.). (1970). *Personality tests and reviews.* Highland Park, NJ: Gryphon Press.

Burt, C. (1945). *The Rorschach test.* Unpublished manuscript, University College, London.

Callan, M. F., & Yeager, D. C. (1991). *Containing the health care cost spiral.* New York: McGraw-Hill.

Cerney, M. S. (1984). One last response to the Rorschach test: A second chance to reveal oneself. *Journal of Personality Assessment, 48,* 338–344.

Chassan, J. B. (1960). Statistical inference and the single case in clinical design. *Psychiatry, 23,* 173–184.

Chassan, J. B. (1961). Stochastic models of the single case as the basis of clinical research design. *Behavioral Science, 6,* 42–50.

Coan, R. W. (1965). Review of the Holtzman inkblot technique. In O. K. Buros (Ed.), *The sixth mental measurements yearbook.* Highland Park, NJ: Gryphon Press.

Codkind, D. (1966). Attitudes toward the imaginary: Their relationship to level of personality integration (Doctoral dissertation, University of Kansas, 1964). *Dissertation Abstracts International, 27,* 1616B.

Craddick, R. A. (1972). Humanistic assessment: A reply to Brown. *Psychotherapy: Theory, Research and Practice, 9,* 107–110.

Craddick, R. A. (1975). Sharing oneself in the assessment procedure. *Professional Psychology, 6*, 279–282.

Cronbach, L. J. (1949). Statistical methods applied to Rorschach scores: A review. *Psychological Bulletin, 46*, 393–429.

Cutter, F. (1968). Role complements and changes in consensus Rorschachs. *Journal of Projective Techniques and Personality Assessment, 32*, 338–347.

Cutter, F., & Farberow, N. L. (1968). Serial administration of consensus Rorschachs to one patient. *Journal of Projective Techniques and Personality Assessment, 32*, 358–374.

Cutter, F., & Farberow, N. L. (1970). The consensus Rorschach. In B. Klopfer, M. M. Meyer, F. B. Brawer, & W. G. Klopfer (Eds.), *Developments in the Rorschach technique* (Vol. 3). New York: Harcourt Brace Jovanovich.

Dana, R. H. (1954). The effects of attitudes towards authority on psychotherapy. *Journal of Clinical Psychology, 10*, 350–353.

Dana, R. H. (1978). Review of the Rorschach. In O. K. Buros (Ed.), *The eighth mental measurements yearbook.* Highland Park, NJ: Gryphon Press.

DeAngelis, T. (1992, July). APA aims for equitable spot in new HCFA fee schedule. *APA Monitor*, pp. 22–24.

Dearborn, G. V. (1897). Blots of ink in experimental psychology. *Psychological Review, 4*, 390–391.

Dearborn, G. V. (1898). A study of imaginations. *American Journal of Psychology, 9*, 183–190.

De Vos, G. (1952). A quantitative approach to affective symbolism in Rorschach responses. *Journal of Projective Techniques, 16*, 133–150.

Dorr, D. (1981). Conjoint psychological testing in marriage therapy: New wine in old skins. *Professional Psychology, 12*, 549–555.

Durand, V. M., Blanchard, E. B., & Mindell, J. A. (1988). Training in projective testing: Survey of clinical training directors and internship directors. *Professional Psychology: Research and Practice, 19*, 236–238.

Edell, W. S. (1987). Role of structure and disordered thinking in borderline and schizophrenic disorders. *Journal of Personality Assessment, 51*, 23–41.

Elitzur, B. (1976). Content analysis of the Rorschach in two phases: Imaginary story and self interpretation. *Perceptual and Motor Skills, 43*, 43–46.

Elizur, A. (1949). Content analysis of the Rorschach with regard to anxiety and hostility. *Rorschach Research Exchange and Journal of Projective Techniques, 13*, 247–284.

Ellenberger, H. (1954). The life and work of Hermann Rorschach (1884–1922). *Bulletin of the Menninger Clinic, 18*, 173–219.

Ellenberger, H. (1989). The life and work of Hermann Rorschach: II. Personality of Hermann Rorschach. *Society for Personality Assessment: Fiftieth Anniversary History and Directory.* Separate Issue Number 1, April 1989.

Endicott, N. A. (1972). The Holtzman inkblot technique content measures of depression and suspiciousness. *Journal of Personality Assessment, 36,* 424–426.

Eron, L. D. (1965). Review of the Rorschach. In O. K. Buros (Ed.), *The sixth mental measurements yearbook.* Highland Park, NJ: Gryphon Press.

Evans, R. B., & Marmorston, J. (1964). Rorschach signs of brain damage in cerebral thrombosis. *Perceptual and Motor Skills, 18,* 977–988.

Exner, J. E. (1969). *The Rorschach systems.* Orlando, FL: Grune & Stratton.

Exner, J. E. (1974). *The Rorschach: A comprehensive system* (Vol. 1). New York: Wiley.

Exner, J. E. (1978). *The Rorschach: A comprehensive system* (Vol. 2). New York: Wiley.

Exner, J. E. (1985). *Rorschach interpretation assistance program.* San Antonio, TX: The Psychological Corporation.

Exner, J. E. (1986a). *The Rorschach: A comprehensive system. Volume 1, Basic Foundations* (rev. ed.). New York: Wiley.

Exner, J. E. (1986b). Some Rorschach data comparing schizophrenics with borderline and schizotypal personality disorders. *Journal of Personality Assessment, 50,* 455–471.

Exner, J. E. (1989). Searching for projection in the Rorschach. *Journal of Personality Assessment, 53,* 520–536.

Exner, J. E. (1991). *The Rorschach: A comprehensive system. Volume 2, interpretation* (2nd ed.). New York: Wiley.

Exner, J. E. (1992a). R in Rorschach research: A ghost revisited. *Journal of Personality Assessment, 52,* 245–251.

Exner, J. E. (1992b). Some comments on "A conceptual critique of the EA:es comparison in the Comprehensive Rorschach System." *Psychological Assessment, 4,* 301–302.

Exner, J. E., & Weiner, I. B. (1982). *The Rorschach: A comprehensive system. III. Assessment of children and adolescents.* New York: Wiley.

Finn, S. E., & Butcher, J. N. (1991). Clinical objective personality assessment. In M. Hersen, A. E. Kazdin, & A. S. Bellack (Eds.), *The clinical psychology handbook* (2nd ed., pp. 362–373).

Finn, S. E., & Tonsager, M. E. (1992). Therapeutic effects of providing MMPI-2 test feedback to college students awaiting therapy. *Psychological Assessment, 4,* 278–287.

Fischer, C. T. (1970). The testee as co-evaluator. *Journal of Counseling Psychology, 17,* 70–76.

Fischer, C. T. (1972). Paradigm changes which allow sharing of results. *Professional Psychology, 3,* 364–369.

Fisher, S., & Cleveland, S. E. (1958). *Body image and personality.* Princeton, NJ: Van Nostrand.

Fisher, S., & Cleveland, S. E. (1968). *Body image and personality* (2nd ed.). New York: Dover.

Fisher, S., & Greenberg, R. P. (1977). *Scientific credibility of Freud's theories and psychotherapy.* New York: Basic Books.

Fisher, S., & Greenberg, R. P. (1978). *The scientific evaluation of Freud's theories and therapy: A book of readings.* New York: Basic Books.

Francis-Williams, J. (1968). *Rorschach with children.* London: Pergamon Press.

Frank, G. (1990). Research on the clinical usefulness of the Rorschach: 1. The diagnosis of schizophrenia. *Perceptual and Motor Skills, 71,* 573–578.

Freiberg, P. (1992, July). SSA may postpone rules announcement. *APA Moniter,* p. 24.

Friedman, H. (1952). Perceptual regression in schizophrenia: An hypothesis suggested by the use of the Rorschach test. *Journal of Genetic Psychology, 81,* 63–98.

Friedman, H. (1953). Perceptual regression in schizophrenia: An hypothesis suggested by the use of the Rorschach test. *Journal of Projective Techniques, 17,* 171–185.

Gamble, K. R. (1972). The Holtzman inkblot technique: A review. *Psychological Bulletin, 77,* 172–194.

Gass, C. S., & Brown, M. C. (1992). Neuropsychological test feedback to patients with brain dysfunction. *Psychological Assessment, 4,* 272–277.

Goddard, R., & Tuber, S. (1989). Boyhood separation anxiety disorder: Thought disorder and object relations psychopathology as manifested in Rorschach imagery. *Journal of Personality Assessment, 53,* 239–252.

Goldfried, M. R., Stricker, G., & Weiner, I. B. (1971). *Rorschach handbook of clinical and research applications.* Englewood Cliffs, NJ: Prentice-Hall.

Goldstein, K. (1944). Methodological approach to the study of Schizophrenic Thought Disorder. *Language and Thought in Schizophrenia.* A. Kasanin, (Ed.). New York: Norton. 17–41.

Gregory, R. J. (1992). *Psychological testing.* Needham Heights, MA: Allyn & Bacon.

Grossman, L. S., Harrow, M., & Sands, J. R. (1986). Features associated with thought disorder in manic patients at 2–4-year follow-up. *American Journal of Psychiatry, 143,* 306–311.

Halpern, F. (1953). *A clinical approach to children's Rorschachs,* New York: Grune & Stratton.

Halpern, F. (1960). The Rorschach test with children. In A. I. Rabin & M. R. Haworth (Eds.), *Projective techniques with children.* New York: Grune & Stratton.

Halpern, H. M. (1965). A Rorschach interview technique: Clinical validation of the examiner's hypotheses. In M. Kornrich (Ed.), *Psychological test modifications.* Springfield, IL: Thomas. (Reprinted from *Journal of Projective Techniques,* 1957, *21,* 10–17.)

Hammer, M. (1966). A comparison of responses by clinic and normal adults to Rorschach card III human figure area. *Journal of Projective Techniques and Personality Assessment, 30,* 161–162.

Harrow, M., Adler, D., & Hanf, E. (1974). Abstract and concrete thinking in schizophrenia during the prechronic phases. *Archives of General Psychiatry, 31,* 27–33.

Harrow, M., Grossman, L. S., Silverstein, M. L., Meltzer, H. Y., & Kettering, R. L. (1986). A longitudinal study of thought disorder in manic patients. *Archives of General Psychiatry, 43,* 781–785.

Harrower, M. (1960). Projective counseling—a psychotherapeutic technique. In M. Harrower (Ed.), *Creative variations in the projective techniques.* Springfield, IL: Thomas.

Harrower, M., Vorhaus, P., Roman, M., & Bauman, G. (1960). *Creative variations in the projective techniques.* Springfield, IL: Thomas.

Hayes, S. C., Nelson, R. O. & Jarrett, R. B. (1987). The treatment utility of assessment: A functional approach to evaluate assessment quality. *American Psychologist, 42,* 963–974.

Hayslip, B., Jr., & Darbes, A. (1974). Intra-subject response consistency of the Holtzman inkblot technique. *Journal of Personality Assessment, 38,* 149–153.

Hershenson, J. R. (1949). Preferences of adolescents for Rorschach figures. *Child Development, 20,* 101–118.

Hertz, M. R. (1936). The method of administration of the Rorschach inkblot test. *Child Development, 7,* 237–254.

Hertz, M. R. (1970). *Frequency tables for scoring Rorschach responses* (5th ed.). Cleveland, OH: Press of Case Western Reserve University.

Hertzman, M., & Pearce, J. (1947). The personal meaning of the human figure in the Rorschach. *Psychiatry, 10,* 413–422.

Hill, E. F. (1972). *The Holtzman Inkblot Technique: A Handbook for Clinical Application.* San Francisco: Jossey-Bass.

Hock, R. R. (1992). *Forty studies that changed psychology.* Englewood Cliffs, NJ: Prentice-Hall.

Holt, R. R. (1962). Individuality and generalization in the psychology of personality. *Journal of Personality, 30,* 377–404.

Holt, R. R. (1968). Editor's foreword. In D. Rapaport, M. M. Gill, & R. Schafer, *Diagnostic psychological testing* (rev. ed.). New York: International Universities Press.

Holt, R. R., & Havel, J. (1960). A method for assessing primary and secondary process in the Rorschach. In M. A. Rickers-Ovsiankina (Ed.), *Rorschach psychology.* New York: Wiley.

Holtzman, W. H. (1968). Holtzman inkblot technique. In A. I. Rabin (Ed.), *Projective techniques in personality assessment.* New York: Springer.

Holtzman, W. H., Thorpe, J. S., Swartz, J. D., & Herron, E. W. (1961). *Inkblot perception and personality.* Austin, TX: University of Texas Press.

Howard, J. W. (1953). The Howard Ink Blot Test: A descriptive manual. *Journal of Clinical Psychology, 9,* 209–254.

Huber, J. (1961). *Report writing in psychology and psychiatry.* New York: Harper.

Jaffe, L. (1988). The selected response procedure: A variation on Appelbaum's altered atmosphere procedure for the Rorschach. *Journal of Personality Assessment, 52,* 530–538.

Janis, M. G., & Janis, I. L. (1965). A supplementary test based on free association to Rorschach responses. In M. Kornrich (Ed.), *Psychological test modifications.* Springfield, IL: Thomas. (Reprinted from *Rorschach Research Exchange,* 1946, *10,* 1–19.)

Johnston, M. H., & Holzman, P. S. (1979). *Assessing schizophrenic thinking.* San Francisco: Jossey-Bass.

Jortner, S. (1966). An investigation of certain cognitive aspects of schizophrenia. *Journal of Projective Techniques and Personality Assessment, 30,* 559–568.

Jung, C. G. (1961). *Memories, dreams, and reflections* (A. Jaffe, Ed.). New York: Pantheon Books.

Kessel, P., Harris, J. E., & Slagle, S. J. (1969). An associative technique for analyzing the content of Rorschach test responses. *Perceptual and Motor Skills, 29,* 535–540.

Kessler, K. A. (1987). Benefit design, utilization review, case management, PPOs contain costs. *Benefits Today, 3,* 1–2.

Kirkpatrick, E. A. (1900). Individual tests of school children. *Psychological Review, 7,* 274–280.

Kleiger, J. H. (1992a). A conceptual critique of the EA:es comparison in the comprehensive Rorschach system. *Psychological Assessment, 4,* 288–296.

Kleiger, J. H. (1992b). A response to Exner's comments on "A conceptual critique of the EA:es comparison in the Comprehensive Rorschach System." *Psychological Assessment, 4,* 301–302.

Klopfer, B., & Kelley, D. M. (1946). *The Rorschach technique: A manual for a projective method of personality diagnosis.* New York: Collins.

Klopfer, B., Ainsworth, M. D., Klopfer, W. G., & Holt, R. R. (1954). *Developments in the Rorschach technique, I: Technique and theory.* New York: Harcourt, Brace & World.

Klopfer, B., & Davidson, H. H. (1962). *The Rorschach technique: An introductory manual.* New York: Harcourt, Brace & World.

Klopfer, B., Fox, J., & Troup, E. (1956). Problems in the use of the Rorschach technique with children. In B. Klopfer (Ed.), *Developments in the Rorschach technique* (Vol. 2). New York: Harcourt, Brace & World.

Klopfer, W. G. (1960). *The psychological report.* New York: Grune & Stratton.

Klopfer, W. G. (1968). Current status of the Rorschach test. In P. McReynolds (Ed.), *Advances in psychological assessment* (Vol 1). Palo Alto, CA: Science & Behavior Books.

Klopfer, W. G. (1969). Consensus Rorschach in the primary classroom. *Journal of Projective Techniques and Personality Assessment, 33,* 549–552.

Knight, R. P. (1954). Introduction. In E. B. Brody & F. C. Redlich (Eds.), *Psychotherapy with schizophrenics.* New York: International Universities Press.

Korchin, S. J., & Schuldberg, D. (1981). The future of clinical assessment. *American Psychologist, 36,* 1147–1158.

Kornrich, M. (1965). Eliciting "new" Rorschach responses. In Kornrich (Ed.), *Psychological test modifications.* Springfield, IL: Thomas.

Lerner, P. M. (1991). *Psychoanalytic theory and the Rorschach.* Hillsdale, NJ: The Analytic Press.

Lerner, H., Sugarman, A., & Barbour, C. G. (1985). Patterns of ego boundary disturbance in neurotic, borderline, and schizophrenic patients. *Psychoanalytic Psychology, 2,* 47–66.

Leventhal, T., Slepian, H. J., Gluck, M. R., & Rosenblatt, B. P. (1962). The utilization of the psychologist-patient relationship in diagnostic testing. *Journal of Projective Techniques, 26,* 66–79.

Levin, R. (1990). Ego boundary impairment and thought disorder in frequent nightmare sufferers. *Psychoanalytic Psychology, 7,* 529–543.

Levine, M., & Spivack, G. (1964). *The Rorschach index of repressive style.* Springfield, IL: Thomas.

Levitt, E. E., & Truumaa, A. (1972). *The Rorschach technique with children and adolescents.* New York: Grune & Stratton.

Levy, D. M., & Beck, S. J. (1934). The Rorschach in manic-depressive psychosis. *American Journal of Orthopsychiatry, 4,* 31–42.

Levy, J., & Epstein, N. B. (1964). An application of the Rorschach test in family investigation. *Family Process, 3,* 344–376.

Lindner, R. M. (1946). Content analysis in Rorschach work. *Rorschach Research Exchange, 10,* 121–129.

Lipgar, R. M. (1992). The problem of R in the Rorschach: The value of varying responses. *Journal of Personality Assessment, 58,* 223–230.

Loveland, N. (1967). The relation Rorschach: A technique for studying interaction. *Journal of Nervous and Mental Disease, 145,* 93–105.

Lubin, B., Larsen, R. M., Matarazzo, J. D., & Seever, M. F. (1985). Psychological test usage patterns in five professional settings. *American Psychologist, 40* 857–861.

Lubin, B., Wallis, R. R., & Paine, C. (1971). Patterns of psychological test usage in the United States: 1935–1969. *Professional Psychology, 2,* 70–74.

Marengo, J., & Harrow, M. (1985). Thought disorder: A function of schizophrenia, mania, or psychosis? *Journal of Nervous and Mental Disease, 173,* 35–41.

Martin, D. G. (1968). Test reviews. *Journal of Counseling Psychology, 15,* 481–484.

Meloy, J. R., & Singer, J. (1991). A psychoanalytic view of the Rorschach comprehensive system. *Journal of Personality Assessment, 56,* 202–217.

Meyer, G. J. (1992a). Response frequency problems in the Rorschach: Clinical and research implications with suggestions for the future. *Journal of Personality Assessment, 58,* 231–244.

Meyer, G. J. (1992b). The Rorschach's factor structure: A contemporary investigation and historical review. *Journal of Personality Assessment, 59,* 117–136.

Mindess, H. (1970). The symbolic dimension. In B. Klopfer, M. M. Meyer, F. B. Brawer, & W. G. Klopfer (Eds.), *Developments in the Rorschach technique* (Vol. 3). New York: Harcourt Brace Jovanovich.

Molish, H. B. (1951). The popular response in Rorschach records of normals, neurotics, and schizophrenics. *American Journal of Orthopsychiatry, 21,* 523–531.

Mosak, H. H., & Gushurst, R. S. (1972). Some therapeutic uses of psychological testing. *American Journal of Psychotherapy, 26,* 539–546.

Murstein, B. I. (1968). Discussion for current status of some projective techniques. *Journal of Projective Techniques and Personality Assessment, 32,* 229–232.

Neiger, S., Slemon, A. G., & Quirk, D. A. (1962). The performance of chronic schizophrenic patients on Piotrowski's Rorschach sign list for organic CNS pathology. *Journal of Projective Techniques, 26,* 419–428.

Ogdon, D. P. (1975). *Psychodiagnostics and personality assessment: A handbook* (2nd ed.). Los Angeles: Western Psychological Services.

Parker, K. C. H., Hanson, P. K., & Hunsley, J. (1988). MMPI, Rorschach, and WAIS: A meta-analytic comparison of reliability, stability, and validity. *Psychological Bulletin, 103,* 367–373.

Pascal, G. R., Ruesch, H. A., Devine, C. A., & Suttell, B. J. (1950). A study of genital symbols on the Rorschach test: Presentation of a method and results. *Journal of Abnormal and Social Psychology, 45,* 286–295.

Parsons, C. J. (1917). Children's interpretations of inkblots. *British Journal of Psychology, 9,* 74–92.

Perry, W., & Viglione, D. J., Jr. (1991). The ego impairment index as a predictor of outcome in melancholic depressed patients treated with tricyclic antidepressants. *Journal of Personality Assessment, 56,* 487–501.

Peterson, R. A. (1978). Review of the Rorschach. In O. K. Buros (Ed.), *The eighth mental measurements yearbook.* Highland Park, NJ: Gryphon Press.

Phillips, L. (1953). Case history data and prognosis in schizophrenia. *Journal of Nervous and Mental Disease, 117,* 515–525.

Phillips, L. (1992). A letter from Leslie Phillips. *SPA Exchange, 2,* 9.

Phillips, L., & Smith, J. G. (1953). *Rorschach interpretation: Advanced technique.* New York: Grune & Stratton.

Piotrowski, C. (1984). The status of projective techniques: Or "wishing won't make it go away." *Journal of Clinical Psychology, 40,* 1495–1502.

Piotrowski, C. (1985). Clinical assessment: Attitudes of the Society for Personality Assessment membership. *The Southern Psychologist, 2,* 80–83.

Piotrowski, C., & Keller, J. W. (1978). Psychological test usage in southeastern outpatient mental health facilities in 1975. *Professional Psychology, 9,* 63–67.

Piotrowski, C., & Keller, J. W. (1984a). Attitudes toward clinical assessment by members of the AABT. *Psychological Reports, 55,* 831–838.

Piotrowski, C., & Keller, J. W. (1984b). Psychodiagnostic testing in APA-approved clinical psychology programs. *Professional Psychology: Research and Practice, 15,* 450–456.

Piotrowski, C., & Keller, J. W. (1989a). Psychological testing in outpatient mental health facilities: A national study. *Professional Psychology: Research and Practice, 20,* 423–425.

Piotrowski, C., & Keller, J. W. (1989b). Use of assessment in mental health clinics and services. *Psychological Reports, 64,* 1298.

Piotrowski, C., Sherry D., & Keller, J. W. (1985). Psychodiagnostic test usage: A survey of the Society for Personality Assessment. *Journal of Personality Assessment, 49,* 115–119.

Piotrowski, Z. A. (1937). A comparison of congenital personality structure and intelligence. *Proceedings of the American Association of Mental Deficiency, 42,* 78–90.

Piotrowski, Z. A. (1957). *Perceptanalysis.* New York: Macmillan.

Pope, K. S. (1992). Responsibilities in providing psychological test feedback to clients. *Psychological Assessment, 4,* 268–271.

Potkay, C. R. (1971). *The Rorschach clinician.* New York: Grune & Stratton.

Powers, W. T., & Hamlin, R. M. (1957). The validity bases, and process of clinical judgment, using a limited amount of projective test data. *Journal of Projective Techniques, 21,* 286–293.

Pyle, W. H. (1913). *Examination of school children.* New York: Macmillan.

Pyle, W. H. (1915). A psychological study of bright and dull pupils. *Journal of Educational Psychology, 6,* 151–156.

Quinlan, D., & Harrow, M. (1974). Boundary disturbance in schizophrenia. *Journal of Abnormal Psychology, 83,* 533–541.

Quinlan, D., Harrow, M., Tucker, G., & Carlson, K. (1972). Varieties of "disordered" thinking on the Rorschach. *Journal of Abnormal Psychology 79,* 47–53.

Rapaport, D., Gill, M., & Schafer, R. (1946). *Diagnostic psychological testing* (Vol. 2). Chicago: Year Book.

Reznikoff, M., Aronow, E., & Rauchway, A. (1982). The reliability of inkblot content scales. In C. D. Spielberger & J. D. Butcher (Eds.), *Advances in personality assessment* (Vol. 1). Hillsdale, NJ: Erlbaum.

Richman, J. (1967). Reporting diagnostic test results to patients and their families. *Journal of Projective Techniques and Personality Assessment, 31,* 62–70.

Ritzler, B., & Alter, B. (1986). Rorschach teaching in APA-approved clinical graduate programs: Ten years later. *Journal of Personality Assessment, 50,* 44–49.

Ritzler, B. A., Wyatt, D., Harder, D., & Kaskey, M. (1980). Psychotic patterns of the concept of the object on the Rorschach. *Journal of Abnormal Psychology, 89,* 46–55.

Rorschach, H. (1921/1942). [*Psychodiagnostics*] (5th ed.). (P. Lemkau & B. Kronenberg, trans.). Berne, Switzerland: Verlag Hans Huber.

Rorschach, H., & Oberholzer, E. (1924). The application of the interpretation of form to psychoanalysis. *Journal of Nervous and Mental Disease, 60,* 225–248 & 359–379.

Roth, L. H., Wolford, J., & Meisel, A. (1980). Patient access to records: Tonic or toxin? *American Journal of Psychiatry, 137,* 592–596.

Sager, C. J. (1976). *Marriage contracts and couple therapy.* New York: Brunner-Mazel.

Schachtel, E. G. (1966). *Experiential foundations of Rorschach's test.* New York: Basic Books.

Schafer, R. (1948). *The clinical application of psychological tests.* New York: International Universities Press.

Schafer, R. (1954). *Psychoanalytic interpretation in Rorschach testing.* New York: Grune & Stratton.

Schlesinger, H. J. (1973). Interaction of dynamic and reality factors in the diagnostic testing interview. *Bulletin of the Menninger Clinic, 37,* 495–517.

Schuldberg, D., & Boster, J. S. (1985). Two types of distance in Rapaport's original Rorschach thought disorder categories. *Journal of Abnormal Psychology, 94,* 205–215.

Sen, A. A. (1950). A statistical study of the Rorschach test. *British Journal of Psychology Statist. Sect., 3,* 21–39.

Sharp, S. E. (1899). Individual psychology: A study in psychological method. *American Journal of Psychology, 10,* 329–391.

Shontz, F. C., & Green, P. (1992). Trends in research on the Rorschach: Review and recommendations. *Applied and Preventative Psychology, 1,* 149–156.

Singer, M. and Larson, D. (1981). Borderline Personality and the Rorschach Test. *Archives of General Psychology.* Vol. 38, 693–698.

Singer, M. T., & Wynne, L. C. (1966). Principles for scoring communication defects and deviances in parents of schizophrenics: Rorschach and TAT scoring manuals. *Psychiatry, 29,* 260–288.

Smith, B. L. (1992). An American in Paris. *Bulletin of the International Rorschach Society, 2,* 5–6.

Solovay, M. R., Shenton, M. E., Gasperetti, C., Coleman, M., Kestenbaum, E., Carpenter, J. T., & Holzman, P. S. (1986). Scoring manual for the Thought Disorder Index. *Schizophrenia Bulletin, 12,* 483–496.

Stein, E. J., Furedy, R. L., Simonton, M. J., & Neuffer, C. H. (1979). Patient access to medical records on a psychiatric inpatient unit. *American Journal of Psychiatry, 136,* 327–332.

Stevens, S. S. (1951). *Handbook of experimental psychology.* New York: Wiley.

Sundberg, N. D. (1961). The practice of psychological testing in clinical services in the United States. *American Psychologist, 16,* 79–83.

Swartz, J. D. (1970). Pathological verbalization in normals, psychotics, and mental retardates. *Dissertation Abstracts International, 30,* 5703–5704B. (University Microfilms No. 70-10, 872.)

Symonds, P. M. (1955). A contribution to our knowledge of the validity of the Rorschach. *Journal of Projective Techniques, 19,* 152–162.

Tallent, N. (1992). *The practice of psychological assessment.* Englewood Cliffs, NJ: Prentice-Hall.

Tallent, N. (1993). *Psychological report writing* (4th ed). Englewood Cliffs, NJ: Prentice-Hall.

Thelen, M. H., & Ewing, D. R. (1970). Roles, functions, and training in clinical psychology: A survey of academic clinicians. *American Psychologist, 25,* 550–554.

Thelen, M. H., Varble, D. L., & Johnson, J. (1968). Attitudes of academic clinical psychologists towards projective techniques. *American Psychologist, 23,* 517–521.

Tuber S., & Coates, S. (1989). Indices of psychopathology in the Rorschachs of boys with severe gender identity disorder: A comparison with normal control subjects. *Journal of Personality Assessment, 53,* 100–112.

Tulchin, S. H. (1940). The pre-Rorschach use of inkblot tests. *Rorschach Research Exchange, 4,* 1–7.

Urist, J. (1977). The Rorschach test and the assessment of object relations. *Journal of Personality Assessment, 41,* 3–9.

Vincent, K. R., & Harman, M. J. (1991). The Exner Rorschach: An analysis of its clinical validity. *Journal of Clinical Psychology, 47,* 596–599.

Wade, T. C., Baker, T. B., Morton, T. L., & Baker, L. J. (1978). The status of psychological testing in clinical psychology. Relationships between test use and professional activities and orientations. *Journal of Personality Assessment, 42,* 3–10.

Watkins, J., & Stauffacher, J. (1952). An index of pathological thinking in the Rorschach. *Journal of Projective Techniques, 16,* 276–286.

Werner, H. (1948). *Comparative psychology of mental development* (rev. ed.). Chicago: Follett.

Werner, H. (1957). The concept of development from a comparative and organismic point of view. In D. B. Harris (Ed.), *The concept of development* (pp. 125–148). Minneapolis: University of Minnesota Press.

Wheeler, W. M. (1949). An analysis of Rorschach indices of male homosexuality. *Rorschach Research Exchange and Journal of Projective Techniques, 13,* 97–126.

Whipple, G. M. (1910). *Manual of mental and physical tests*. Baltimore, MD: Warwick & York.

Wiener-Levy, D., & Exner, J. E. (1981). The Rorschach EA-ep variable as related to persistence in a task frustration situation under feedback conditions. *Journal of Personality Assessment, 45,* 118–124.

Willi, J. (1969). Joint Rorschach testing of partner relationships. *Family Process, 8,* 64–78.

Willock, B. (1992). Projection, transitional phenomena, and the Rorschach. *Journal of Personality Assessment, 59,* 99–116.

Wilson, A. (1985). Boundary disturbance in borderline and psychotic states. *Journal of Personality Assessment, 49,* 346–355.

Winslow, R. (1989, December 13). Spending to cut mental health costs. *Wall Street Journal,* p. A1.

Zimmerman, I. L., Lambert, N. M., & Class, L. (1966). A comparison of children's perceptions of Rorschach cards III, IV, and VII with independent ratings of parental adequacy, and effectiveness of school behavior. *Psychology in the Schools, 3,* 258–263.

Ziskin, J., & Faust, D. (1988). *Coping with psychiatric and psychological testimony* (4th ed.). Marina del Rey, CA: Law and Psychology Press.

Zubin, J. (1956). The non-projective aspects of the Rorschach experiment: I. Introduction. *Journal of Social Psychology, 44,* 179–192.

Zubin, J., Eron, L. D., & Schumer, F. (1965). *An Experimental approach to projective techniques*. New York: Wiley.

Zulliger, H. (1941/1969). *[The Zulliger individual and group test.]* (F. Salomon, Ed., & D. Dubrovsky, Trans.). New York: International Universities Press.

Name Index

Subject Index

DATE DUE

MAY 1 8 1998		
JUN 2 8 1999		
NOV 0 7 1999		
APR 2 8 2000		
MAY 0 7 2001		
APR 2 3 2003		
		Printed in USA